The Arrogant Connoisseur

for FRANCIS HAWCROFT

editors MICHAEL CLARKE & NICHOLAS PENNY

The Arrogant Connoisseur:
RICHARD PAYNE KNIGHT
1751–1824

essays on RICHARD PAYNE KNIGHT

together with a
catalogue of works exhibited at the Whitworth Art Gallery, 1982

Manchester University Press

Collection of essays
© *Manchester University Press 1982*

Catalogue of the works exhibited at the Whitworth Art
Gallery 1982
© *Whitworth Art Gallery 1982*

Copyright in the individual chapters belongs to their
respective authors, and no chapter may be reproduced
whole or in part without the express permission in
writing of author, editors and publisher

British Library cataloguing in publication data

The Arrogant Connoisseur: Richard Payne
    Knight 1751–1824.
    1. Knight, Richard Payne   2. Art—
Collectors and collecting—Great Britain
—Biography
I. Clarke, Michael   II. Penny, Nicholas
707.5'092'4   N5247.K/

ISBN 0-7190-0871-9

Filmset by August Filmsetting, Reddish, Stockport

Printed in Great Britain
by The Alden Press, Oxford

Contents

Colour plates

The colour plates appear between pages 118 and 119

Monochrome plates

*Plates listed above appear in the Essays section of this book.
A great many of the Catalogue entries are also illustrated.*

Acknowledgements

We are extremely grateful to the present proprietor of Downton Castle who has allowed his home to be explored and who has so generously supported the publication of the catalogue; to Denis Lennox, who has not only lent a great many paintings to the exhibition, but has shared his knowledge of the Castle and its grounds and has permitted quotation from the Downton Castle papers; and to Dr David Wilson, Director of the British Museum, for his enthusiastic response to the idea of the exhibition. The Keepers of the Departments of Prints and Drawings, of Coins and Medals, and of Greek and Roman, Medieval and Later, Prehistoric and Romano-British, Oriental, and Egyptian Antiquities have all been unfailingly encouraging and helpful. We are indebted to the Mellon Foundation for a handsome grant towards the cost of this publication and for support given to Claudia Stumpf in her research. The British Council generously funded a study trip to East Germany by Michael Clarke.

In its initial stages the preparation for this exhibition was in the hands of Francis Hawcroft and despite ill-health he has continued to keep a paternal eye upon its progress. Several of the essays have benefited from the criticism and the knowledge of Professor Francis Haskell. Dr John Newman was of great assistance during the research for Chapter Three. We are indebted to the staff of many libraries and in particular to Miss Hubbard of Herefordshire Record Office, Miss Hart of Kidderminster Public Library, and the archivists of Lancashire Record Office, Preston, of the Goethe – Schiller Archiv, Weimar, of the Bodleian Library, Oxford, and of the British Library and the Society of Antiquaries, London. Her Majesty the Queen has graciously permitted us to quote from the Farington Diaries, and the Pierpont Morgan Library have let us quote from a letter in their possession – although not from the highly important correspondence between Sir Uvedale Price and Sir George Beaumont which is reserved for Professor Marcia Allentuck, who will publish it shortly, she assures us.

Among the numerous individuals who have assisted us we are especially grateful to Donald Bailey, Joanna Banham, Hugh Belsey, Deborah Berkeley, Professor Anthony Blunt, Lady Bromley-Davenport, Dr David Brown, Herbert Cahoon, Andy Carson, Marjorie Caygill, Brian Cook, Anita Coombes, John Cornforth, Diana Dethloff, Diana Donald, Michael Downing, Brinsley Ford, Peter Fullerton, Dr Kenneth Garlick, Charlotte Gere, John Gere, Robin Gibson, David Griffiths, Professor Karl Heinz Hahn, John Hammond, Craig Hartley, Dr John Hayes, Evelyn Joll, Roger Jones, John Kenworthy-Browne, Richard Kingzett, Professor Michael Kitson, Dr Roger Ling, Ian Longworth, the Lady Dorothy Lygon, Jacyntha Macmahon, Gillian Malpass, Mark Murphy, Felicity Owen, William Mostyn Owen, Dr Alex Potts, Dr Martin Price, Simon Pugh, Shelagh Ranger, Dr Tom Rasmussen, Bruce Robertson, Martin Royalton-Kisch, Caroline Scholl, Gertrude Seidmann, Susan L. Silber, Professor Seymour Slive, Lindsay Stainton, Judith Swaddling, Hugh Tait, Nicholas Turner, Dr Richard Verdi, Dr Susan Walker, Margaret Warhurst, Professor Sir Ellis Waterhouse, Professor Christopher White, Dr Jon Whiteley, Imogen Wilde, Reg Williams, Tim Wilson, Sarah Wimbush, Ian Wolfenden, Dr Simon Towneley, Antonia Yates and Wladimir Zwalf.

We are grateful to the following for permission to reproduce photographs: Visitors of the Ashmolean Museum (61); *Country Life* (16, 25); The Courtauld Institute (2, 6, 7, 13, 28, 44–6; Cat. nos. 115(i), (iii), (vi), 181, 182, 185, 194, 203, 204, 207); The Trustees of the British Museum (8–11, 32, 36, 39, 41; Cat. nos. 1, 4, 15, 21, 29, 30, 42, 47, 48, 50, 64, 71, 99, 108, 116, 123, 125, 129, 130, 141, 142, 144, 148, 150, 151, 152, 156, 157, 159, 164, 167, 173; Colour Plates I–V, IX, X); Leicestershire Museum and Art Gallery (Colour Plate XI); The Paul Mellon Foundation (3, 4); Merseyside County Museums (Cat. nos. 52–4); National Gallery of Scotland (47); National Portrait Gallery (Cat. nos. 172, 193, 208); Sotheby's (42); BBC (Colour Plate VIII); City Art Gallery, Manchester (174); National Monuments Record (26).

At Manchester University Press our Editor, John Banks, has carefully ushered the catalogue through its various stages, and it has been designed by Max Nettleton. The exhibition has been designed by Alasdair Hamilton of the University's Audio-Visual Service.

Michael Clarke & Nicholas Penny

Preface

In the last years of the eighteenth century and the early years of the nineteenth Richard Payne Knight was *arbiter elegantiarum* of London society. He lost this rôle because of his arrogance — his refusal to acknowledge the merits of Lord Elgin's marbles. However, this in no way detracts from the superlative quality of Knight's own collections of ancient gems, coins, bronzes and Old Master drawings or from his generosity in bequeathing them to the British Museum. A selection of these has been assembled for this exhibition from the different departments of the British Museum and paintings have been borrowed from other collections, both public and private, together with an exquisite set of watercolour drawings by Hearne of the landscape which Knight shaped at his country seat, Downton Castle.

Hearne's watercolours and the views of the Alps and of Sicily which Knight commissioned from Cozens, are particularly appropriate items to show in the Whitworth Art Gallery, but the emphasis in this exhibition is on the variety of Knight's interests — a variety which was remarkable even in his own day when an enthusiasm for the silver coins of Greek Sicily and for Etruscan bronze figures was seldom combined with one for drawings by Raphael, Rubens, Rembrandt and Claude. Knight was also a man with ideas which he was not disposed to keep to himself and this emerges in Lawrence's portrait of him in the Whitworth Art Gallery.

Some of the items in this exhibition have been selected because of Knight's interpretations of them. Portraits have been included, both of friends such as Charles Townley and Emma Hamilton and of allies and enemies in the 'paper wars' of that period such as Repton, Haydon, Byron and Elgin. Unfortunately, we cannot do justice in this exhibition to Knight's work as a landscape gardener and amateur architect, or to his investigations of primitive symbolism, or to his theories of the psychology of vision; but the preliminary essays in this catalogue attempt to assess some of his intellectual achievements and something of his versatility. These are the work of Peter Funnell and Claudia Stumpf who are researching at the Universities of Oxford and London, and of Nicholas Penny and Michael Clarke of the History of Art Department and the Whitworth Art Gallery of the University of Manchester. The section of the catalogue devoted to the watercolours of Sicily was supplied by Miss Stumpf. That devoted to 'other drawings and watercolours' is almost all the work of Mr Clarke as are many of the entries for oil paintings. The other entries are by Dr Penny. The kind of collaboration represented by this exhibition is one which Manchester is particularly well suited to encourage.

I offer the grateful thanks of the Gallery to the above-named scholars and to all the individuals and institutions whose loans and whose help have made the exhibition possible. We are, as ever, deeply indebted to the Greater Manchester Council for their support without which this exhibition would have been impossible.

PROFESSOR C. R. DODWELL
Director

CHAPTER ONE—*Richard Payne Knight: a brief life*

Herefordshire and South Shropshire must count amongst the least 'spoilt' areas of England, but in the eighteenth century the countryside was much more populated and much less peaceful. To the east of Ludlow the Clee Hills, now exhausted, then yielded not only abundant supplies of coal but also iron ore. To the west by the banks of the Teme was the busy Bringewood iron works whence the ore had been carried since the late sixteenth century by pack mule to be smelted with charcoal from the rich woods of the Bringewood Chase.[1]

In 1698 Bringewood forge, furnace, and chase were leased by Richard Knight, grandfather of the subject of this book. The fifth child of a landowner 'of narrow and embarrassed circumstances', he was born thirty years earlier in the substantial farm house of Castle Hill at Madeley, Shropshire; received a 'liberal education' at Shiffnall School and was then employed as a clerk and afterwards as a manager of ironworks, first at Coalbrookdale and then at Withyford, in Shropshire, by the Wellington and Corbett families. He was able to move to Bringewood and establish himself as an ironmaster by adding to his savings and the dowry of his bride Elizabeth Payne (daughter of the squire of Shawbury, not far from Withyford) a loan of a thousand guineas 'made on no other security than that of his character'.[2] He improved the works — adding a tinplate rolling mill — and quickly prospered. Before long he was able to purchase the lease from Lord Craven, and during the 1720s he acquired for his family a controlling interest in a chain of forges and furnaces on the Stour in Shropshire, Staffordshire and Worcestershire.[3] Between 1710 and 1740 he spent over £45,000 acquiring the manors around Bringewood — Burrington, Elton, Leinthall Starkes, Leintwardine, Downton and Wharton.[4]

Richard, the ironmaster's eldest son, who settled in a large house, Dynham, near Ludlow and acquired two large estates, Croft Castle and Stannage Park, together with Edward, the third son, who was eventually established at Wolverley and Cookley, Ralph, the fourth son, and their brother-in-law, Abraham Spooner, a prominent Quaker iron merchant, are all mentioned as partners in the Stour iron works,[5] and although Richard seems to have been a lawyer, the others were ironmasters. The cuckoo in the nest was Thomas, the second son.

Thomas Knight was appointed domestic chaplain to Francis, Lord Deloraine in 1730[6] and later presented with the livings of Ribbesford and Bewdley in Worcestershire by Lord Powis[7] (whose estates at Oakly bordered upon Bringewood Chase). Whereas his brothers married well,

Thomas, unexpectedly and in middle age, wedded Ursula Nash, his servant, apparently a milkmaid, the daughter of a 'working carpenter' — their 'connections', it was observed, 'will not contribute much to adorn a pedigree' but Mr Nash and his daughter possessed 'respectable moral characters'.[8] Pastoral responsibilities had been delegated to curates, and the couple lived at Wormsley Grange, a large manor house nine miles north-west of Hereford where, on 11 February 1751, when Ursula was aged 37 and her husband 54, their first child was born.[9] He was baptised Richard, after his grandfather, and Payne, the maiden name of his grandmother, and was always known by all three names to distinguish him from the other Richards in the family. Grandfather Richard, the iron-master, had died in 1745 and is buried at Burrington beneath an elegantly lettered cast iron ledger (Plate 1). The Bringewood estates were entailed and passed to the eldest son, Richard, who, however, died without a son soon afterwards. The heir was thus Richard Payne Knight.

Richard Payne Knight had two sisters, Barbara, born 1756, who died aged 19, and Ursula, born 1760, who died aged 17. And he had a younger brother Thomas Andrew, born in 1759[10] who was to be elected a fellow of the Royal Society in 1805 and of the Linnean Society in 1807 and was President of the Horticultural Society, of which he was a founding member, from 1811 until his death in 1838. He was the author of *A Treatise on the Culture of the Apple and Pear* and of *Pomona Herefordiensis* as well as over a hundred papers on matters such as grafting and mildew, and he raised numerous new varieties of fruit and vegetable. The range of his interests is well conveyed by his correspondence between 1809 and 1819 with Sir Joseph Banks on the prospects of a new ice age, the taste of giant crab, the cultivation of hermaphrodite strawberries and the ethics of dissecting living rabbits.[11] Richard Payne Knight attained still greater eminence as a philologist, numismatist, collector, arbiter of taste and *philosophe*. The brothers were close and Richard Payne Knight was also curious about natural history as is clear from notes in his works on matters such as the feeding habits of rooks, the smell of the elephant or the sexual life of worker bees.[12]

Whereas his younger brother was educated at Ludlow Grammar School and then at a boarding school in Chiswick before going up to Balliol College, Oxford, Richard Payne Knight, owing to his poor health as a child, was kept from school until after his father's death in the winter of 1764 when he was sent to a tutor, Mr Blyth of Coleshill, Worcestershire. He was introduced to Greek, of which he became so excellent a scholar, only at the age of 13.[13] To the fact that he was educated, in one or another sense, by himself, we may attribute his independence and originality as a thinker. We should not, however, overemphasize this. His cousins at Wolverley were highly cultivated, especially Edward Knight junior who took a keen interest in landscape gardening and in aesthetics and was already in the 1760s a considerable collector.[14]

Richard Payne Knight never went to University. Instead he made 'the Tours of France and Italy in the years 1772 and 1773'.[15] His health

PLATE 1 *Left*
Iron tombstones made by
the masters of Bringewood
forge, including that of
Richard Knight, Burrington
Churchyard, Herefordshire

PLATE 2 *Right*
Nathaniel Hone, *Richard
Payne Knight* (cat. no. 178)

meanwhile had evidently improved, for his capacity for consuming macarone, turbot, mutton and game puddings was remembered as marvellous. His energy, later in life, whether climbing Etna at the age of 25 or Snowdon and Cader Idris at the age of 49,[16] or simply taking long country walks was frequently commented upon. He rose early and he drank moderately, making himself very strong coffee whilst his guests continued with wine.[17] But according to an autobiographical passage in one of his poems, his youth was dissipated – without 'preceptor's care, or parent's love', he wrote (during his mother's lifetime),

> Ungovern'd passions led my soul astray,
> And still, where pleasure laid the bait for wealth,
> Bought dear experience with the waste of health,
> Consum'd in riot all that life adorn'd,
> For joys unrelish'd, shar'd with those I scorn'd.[18]

Later in life he referred to his youthful acquaintance with 'gentlemen jockeys' whose morals were somewhat lax (although quite 'rigid', he later discovered, when compared with those of 'gentlemen picture dealers').[19] The earliest likeness of him shows a sensitive and scholarly young man, less self-confident then he in fact must have been (Plate 2).

Accounts survive for the celebrations in 1772 at Knight's coming of age. They include breakfast for the bellringers and '55 gallants of Cyder which was gave in ye Streets' (and cost one guinea).[20] Bills for fitting up Maryknowle, an old house to the east of the chase, are dated 1771 and

1772,[21] and it was here that his mother, and, for a while, his brother were settled. By the autumn of that year Knight had decided to build for himself a new house at Downton, a manor his grandfather had purchased in 1727[22] and where he had died. The exterior seems to have been complete in 1778. The boldly displayed irregularity of plan and striking combination of classical elegance within and picturesque castellation without made Downton Castle, as it was called, one of the most original country houses in English architectural history. To its significance we have dedicated a separate essay here.

Whilst building was in progress Knight spent much of his time abroad. In the late summer of 1776 he seems to have been touring Switzerland with the painter John Robert Cozens. In April 1777 together with Charles Gore, a talented amateur, and Hackert, a professional artist, he ventured south from Naples to Paestum and then on to Sicily, keeping a journal (a version of which has recently been discovered by Claudia Stumpf) probably with an eye to publication. In the conventional manner of English travellers Knight provides a censorious and patronizing, if also forcefully argued, analysis of the society, economy and politics of this part of modern Italy – he is (although a parson's son) particularly contemptuous of 'priestcraft'. His chief interest is in the remains of Greek art and he ignores or dismisses the subsequent embellishments of the island whether Norman or Baroque. The thoroughness of his investigation of ancient architecture and his extensive knowledge of ancient topography are impressive. The records, written and drawn, of the expedition are discussed in detail in Chapter Two.

Knight seems to have been in Paris in the winter of 1777 where he was profoundly disturbed by the torture and execution of Desrues and the incarceration of his widow and the false confession forced from her.[23] He was almost certainly back in England by 1778 and two years later in 1780, aged 29 and properly resident in the country, he was returned as Member of Parliament for Leominster. In the following year he was, together with Charles Gore, elected to the Society of Dilettanti.[24] He was elected as a Whig in Leominster and would have been less welcome in the Dilettanti had he been a Tory. We know little of the political affiliations of the Knight family but Knight's cousins at Wolverley were allied in Whig politics and in the iron industry with Lord Lyttleton. Another cousin, Thomas Johnes, and his friend Uvedale Price, a Herefordshire squire, had been friends at Eton with Charles James Fox and William Windham[25] and Knight must already have belonged to the circle of young Whigs centred on these brilliant men.

The Society of Dilettanti was founded as a dining club for gentlemen who had travelled to Italy and had adopted the cultivated tastes which this encouraged. In 1742 the Society's committee had resolved unanimously that 'whoever shall descend to be serious in earnest thereby deviating from the Originall constitutional sense and spirit of the Society, shall be severely reprimanded',[26] but the Society had, without ceasing to be convivial, become, well before the time Knight joined it, 'serious in earnest' and in particular a lavish patron of expeditions to Greece and the eastern Mediterranean. The standards set by the archaeological publications which were the fruit of these expeditions were without precedent and had no doubt already influenced Knight in his investigations in Sicily. The sympathies of the members in the 1770s were predominantly Whig.

When, in 1777, exhausted and freezing on the summit of Etna, Knight had taken careful samples of the ash, he perhaps had the interests of Sir William Hamilton, the British envoy in Naples and a keen volcanologist, in mind. He could certainly have met him on his first visit to Italy. Hamilton had been enrolled in the Society of Dilettanti not long before Knight (Plates 3 and 4) and at the end of 1781 he wrote to Sir Joseph Banks (President of the Royal Society as well as Secretary of the Dilettanti) concerning the survival of pagan phallic cults in a Roman Catholic festival at the remote town of Isernia. The Society was responsible in 1786 for the publication of this letter together with a learned discourse on the significance of the 'worship of Priapus' in antiquity written by Knight, under whose direction plates of erotica were also engraved. He was somewhat apprehensive of scandal and the edition was limited,[27] but copies were not, it seems, as has often been alleged, withdrawn.

A good deal of armchair anthropology and comparative mythology is here combined with a thesis concerning the 'mystic theology' of the Greeks – mysteries concerning the elementary and polar forces of generation, creation and destruction – which Knight believed to be originally

PLATES 3&4
Sir Joshua Reynolds, *Members of the Society of Dilettanti Celebrating the Introduction of Sir William Hamilton* (Society of Dilettanti)

expressed by the 'symbolical language' of ancient art and mythology. The exposition conceals a polemic against the orthodox prejudices of those who 'think they know, because they are sure they feel'.[28] It provides an ironic account of the practices of the early Christians and attacks some of the fundamentals of the Christian faith, defining 'Dogmatical Theology, and its consequent Religious Persecution' as 'two of the greatest curses that ever afflicted the human race'.[29] The theories of the 'Symbolical Language' of ancient art which so attracted Knight are traced in detail in a subsequent chapter.

Several of the works of art Knight refers to in this work were in the collection of a friend and fellow member of the Society, Charles Townley, and had been discussed in a slightly earlier publication by a protégé of both Hamilton and Townley — the Baron d'Hancarville to whose 'great and elaborate work' Knight refers with respect (although not always agreement).[30] Townley was one of the greatest collectors of ancient art in Europe at that date and Knight's friendship with him must have encouraged his own collecting which seems to have commenced in 1785, and was thereafter an unremitting passion. According to one report in

PLATE 5
John Samuel Agar, *Colossal Marble Head of Apollo*, from *Specimens of Antient Sculpture* (cat. no. 85)

1806 he received an annual income of about £6000; according to another it was not more than £4000, but he saved nothing[31] – in fact his Rent Roll for the year 1790 was a little less than £5000[32] and there would have been additional income from the sale of timber, from interests in coal mining and from investments. This made him a rich man, but the leading aristocratic collector of ancient marbles, the first Marquis of Lansdowne, was said to receive £30,000 a year and William Beckford over three times that sum from his Jamaican plantations.[33]

Townley's determination to leave his collection to the British Museum altered at the end of his life and he then revived the idea of establishing a family museum at Towneley Hall, his ancestral home in Lancashire,[34] in the manner of a rival Lancashire collector, Henry Blundell. But, after his death in 1804, his family found that they could not meet the conditions upon which he had insisted and the collection was in fact acquired for the nation by Act of Parliament. Knight was a leading agent in the negotiations that made this possible.[35] He was also responsible for completing, for the Dilettanti Society, the first volume of the folio *Specimens of Antient Sculpture selected from Several Collections in Great Britain* which he had commenced with Townley in 1799 and which was in large part devoted to illustrations of the masterpieces in their collections. The plates made under their direction are of extraordinary quality (Plate 5) and represent the transfer to the field of sculpture of the standards pioneered by the Society's earlier volumes on ancient architecture. Knight's Preliminary Dissertation to the first volume represents the first substantial contribution to the history of ancient sculpture in English.

On 9 April 1814, Knight, who had not formerly entertained a high opinion of the way the British Museum was managed,[36] was appointed a Trustee (representing the Towneley family) and on 30 June of the same year he made a will revoking his earlier resolution of 1809 to bequeath his collection to the Royal Academy. Now 'all coins and medals, and all wrought or sculptured articles in every kind of metal, ivory and gems, or precious stones, together with all descriptive catalogues of the same and all drawings, or books of drawings of every kind which shall be found in the Gallery or Western Room of my house in Soho Square' were to be given to the British Museum.[37] He mentioned that he had no disrespect for the Academy but wished his collection to join that of his late friends – Townley and 'Cratchrode'. The latter was Clayton Mordaunt Cracherode who had bequeathed his library, his portfolios of drawings and prints and his cabinets of coins and gems to the Museum in 1799.[38] Letters reveal that even in 1821 Knight was not sure that he was doing the right thing,[39] but he did not change his will and his collection went fortunately to the Museum – except the paintings which his brother inherited and which were kept until recently at Downton Castle – and his condition, that a Knight family trustee be appointed, was accepted by Act of Parliament on 9 June 1824.

The gallery which housed Knight's museum, also apparently his library, in his house at 3 Soho Square was specially built for him to be 'secure from fire', certainly by 1809[40] — and it is probably the room 'with its iron roof and skylights' which Mary Berry noted as 'impossible to warm' in 1808.[41] An attraction was his friend Sir Joseph Banks, seven doors away at no. 32. The area was respectable, but no longer fashionable, as it had been when no. 3 was built in 1735. It has not survived but was a three-storyed, three-bayed plain stockbrick house similar in character to no. 2.[42] It seems that Knight entertained there more than one would suppose likely in so dedicated a scholar.

Throughout the 1780s Knight had been at work on his *Analytical Essay on the Greek Alphabet*. It appeared in 1791. Porson considered Knight's scheme narrow and his notions of how sounds and words changed limited, but he 'perused his essay generally with entertainment, sometimes with instruction and approbation' and reviewed it in detail.[43] The sixth section of the book was the most sensational. It is a 'free and candid examination' — that is, a thorough and merciless exposure — of the 'inscriptions said to have been discovered in the neighbourhood of Lacedaemon, by the Abbé Fourmont, during a journey through Greece', published by the French Académie des Inscriptions et Belles Lettres and 'cited as authoritative by every writer upon the subject'.[44] Quite apart from the inherent inconsistencies in Fourmont's 'discoveries', Knight was able to report that James Stuart had found that he had smashed up genuine inscriptions 'so that future travellers might not detect his errors and frauds'.[45]

Much of the second, third and fourth sections of this *Essay* are devoted to Homer whose poetry was, Knight believed, 'defaced by the varnishes of criticks, grammarians and transcribers', marred by 'articles, particles, and prepositions . . . omitted, transferred, and inserted' and by some interpolations, but none the less better preserved than was suggested by the 'ingenious arguments' of other scholars.[46] In the same year, 1791, Knight acquired from Thomas Lawrence a painting of Homer reciting in a forest clearing to an enraptured audience (Plate 6). It is not the vision of a pedant, and Homer excited something like religious enthusiasm in Knight. He stressed the 'great influence' of Greek poetry 'in expanding and elevating' the minds of the Greeks 'and in forming and polishing their taste' and noted that this

appears to have been owing to the transcendent genius of one individual; from whom all that is splendid, or elegant, or exalted in the production of man seems to have flowed. Born in an age of which we know nothing; and not only his country, his family, and his fortunes, but even his name uncertain, the effulgence of his mind still bursts upon us like the rays of the sun, which traverse the immensity of space with undiminished brightness, and diffuse life and motion through the universe, though we know not the nature of the body, which emits them, nor the regions of inanity, through which they pass.[47]

Knight seems to have completed a draft of a *Prolegomena* to an edition of Homer in 1805[48] and he had fifty copies privately printed in 1808 and then reprinted in *The Classical Journal* in 1813 soliciting criticism. He wrote

PLATE 6
Sir Thomas Lawrence,
Homer Reciting his Poems
(cat no. 183)

in Latin the better to address the international scholarly community – and the Germans in particular – but a précis in English appeared in the *Gentleman's Magazine*.[49] The edition proper finally appeared in 1820. 'Whatever may be thought of my system of restoring the ancient forms to the words, future Editors of the Common Form may be supplied with a purer Text than has hitherto appear'd', he wrote to a friend.[50] 'The ordeal of time', as Gladstone noted, proved 'decidedly unfavourable to his text as a practical attempt at reconstruction' but it was agreed to be a 'remarkable performance', and modern authorities concede that it is 'able though perverse', 'acute but undisciplined'.[51] The *Prolegomena* is certainly the most important English contribution of its period to the 'Homer question'. Knight argued for Homer as the author of the *Iliad*, but not the *Odyssey* which was, he supposed, written about a century later. He proposed that Homer was among the Greeks driven into exile in Asia after the Dorian invasion and that both Hesiod and the author of the *Odyssey* also came from the Asian colonies. He argued against Wolf's idea that the *Iliad* was a patchwork, and that a simpler, more unified poem upon the Anger of Achilles was buried in it, and against Heyne's objection to digressions and inconsistencies, pointing out that Homer's audience was not composed of academic critics. He entirely rejected Heyne's suspicion that the famous description of the shield of Achilles was an interpolation by Pisistratus.[52]

Knight had no university degree and was proud of his independent status as a scholar. He was scathing in the *Edinburgh Review* about the inadequacies of the edition of Strabo prepared by Falconer for the Oxford University Press, and contributed to the devastating reply made by the *Edinburgh* to Bishop Copleston's pamphlet defending the University.[53] It is surprising that he had time to develop his interests in — and his collection of — ancient art. But it was hardly possible for him to dissociate his numismatic from his philological pursuits, and he was always looking for reflections of Homer in Greek sculpture. What is more extraordinary is that Knight was also an expert judge and a keen collector of paintings by Old Masters such as Rembrandt, Ruysdael, Elsheimer and Claude — as well as by British contemporaries — and more importantly a connoisseur of Old Master drawings. The collection of these that he bequeathed to the British Museum is one of the most distinguished ever formed in this country. Oil painting was for him the triumph of modern art — the 'one perfection, e'en to Greece unknown' — and the ancients, he conceded, never had 'a complete relish for those gratifications which come from landscape painting'.[54]

It was not on account of his theories about the Greek alphabet or the worship of Priapus, or on account of his collection of coins, sculpture and drawings that Knight's name was a familiar one during the last decade of the eighteenth century and the first of the nineteenth, but because of *The Landscape* — a 'Didactic Poem' which he wrote in 1793 and published in 1794, attacking the style of landscape gardening which Lancelot 'Capability' Brown (who died a decade earlier) had practised all over England in the mid eighteenth century, and advocating far more roughness, richness, variety and intricacy in the planting of parks and irregularity not only in them but in the houses established in them. The poem, together with the more substantial book on the picturesque by his friend and neighbour Uvedale Price, and the replies of Humphry Repton, a practising landscape gardener who defended Brown, and others[55] stimulated much controversy in the reviews and was, for more than a decade, a popular subject of debate in educated society.

Knight, unlike Price, was never generous in his polemics and this, combined with his apparent admiration for disordered nature, led some to react politically. To Horace Walpole, Knight appeared as one who 'Jacobinacally would level the purity of gardens, would as malignantly as Tom Paine or Priestley guillotine Mr Brown'.[56] The passage is highly revealing of the temper of the time since it was made by a Whig of the old school who should have realized that Paine and Priestley were no lovers of the guillotine. The revolution in France was polarizing society violently and Knight was suspected of being on the wrong side because he was not violently against it. Perhaps for this reason he was black-balled at the Literary Club.[57]

The Progress of Civil Society, another poem of greater length which Knight published in 1796, imitates the manner and develops some of the themes of Lucretius and incorporates an elegant translation of the consular oration of Themistius to the Emperor Jovian pleading for freedom of conscience. But Knight's knowledge of the discoveries of Captain Cook and Sir Joseph Banks is quite as obvious as his knowledge of classical literature. There is nothing controversial about his reflections on the origins and consequences of language, huts, food-storage, domestic animals, crops, iron-forges, writing, minting, navigation and colonization. But Knight concludes with his view of the French Revolution – condemning the Terror but also reminding his readers of the terrible cruelties of the Ancien Régime.[58] When the Whigs had divided over the Revolution Knight gave up literature to investigate the matter for himself and decided that Charles James Fox was right – indeed it was only with 'great diffidence' that he ever dissented from Fox in a 'question of general politics'.[59] After the Terror he saw no justification for war with the French Republic. If left alone it would ruin itself but if provoked would develop a formidable because desperate military dictatorship – which of course it did.[60]

These views were considered dangerous, and the Tories were quick to detect other signs of 'Jacobinism' in the poem. There was a note deploring the indissolubility of marriage and suggesting that there are 'many causes which ought to justify divorce, as well as that of adultery on the part of the woman'.[61] Worse still was Knight's profession in the Preface that he was bewildered as to what Christian morality was since it seemed to mean something different at different times and places. And there was the opening passage of the poem which implied that it was but 'learned folly' to seek for 'the sovereign mandates of almighty will' in 'mechanic nature'.[62] The poem was violently attacked by the Tory *British Critic*[63] and was parodied by Canning and others in the *Anti-Jacobin* – they captured perfectly the ludicrous effects into which Knight, endeavouring to decorate a platitude, sometimes stumbled.

> First – to each living thing, whate'er its kind
> Some lot, some part, some station is assign'd
> The feather'd race with pinions skim the *air* –
> Not so the mackerel, and still less the bear.[64]

As has been mentioned already, Knight was returned as Member for Leominster in 1780. He was never active in debate and did not seek 'the senate's loud applause'[65] but was firmly attached to Fox, against whom there was such feeling in Leominster that Knight was returned in 1784 as Member for Ludlow instead – this borough being in the pocket of his neighbour, Lord Clive (later Earl of Powis) of Oakly Park. He retained this seat until 1806 when he began to feel parliamentary duties to be 'injurious to his Health and incompatible with the prosecution of other studies'[66] and it was required by the patron's son. Fox died in the same year and Knight closed his parliamentary career with a monody in honour of his friend. At the end of the *Progress of Civil Society* Knight gloomily contemplated the possibility of emigrating to America where political freedom would perhaps survive but where the landscape was less likely to console him than the woods of Herefordshire – 'No Muses drink at Appalachian springs'.[67] Ten years later things were no better. Britain has 'despis'd' Fox's 'warning voice' and 'madly hurl'd / In Slavery's yawning gulf a frantic world'.[68] Meanwhile, if not too preoccupied by the 'doleful clink' of slavery's chains, we could join Knight in envisaging Fox greeted by Timoleon, Washington and Epaminondas in the 'eternal mansions of the blest'. That is hyperbole, but the poem also includes a sincere profession of faith in an 'Almighty Universal Soul'.[69]

Knight remained friends with some Tories. He was, for instance, a close friend of the Marquis of Abercorn and a frequent guest at the Priory, Stanmore. He also formed important new friendships with two protégés of Pitt — Charles Long (later Lord Farnborough) and the much younger George Hamilton Gordon, fourth Earl of Aberdeen, who later married one of Lord Abercorn's daughters. Uvedale Price, although even closer to Fox than Knight, was a more conciliatory character and provided Sir George and Lady Beaumont with a jocular account in 1798 of the solemn cutting off of Knight's pig-tail by Lady Oxford, who was, he warned them, in favour of cutting off all their friends' heads.[70] Price seems to have feared that Knight might be excommunicated, and there must have been tensions.[71] Nevertheless, in 1799 he managed to get Beaumont and Knight and Fox to write criticisms of plays together[72] and Knight was a welcome guest of the Beaumonts at Benarth, near Conway, in 1800[73] and evidently remained a good friend.

The friendship and esteem of Beaumont and Long accounts for Knight's appointment in 1802 to the 'Committee of Taste' convened, with Long as Chairman, to superintend the national monuments in St Paul's Cathedral[74] — a government appointment which may seem surprising in view of Knight's attachment to the Opposition. In 1805, and again together with Long, Knight was one of the founders of the British Institution and was elected a governor, one of the committee of managers and a director.[75] In the same year his *Analytical Inquiry into the Principles of Taste* was published. It was a great success, passing rapidly through three editions, and was even praised (although also blamed) by the *British Critic*.[76]

Some of the material in this book — both general reflections on the sublime and particular prejudices and enthusiasms (against Michelangelo and for Salvator Rosa, for instance) — may be found in notes Knight had made thirty years before when he was planning a treatise on the human mind.[77] The immediate pretext for the work, however, was Knight's desire to convince his friend Samuel Parr of the inadequate aesthetics of Price.[78] Knight is indeed most brilliant when least positive, gaining impetus from the investigation — and, invariably, the ridicule — of the errors or inconsistencies into which other authors, most of whom he professed to esteem, had stumbled. Price and Burke were the chief victims but there are many others. The argument, although sustained, moves at an unexpected pace, and we tend to forget it on account of the examples — always entertaining, often startling and once or twice in dubious taste — with which it is illustrated. If a man supposes that it is the form alone of a female breast that he admires, let him consider his reaction to a plum pudding cast in a mould taken from such a breast.[79] If astonishment and terror are invariably causes of sublimity, then would the spectacle of Burke, without his breeches and bearing a loaded blunderbuss, be sublime?[80] The incidental literary criticism in the book is invariably pointed, as we would expect from the brief observations on Pope in the preface to the *Progress of Civil Society* and contributed greatly to its success. Knight's admiration for Shakespeare and Homer – also Fielding – was, it seems, unqualified, but he had reservations, which he expressed as provocatively as he could, concerning Virgil and Milton. For the benefit of the indiscriminate admirers of the latter, he printed a slab of *Paradise Lost* as prose.[81]

'The Abbé Winckleman', Knight declared coolly in his *Analytical Essay*, had 'no knowledge of coins.' Here, in the *Inquiry*, he announces that Wincklemann 'understood nothing of the Greek language'.[82] If Knight could make such assertions in print, it is not hard to hear him declaring at a dinner given by the Duke of Sutherland in 1806 that Lord Elgin had 'lost his labour' in bringing to England the sculptures of the Parthenon.[83] The first batch of these had arrived and Knight, although he had not seen them, was reported to have declared them to be 'of the time of Adrian'. After viewing the frieze, he found the 'principal fragments' to be 'interesting'. He was eventually prepared to praise them more, but he never acknowledged the superlative quality of the sculpture – unless we credit the story that he visited the British Museum shortly before his death in Elgin's company and confessed his error.[84] One problem was probably Elgin himself, who was not liked by Knight's circle. Things might have been very different had Knight succeeded in negotiating the purchase of Elgin's coins.[85] The other problem was Knight's stubborn and dictatorial public manner. Friends lamely claimed that he could sometimes be more flexible in private.[86]

In the evidence he gave to the Select Parliamentary Committee established to look into the question of the British Museum acquiring the marbles, Knight's voice was solitary in its lack of enthusiasm (although it is clear that both Lord Aberdeen and Wilkins were reluctantly enthusiastic).[87] Against him were ranged all the leading British artists of the day – including Flaxman, Lawrence and West – and Canova and Visconti, the leading sculptor and the leading antiquarian in Europe. Knight was not only abused in a personal attack in *The Examiner* signed by the fanatical Haydon but 'slashed' anonymously by Croker in the Tory *Quarterly Review* in 1816.[88] In the same year he was ridiculed as 'Sooton' in Smirke's anonymous satire on the British Institution.[89] In the spring of 1818 he was passed over for the honorary post of Professor of Ancient Literature at the Royal Academy in preference for the Bishop of London.[90] The Prince Regent would in any case not have favoured him for this post, for Knight was a supporter of Princess Caroline and was the author of an astonishing attack on the Regent's meretricious taste in the *Edinburgh Review*.[91]

Knight did not, however, lose his influential friends, although most of them thought him wrong over the Elgin marbles, and he continued to occupy privileged positions. He was, for instance, with Beaumont and Long, a member of the 'committee for National Monuments' (essentially the old Committee of Taste) given the task in 1816 of deciding on a war memorial,[92] and Lord Aberdeen who had, with Knight's assistance, captured the presidency of the Society of Antiquaries in 1812, appointed Knight Vice-President in 1819.[93] Knight had, however, certainly lost the reputation that he had once enjoyed, and even today most people who have heard of him know him only as the 'expert' who failed to appreciate the work of Phidias.

Knight was not humbled by the reaction to his views on Elgin's marbles. He promptly published a spirited pamphlet replying to the attack in the *Quarterly*.[94] Thereafter, however, his chief concerns were too learned to be controversial. In 1818 he published his *Inquiry into the Symbolical Language of Ancient Art and Mythology*, which was intended as the preliminary essay in the delayed second volume of *Specimens of Antient Sculpture*. Here, as in his earlier essay on Priapus, we are entertained with comparisons between native Americans and ancient Scandinavians, the English Maypole dance and the phallic ceremonies of the Hindus, the gestures made by erotic bronze figures found at Herculaneum and made by contemporary Italians,[95] but much of the analysis of ancient mythology reminds us of the sterile labours of Casaubon in George Eliot's *Middlemarch*. The destruction of Bryant's naive theories comes as an

PLATE 7
? John Opie, *Thomas Andrew Knight* (cat. no. 190)

enjoyable parenthesis, however, and in the final pages Knight has some provocative reflections on the inadvertent contribution likely to be made by Christian conversion to the overthrow of British rule in India.[96] He also continued to work on Homer.

After 1812, when he visited Scotland, Knight seems to have devoted fewer of the summer months to touring Britain. But he never tired of Herefordshire. In 1808, two years after he had ceased to sit as Member for Ludlow, he gave up Downton Castle to his brother (Plate 7) who, after his marriage in 1791, had lived at Elton Hall. Thomas Andrew Knight now had four children and was in any case more in the country than his brother who, however, was still involved in managing the estate, at least in September and October, his 'months of business' at Downton.[97] Payne Knight continued to entertain occasionally at the Castle, but when alone he lived in a much more modest dwelling — Stonebrook Cottage, which had formerly been let at a mere two shillings per annum.[98] It had only one living-room, which was hung with green baize. 'I want nothing but a long beard, a skull and a rosary to be a complete Hermit', he wrote.[99] His friends could appreciate the charm of the little dell in which it was set, but found it depressingly damp and gloomy in bad weather and marvelled at his capacity to endure such solitude.[100] But Knight declared himself happy to remain alone for weeks 'wandering thro' my romantic woods, planning and executing Improvements every morning, and enjoying my old books in undisturbed tranquility every evening'. He pitied the 'grumbling Englishmen' who slept or dined or 'toiled through Turnip Fields and Stubble in pursuit of partridges' whilst he enjoyed the landscape. Although he thought that his respectable neighbours considered him mad,[101] we know that he enjoyed walking and pointing out natural beauties to the daughters of Sir George and Lady Cornewall of Moccas.[102] In London they sang at his musical evenings.[103]

His interest in these girls was of course avuncular. In giving up the Castle he had renounced any idea of marriage and 'love', he explained to Lord Aberdeen, 'such as poets and novel-writers have imagined and described never frequented any cottages but those ideal ones of their building. At least my experience, which has been very long and extensive, never found any in them, but of a sort which was to be bought ready made. Of this last I get enough to keep my thoughts at Home, (and a little now sufficing) in a very secret and comfortable way — not of course without some suspicions, but without any glaring scandal.'[104] Of earlier unmercenary attachments we know little, but a mistress was reported as dying of consumption in November 1794.[105] And in the summer of 1801 he was described as 'philandering Lady Oxford down the Wye'.[106]

The fifth Earl of Oxford, who inherited in 1790 had married his beautiful Countess four years later. Among his property was a string of farms stretching from Eywood, his seat, to the neighbourhood of Downton and including the picturesque ruins of Wigmore Castle. In 1797 Knight exchanged land with him to a considerable value[107] and he clearly knew the couple well. It was Lady Oxford who cut off his pig-tail in 1798. In

1800 Lady Holland observed how Knight, whose former favourite had been Lady Hamilton, greatly admired Lady Oxford, and in March 1801 when Lady Oxford stayed at Holland House she claimed that Knight had 'to use a vulgar phrase . . . corrupted her mind by filling her head with inumerable vain conceits, and teaching her to exclaim against institutions, especially that of marriage, to which she says she has been a helpless victim'.[108] She was, however, 'the prey' of Sir Francis Burdett. Their liaison was notorious as early as 1798. She was later connected with the Marquess of Douglas and Lord Byron, among others, and her children were named the 'Harleian miscellany' on account of their doubtful paternity.[109]

Of Knight's domestic arrangements in London in later life we know little. And nothing whatever of the 'Caroline Elizabeth Gregory commonly called Ford of 44 Wells Street Oxford Road' who received a generous pension of £3 per week in his will – 'a reward for the affectionate kindness and sincerity with which she has always behaved toward me'.[110]

The late summer and autumn of 1817 were spent by Knight removing iron forges and a furnace, and converting a canal connected with them into a pool fed by the river supplying 'a small but very beautiful waterfall'.[111] Six years later he was converting the site of a forge into cottage gardens.[112] Industry, however, had not retreated from the area. His family were involved in the Clee Hill mines – in fact in 1821 Knight, together with his niece's husband W. E. Rouse Boughton, Lord Powis and Thomas Botfield were the chief proprietors.[113] In 1809 he reported that the colliers were agitated because 'holy bretheren' (non-conformist ministers, I suppose) had convinced them that the 'bad Harvest and consequent Dangers of Famine were entirely owing to the profligacy of certain branches of the royal Family and the wickedness of Government in protecting them'.[114] Ten years later as a magistrate he organized a charge of cavalry against the colliers 'which they sustain'd most sturdily with their pike axes and iron crows; but after many hard blows and cuts were overpowered, their leaders taken and transported, without any loss of life' – the operation was, he considered, far more worthy than that of the 'drunken Boobies of Manchester' who acted (in the 'Peterloo Massacre') with 'silly and lawless precipitation' against a larger, but less formidable, mob.[115]

As an historian, Knight was much preoccupied by the slave rebellions of ancient Rome, and he realized that the concentration of the labouring poor in manufacturing towns was liable to give 'a dreadful momentum to popular commotion' and perhaps 'replunge Europe into Barbarism'.[116] But he was equally alert to the consequences of depending for the preservation of order upon an army.[117] Now at the age of 70, after his successful 'campaigne' against the colliers, he was horrified by the Government's proposal to enlarge the army to deal with civil emergencies, for all recruits whether veterans or novices

must alike come from the lowest class of the redundant population of the Manufacturing Districts . . . as Ingredients of a Mob they are utterly contemptible, but as those of an army they will be dreadfully formidable indeed . . . I have never felt any serious alarm from internal commotion, except during the Revolt of the Fleet, till now, but if the measure announced by [*sic*] carried into effect, I shall feel it prudent, in common with many others, to convert some of my capital into foreign stock.[118]

On 2 November 1819, when he wrote this, Knight noted that he was still in good health but liable to a 'chronical cough'. His way of life in the country seems to have been little changed. It was his habit to go about his woods with a saw at the end of a long pole for pruning and, in September 1821, a bough that he had sawed off dropped on the nape of his neck.[119] A gigantic carbuncle swelled up there – the 'village aesculapius thought the brain and spine effected' – and he passed a night in delirium prior to the discharge.[120] However he made an astonishing recovery and was soon walking five miles a day and capable of eating almost a whole goose at a single sitting.[121]

In 1823 his long poem *Alfred*, a 'Romance in Rhyme', was published. It is not good, but it shows him to have been capable of a brisk narrative style as well as a pointed polemical one in poetry. In the conclusion he surveys modern Europe, refers to the massacre at Chios, to the Slave Trade, to the recent war with the 'little despot' Napoleon[122] – the most contemptible, he explained in the preface, of all the personages who have 'successively disturbed, dazzled and desolated mankind'.[123] The preface also includes a defence of *Cain* by Lord Byron, 'a noble poet' who 'has squandered more talent than most others ever possessed' and some reflections on the various forms Christianity has taken over the centuries. Knight considered it extraordinary to believe in a god who creates 'millions upon millions of his creatures' only to damn them to eternal torture, and thought that Providence had given 'what, well employ'd, may lead alike to heaven' to 'Pagans, Mussulmen and Jews' as well as to Christians.[124]

In the early months of this year he was at Downton in very bad shape but in March he was back in London planning to add to his edition of Homer yet dreading that he might become incapable of intellectual exertion and be good for nothing but playing cards and reading novels.[125] In a short note of 26 July he described 'long life' as 'long death, the greatest of all miseries'.[126] In November he was 'full of blue pills and blue (not to say black) devils'.[127] From this he was released on 23 April 1824 by 'an apoplectic affection' according to the *Gentleman's Magazine*,[128] by means of prussic acid according to Rogers.[129] He was buried at Wormsley on 11 May beneath a large but simple tombchest with a fine Latin epitaph. In accordance with his will £300 was distributed to the poor of the parishes of Downton, Burrington, Aston, Elton, Leinthall Starkes and the northern division of Leintwardine.

Thomas Andrew Knight, who in no way resented the bequest of his brother's collection, valued at the lowest estimate at £30,000, to the British Museum, inherited the estates and his brother's personal wealth which principally consisted of the pictures, wine and 'money lent by him at interest to a partner of a country Bank which failed soon after his death'.[130] Thomas Andrew Knight's only son, also named Thomas Andrew, was accidentally killed by a friend with whom he was shooting pheasants in the woods at Downton on 29 November 1827. Pious obituaries claimed that he had inherited the tastes and interests of his uncle[131] but his amusing letters from Eton show that he thought of his uncle as a source of pocket money[132] and in a letter written from Paris to one of his sisters in 1820 he is impatient with a companion for spending so long looking at pictures.[133] He was, however, an intrepid traveller in the arctic regions. After his death his father wrote that he had no wish to live, or at least did so 'only from the horror I felt at leaving my unhappy family in the jaws of the Court of Chancery'.[134] The problem was that Knight had written his will unassisted by a lawyer. Now the grandson of Edward Knight ironmaster of Wolverley (third son of Richard Knight, founder of the family's fortunes), John Knight of Lea Castle, Cookley in Worcestershire, then living at Lynton in Devon and attempting to reclaim Exmoor, claimed that the estates should be his.[135] These two branches of the family seem to have quarrelled half a century earlier.[136]

Thomas Andrew Knight died in 1838 and only two years later judgement was given in favour of his family and the estates secure in the possession of his daughter Charlotte's husband Sir William Edward Rouse Boughton.[137] His chief residence remained Downton Hall in Shropshire, half-a-dozen miles to the east of Downton Castle, but he added at least one tower and made other alterations to the castle.[138] On his death the castle passed to his second son Andrew Johnes Rouse Boughton (who added the name of Knight by Royal licence in 1856). He took his wife to Downton Castle in 1858. A new parish church was built at his expense and opened in April 1862 – terminating an avenue from the house – and he also established a new parochial school.[139] In the following decade further alterations were made to the castle. A domestic chapel was added, also a ball-room, a nursery, and increased accommodation for servants. Boughton Knight, however, lived long enough to see the family prosperity decline and on 30 April 1909 he wrote to the National Gallery with the suggestion that they might be interested in two pictures in the house.[140] It is, however, only in the last decades that the paintings have been dispersed and it was only a few years ago, when work was starting on this exhibition, that the house was sold out of the family.

CHAPTER TWO—*The 'Expedition into Sicily'*

Throughout his life Richard Payne Knight was an insatiable reader. Although his schooling had begun at a comparatively late age, he was soon steeped in the classics, as can be gathered from the extensive references to Homer, Theocritus, Euripides, Strabo and Virgil in the journal he wrote of an 'Expedition into Sicily' in 1777.[1] At the same date and partly inspired by his reading, he also developed a predilection for poetic landscape which manifested itself in his special liking for Claude, and became a decisive factor in the creation of Downton Castle. His journey to Sicily itself may be seen as a search for the original setting of Greek pastoral poetry: idyllically fertile plains, streams rippling through flowery meadows, caressed by mild breezes and bounded by shadowy groves.

Sicily had, of course, more 'sublime' attractions: the fascinating and dangerous heights of Mount Etna, news of whose eruptions had alarmed Europe since 1693, or the legendary eddy of Scylla and Charybdis near Messina. But the possibility of plague, plundering banditti, a hostile climate[2] and primitive transport made travelling on the island a rare occurrence. And accounts by those who had visited the island earlier in the century – among them John Dryden (the poet's son), d'Orville and Brydone[3] – did nothing to establish it on the itinerary of English Grand Tourists. But the outlook had changed radically since the 1750s. With Winckelmann's friend, Baron von Riedesel,[4] and Sir William Hamilton,[5] a new generation of travellers had made their appearance, enterprising and fired by a passion for scientific exploration and archaeological investigation, inspired by the pioneering example of Stuart and Revett's survey of the remains of Greek architecture in Athens.[6]

It was in the wake of this movement that the remains of Greek civilisation in southern Italy were to become famous in the following decades. Knight, however, anticipated most of the promoters of the 'gusto greco', and travelled to Sicily at a time when Henry Swinburne could still write that although 'Our earliest education has made us acquainted with those classic regions; Poetry and History have rendered their topography familiar to us', the English public knew little of their present condition save through 'the inaccurate work of Mr Brydone'.[7] Knight was surely as aware of this opportunity for scholarly distinction as he was attracted by arcadian visions or the prospect of adventure.

The reader may expect to find an explanation for Knight's intentions in his account of the journey, a handwritten diary, 120 pages long, preserved in the Goethe–Schiller-Archiv in Weimar. Turning the pages, densely covered by an immaculate calligraphic hand,[8] he will be impressed by the author's accuracy of observation, his readiness to voice an opinion on social matters, his ironic humour and display of literary and historical knowledge, but he will not discover a statement of the traveller's motives. The manuscript does, in fact, pose more questions than it answers. We cannot be sure whose hand it is written in, or when or where it was made. It was partly translated and published by Goethe in 1810 and since then has been thought of as lost.[9] Its rediscovery in 1980 has led to a re-examination of the circumstances of its creation, its subsequent history and its relationship with the thirty-nine drawings apparently illustrating it to be found in Knight's Bequest to the British Museum.[10] Most of these are watercolours made by Knight's travelling companions Charles Gore and Jakob Philipp Hackert, the rest copies after their sketches commissioned after the journey from John Robert Cozens and Thomas Hearne.

Knight left England in the late summer of 1776 for a second visit to the Continent. He was almost certainly accompanied by Cozens, with the help of whose sketches we can follow their route via Switzerland (cat. nos. 129–32) to Italy.

On the 24 November – after their arrival in Rome – Knight wrote a long letter, to the painter George Romney. After a dissertation 'upon the different modes of interesting the passions in painting' he explained that he had found 'the subject so difficult, and the passions so involved with other faculties of the mind, that I almost despair of being able to reduce them to any certain rules'. And he concluded: 'It is now some years since I have quitted these kind of speculations, and devoted the little time I give to study, to history and morality, sciences that are more likely to be useful to me.'[11] This is the only hint of Knight's motive for the journey: it was perhaps intended to be an exercise in these empirical 'sciences', history and morality, that is, an investiation of ancient remains and of modern manners.

The young traveller could hardly have chosen better partners for the venture than the fashionable German landscape painter Jakob Philipp Hackert[12] and his amateur pupil, the wealthy English marine architect and collector Charles Gore,[13] both of whom had settled in Rome before Knight's arrival. The two men shared a passion for travelling and topographical representation, were interested in contemporary archaeological investigation and saw to it that their scholarly and artistic endeavours were also, wherever possible, financially rewarding.

As will become clear, the relationship between the drawings by Hackert and Gore with Knight's text is close and evidently calculated. The travellers may have been friends, but their relationship was also certainly business-like and the trip was most unlikely to have been a spontaneous adventure but was probably planned well in advance – a point to which we will return. Their eventual purpose was surely to publish a learned account of the island, fully and attractively 'documented' visually, which would both make a profit and establish their reputations as scholars.

The journey began on 12 April 1777, when the party left Naples on board ship 'with an intention of making the turn of Sicily and visiting

Paestum and the Lipari Islands on our way'.[14]

> As soon as one is out of the Port of Naples, the most magnificent scene opens itself on every side. The city rising gradually from the shore, Mount Vesuvius smoking on one side, with Sorrento, Capri, Ischia, and Procida extending round to Cape Miseno in the form of an Amphitheatre, enriched with Palaces, Gardens, Woods and Ruins, are such an assemblage of objects, as are no where else to be seen. We enjoyed it in the utmost perfection, as the weather was extremely fine and the Spring in its bloom. The infinite variety of tints were all harmonized together by that pearly hue, which is peculiar to this delicious climate.[15]

After leaving the Bay of Naples the companions sailed southwards along the coast to Paestum, an obvious intermediate station on their way to similar Doric edifices in Sicily. Knight continues his account with a detailed description of the structure, style and history of the massive temples and strikes an unexpectedly progressive note in his concise assessment of the buildings: 'When one examines the Parts near, they appear rude, massive and heavy; but seen at a proper distance, the general effect is grand, simple and even elegant.'[16] Few of his contemporaries could appreciate Doric architecture so spontaneously. Lord North of Wroxton writing to his tutor Charles Dampier described the massive columns as 'short, clumsy & ill-shaped' and thought that 'they resemble in shape pretty much those props, on which our peasants in England sometimes put their corn, to prevent being eaten by vermin', and Goethe in 1787 could still consider these 'obtuse, dull cramped masses of columns' to be 'cumbersone and even terrifying'.[17] Knight is at once the aesthete and the archaeologist. His analytical turn of mind is evident even in his descriptions, as in the account just quoted of the bay of Naples to which he added a marginal note comparing the 'pearly hue' to the 'coloring' of Claude.

PLATE 8
Charles Gore, *The Lipari Islands from the North* (cat. no. 98)

From Paestum the party sailed further south during the night and landed at Porto Palinuro where they were detained 'eight days by bad weather and the Cowardice of Neapolitan seamen, and repented much of having

left Paestum, where we could have passed our time so agreeably among the Ruins'.[18] It was not until 22 April that they finally set sail and reached the Lipari Islands, a small archipelago north of Sicily, the following evening. On approaching Stromboli, the only active volcano of the group, Charles Gore made a number of sketches from consecutively closer viewpoints, two of which Knight kept later in his collection, as illustrations to his diary. The one exhibited here (Plate 8) is carefully inscribed and dated: 'L'isles de Stromboli, Panaria, La Saline: prise de cote de Nord douze Miles de distance en voyant la Stromboletta. 1777.' Gore depicts the cool, transparent beauty of the scene — the volcano emerging slowly from the evening haze over the sea — with a sensitive understatement characteristic of the cautious precision of topographical artists. Knight's written account — elucidated by Gore's illustrations — is dominated by his disappointment at being prevented from disembarking and examining the crater by a quarantine imposed by the King of Naples, 'a ceremony which we had no inclination to go thro'.

After spending a day on the neighbouring island of Lipari, the party set sail for Milazzo, on the north-east promontory of Sicily and arrived there on 25 April. From there the expedition had to be continued on horseback 'with a Mulateer recommended to us by the Governor'.[19] 'We pursued our journey along the Shore, and sometimes among the Mountains. Thro' the worst roads I ever travelled, but the richness & beauty of the Country made ample amends for every inconvenience of this kind.'[20] Their route was along the north coast via Tindaro, Patti, Aqua dolce and Cefalù where only scattered remains of the Greek settlements, familiar from classical literature, were accessible. But excitement was provided by their first encounter with the local population.

The inhabitants of Patti took them for spies when they were drawing the surroundings of the village. They had to appear before the magistrate 'who dignified himself with the title of Governor' and were charged with

> having drawn a small watch-tower . . . which he call'd a fortress . . . Mr. Hackert, the principal offender, went & found the Magistrate surrounded by Lawyers who had composed an Indictment of several sheets of Paper. He told them that we were only dilettanti, who travelled only for amusement, & that, had he known of any fortress, he certainly should not have ventured to draw without permission; but he was so far from thinking the tower in question one, that he had taken it for a Building to bake Earthen Pots . . . The Magistrate was extremely dissatisfied with this answer, and the Lawyers all pronouncing it impossible that we should have come so far without some very important designs, were unanimous for detaining us, when Mr. Hackert took some Letters from his Pocket, which he desired them to read. These being recommendations to the Vice-roy . . . threw the whole process into confusion, & he was dismissed with a number of apologies . . .'[21]

The incident testifies not only to Hackert's influence with the Neapolitan court[22] — the depiction of Sicilian territory was, for strategical reasons, strictly forbidden, unless by the King's special permission[23] — but it also gives the first indication of Knight's low opinion of the education and

manners of the Sicilians. At Palermo, where they arrived on 1 May, Knight noted the 'excellent conveniency for pleasure and debauchery' which the Festa offered – these 'it may be imagined . . . are not neglected by People so lively as the Sicilians'.[24] On the other hand 'objects of curiosity' there were 'not very numerous'.[25] Dismissing the Byzantine mosaics of the Capella Palatina as 'barbarous' and the late-baroque eccentricities of the Prince of Palagonia's palace as of 'absurd taste',[26] and having admired the Greek bronze rams the party proceeded southwards.

Two days later they finally arrived at one of the magnificent Greek temples, at Segesta – a sight anticipated since the beginning of the journey. 'On approaching one is struck with a view of a noble temple, which stands alone upon a small Hill surrounded by high Mountains . . .'[27] and again Knight continues with a detailed description of the building's structure, style, proportions, material and state of preservation, the archaeological accuracy of which is matched by Hackert's illustration (cat. no. 99), where the temple is seen obliquely, so that front and side views are equally well documented; its position on the hill is indicated by the low viewpoint and its height defined by several figures who are seen examining the edifice. Even details like the corrosion of the stone and damage to the pediment are carefully recorded. The same organized and methodical approach is apparent in the documentation of the ruins of Selinus, on the south coast of Sicily, where they arrived on 6 May.

It soon became evident that archaeological stock-taking would be incomparably more complicated there than at Segesta. The site consisted of the remains of six massive temples 'all prostrate upon the ground',[28] and furthermore divided into two groups of three with about one mile distance between the sites. This diffusion of the ruins made it impossible for Hackert and Gore to depict the site as a whole and the illustrations consequently show different parts of the area from various angles and numerous details (Plate 9) – and the difficulties of recording the vast site are no less apparent in Knight's descriptions and reconstructions. An extract from his account of the 'Temple of Jupiter Forensis' (Temple G), 'the largest and most northern one'[29] has to suffice as an example of his style:

> The stupendous Ruins of it, which still cover a great share of ground, prove it to have been one of the most magnificent Edifices ever built. It had eight columns in front and seventeen deep, each ten feet diam! at base & six at the Capital, & about fifty feet high. Each round is a single Stone of which there are seldom more than eight in a Column, & in many less. The Capitals are like those of the great Temple or Basilica at Paestum & the Columns diminished regularly from bottom to top. The Abacus is twelve feet, ten Inches square, & the trigliffs four feet long and every other number of the entablature in proportion. The intercolumnation was a little more than a diameter . . .[30]

Looking at Charles Gore's illustration of this scene (cat. no. 103), we are reminded that this information is pieced together painstakingly from measurements taken from the scattered ruins.

In his account of the history of Selinus Knight ponders on the city's destruction by Hannibal:

> Thus fell Selinus about 240 years after its foundation, a memorable monument of the vanity & greatness of human Genius & Industry. Perhaps of all buildings that have ever been erected in the World, the great Temple of Selinus [was] (next to the Pyramids of Egypt) the best calculated for duration; but by the destructive Ambition of a neighboring State, it was thrown down almost at the moment of being finished. Even this Calamity could not totally destroy it, for its ruins still remain a testimony of its greatness, when those of Carthage have long since perished.[31]

Here, as so often in the diary, Knight's archaeological and historical investigations have enhanced the already sublime appearance which is well recorded in the watercolours.

The next station on the journey – Agrigento – was the last major archaeological site they visited. Unlike Segesta and Selinus this city was still inhabited and Knight seized the opportunity to investigate the survival of ancient customs in contemporary life – every aspect of which, from burial rites to the sewage system, underwent a close scrutiny. Detailed records of 'some remains of about fourteen Temples, all of the old Doric order, with great numbers of Sepulchral Grotto's, Magazines for Grain, hollowed in the Rock etc . . .' were, of course, also made. Among them the 'Temple of Juno' whose 'present appearance . . . is the most pictoresque that can be imagined',[32] the Temples of 'Concord', Jupiter Olympus and a 'small pyramidal Building said to be the Tomb of Hiero'[33] (cat. nos. 104–8).

In Agrigento the contrast between the remains of ancient splendour and contemporary poverty was accentuated by their immediate juxtaposition, and in his historical analysis Knight gives a detailed account of the downfall of the city. The Agrigentines, of whom 'Empedocles used to say, that they ate and drank as if they were to die tomorrow, and built as if they were to live for ever',[34] became the envy and consequently the victims of Carthaginian and Roman leaders alternatively, and their 'luxury and refinement soon proved their destruction'.[35] The present state of Agrigento and other poverty-stricken areas in Sicily, however, had to be blamed on their ruthless exploitation by the representatives of the Church: 'Bigotry and oppression and a false system of political economy have done more in laying waste Sicily, than the worst effects of War & tumult could have produced . . .', Knight argued, and he found more evidence for these allegations on his way along the south coast 'which once maintained so many flourishing Cities in all the elegances and luxuries of life, [and] can scarcely now produce necessaries for its miserable Inhabitants'.[36]

They reached Syracuse on 20 May. Knight had regained his ironic humour by then: after their arrival 'we went immediately to view the fountain of Arethusa, which still flows in abundance, but the prayer of Virgil (Sic tibi, cum fluctus subterlabere Siranos / Doris amara suam non intermisceat undam) has not prevailed, for since the Earth-quake of 1693

PLATE 10
Jakob Philipp Hackert,
The 'Ear of Dionysius' (cat.
no. 109)

it has been brakish, & only served for a Wash-pool. We found it frequented by Nymphs somewhat different from those described by Theocritus and Virgil, — no other than a company of the most dirty old washer-women I ever beheld.'[37] Other antiquities in Syracuse he found hardly more inspiring, but not far from the remains of the Greek theatre was the entrance to the 'Latomiae of Epipola . . . anciently the Public Prisons . . . They are immense quarries of Stone, sunk to a great depth & in some places hollowed into immense vaults . . . Many of these have given way and enormous Masses have faln down, which being cover'd with Shrubs and herbage form the most wild and beautiful Scene that can be imagined.'[38]

He was most fascinated by a cave called the 'Ear of Dionysius', the strong echo of which was said to have been created artificially by the tyrant Dionysius in order to overhear the secrets of his prisoners deep inside (Plate 10). 'These tremendous Palaces of Vengeance, on[c]e the Receptacles of crimes and misery . . . the gloomy Caves, where so many Wretches have linger'd away their Lives in horror and despair, now form the most pleasing and romantic retreats . . .'[39] After a visit to the two mutilated Doric Columns, which were . . . 'with some subterraneous Aquaducts and Sepulchral Grotto's . . . all the remains of the mighty City of Syracuse, once so exquisitely beautiful, that e'en Marcellus in the Career of his Conquests, could not help bursting into tears and cursing the fatal lust of Empire, that obliged him to ruin the Glory and envy of the Universe . . .',[40] the party proceeded to Catania, from where they were to set out for the top of Mount Etna on 27 May.

After a visit to the collections of the Prince of Biscari — the only Sicilian landowner, indeed the only single person in Sicily, of whom Knight seems to have approved, and who was widely acknowledged as a solitary representative of the Enlightenment in southern Italy — they began the ascent to the village of Nicolosi, half way up the volcano. From there they continued their journey 'attended by a Peasant of the Village call'd Blasio, who usually serves as a Guide to those, who visit the Mountain . . .'.[41] Knight included an amusing illustration of their departure in his collection (Colour Plate I), showing the small party, Hackert, Gore and himself, their mules urged along by the muleteer while the guide leads on in front. They proceeded leisurely through the lower regions of the mountain until '. . . the ascent become very steep, and the change of climate very perceptible'. Whilst in Catania 'they were in the midst of the Corn harvest, at Nicolosi every thing was in the bloom of may, but when we came near the Grotta del Capro, the trees were just putting their leaves and the Air felt extremely cold & piercing. We kindled a fire in this little Cave and reposed ourselves till midnight, and then proceeded towards the Summet, thro' bare Cinders and fragments of Lava.'[42]

It is this moonlit encampment that is hauntingly illustrated in a watercolour by J. R. Cozens (Plate 11). The sublime bareness of the landscape and towering presence of Mount Etna are emphazised and the small figures huddled around the fire. The scene certainly strikes a different chord to those of their archaeological investigations. Forced to complete

the last stretch of the ascent on foot, they arrived at the edge of the crater 'after climbing about two hours with infinite labor and difficulty'[43] and the awe-inspiring impression of the scenery can be felt vividly through the measured prose of Knight's diary:

The View, that here presents itself, is beyond all description or Imagination. The whole Island of Sicily, Malta, Calabria, & the Liparis appear just under one as in a map. The parts were all obscured in the blue tint of the morning and the whole together seemed wrapt in Silence and repose. I felt myself elevated above humanity, & looked down with Contempt upon the mighty objects of Ambition under me. The Scenes where so many mighty Cities have florished in Art and Arms, where so many numerous fleets and Armies have fought for universal Empire, seemed no more than a spot, 'E luí, ch'or Ocean chiamat'è, or Vasto, / nulla equale a tai nomi ha in sé dí magno / ma è bassa palude, e breve Stagno' Tasso.[44]

Having regained his equilibrium Knight resolved to look into the crater despite the warnings of their guide, who, however, after a little persuasion and a number of prayers to St. Agatha, . . . led us to a place that had already been tried by some adventrous Stranger. From hence I looked into this tremendous Gulf of fire, and saw immense projecting rocks, with vast volumes of Smoke issuing from between them, mixed with a dim glimmering light. I could distinguish no bottom, but the tossing and beating of the waves of melted matter produced a Noise which gave me some idea of the *floods & whirlwinds of tempestuous fire* that rage beneath . . .[45]

The enthusiasm conveyed by such a Miltonic passage, was, however, not such as to let Knight forget to take measurements and samples.

Having recovered from the physical strain of the ascent — Charles Gore wrote, 'I slept in my bed for two days'[46] — they rented a 'Maltese Speronara' and rounding the foot of Mount Etna, arrived at Taormina to survey the remains of the Greek theatre there on 2 June. The following day they sailed towards Messina and entered the Faro — straits leading to the city's harbour — in the afternoon. It was here that Knight formed his final judgement on the state of the island. 'The view', he wrote, in a passage reminiscent of his introductory description of the Bay of Naples, 'is very beautiful and romantic, the Coasts being high and rocky, adorn'd with Towns and Villages . . . a vast range of houses, all uniform . . . form a noble and magnificent scene . . .', but, he continued, 'upon approaching nearer this fine Scene looses all its Splendour, and every object assumes an Air of melancholy and dejection . . . Every thing seemed to declare the fatal calamities that have lately overwhelmed this unfortunate City, and reduced it from the highest State of Wealth and felicity to the lowest depth of misery and despair'.[47] What exasperated Knight more than the actual catastrophies that had befallen the city was the defeatism of its inhabitants, the 'fatal credulity' of the Sicilians and their 'blind attachment to the Place of Nativity'.[48] He had noted this already in Catania, where the population, when faced with inevitable destruction by streams of lava from an eruption of Mount Etna in 1669,

> instead of making Walls or trenches to avert its fury . . . brought out St. Agatha's Veil, & a whole Legion of Saints, each of whom, the Priests assured them, was sufficient to perform much greater Miracles. The consequence of this was, as usual. — A great part of the City was destroyed, its Port filled up and the Inhabitants ruined; but the Saints remained in greater credit, than ever, the People readily believing, that the Calamity arose from their own want of faith and not from any fault in their heavenly Guardians.[49]

Obviously, the representatives of the Church were to blame for this deplorable gullability and Knight dedicated a lengthy postscript to the diary — which ends here with the traveller's departure from Messina on 6 June — to the analysis of this problem.

'I do not know whether so short a stay in the Island will justify my saying any thing of the general character of its Inhabitants. In most other Countries, it is what I should not venture at, till after long experience and mature observation, but here the features are so strong, that it is difficult to miss a resemblance', runs the introduction, and he resumes that the

Sicilians are 'jealous and passionate . . . averse to labor and prone to pleasure, & superstition . . . hospitable and kind to Strangers, fair and honest in their dealings . . . extremely ignorant & Superstition prevails among them to an incredible degree . . .'[50] The reason for this state of affairs, he states, is the overwhelming influence of the 'Ecclesiasticks', by whom 'all inquiry or improvement of every kind is checked. Men, who gain vast emoluments of the blind belief of a few incomprehensible Mysteries, are naturally very jealous of every thing, that can tend to dissipate the cloud of darkness which protects them. Weak as human reason is, it would be sufficient in its lowest state to penetrate the thin veil of Priestcraft, if People only dared think . . . The Ecclesiasticks in Sicily, as everywhere else, are perfectly sensible of this, & therefore oppose every thing, that can possibly imploy the mind.'[51]

With this declaration the theme is set for the ensuing pages: political, economical, sociological and juridical grievances, the decline of the arts and sciences, even the corruption of language, is put at the charge of the 'sour mythology of the Christians'.[52] Knight concludes with an account of how taste was ruined when the Latin language degenerated: 'To determine how far it is ever likely to return to its ancient purity would lead me into too long a discussion at present, but I am inclined to believe, that nothing less than another general Revolution in Europe could effect it, and that does not seem likely to happen.'[53]

The 'Sicilian project' — of which this manuscript and the surviving illustrations[54] bear witness — could have been planned well in advance if Knight had established contact with Hackert during his first trip to the Continent. They could have met in about 1772 if Knight, who was then in Italy, visited (which seems likely) the English Ambassador in Naples, Sir William Hamilton, who employed Hackert in this period and remained a common acquaintance. If an arrangement concerning a future journey to Sicily had been made then, this would explain Knight's second journey south. He had, after all, taken over the management of a considerable fortune only a few years earlier and was furthermore deeply involved in building activities at Downton.

It has been proposed that Knight planned to take J. R. Cozens to Sicily but quarrelled with him[55] (and thus took Hackert instead), but there is no evidence for this. Neither Hackert's dominant rôle in the organization of the venture,[56] nor the fact that Cozens was afterwards commissioned to work on sketches made by Gore and Hackert during the journey indicate that an argument had taken place. And if, as has been suggested, the journey had been arranged several years earlier with Hackert and Gore, Cozens could well have been employed for the tour through Switzerland only. From the choice of subjects passed on to Cozens for completion after the party's return to Rome in July 1777,[57] it seems indeed likely that Knight was following a special purpose with the distribution of commissions, namely his insistence on archaeologically accurate records of the Sicilian journey. Cozens reworked only some of the most poetic scenes — like the 'Grotta del Capro' (Plate 11) — while the main body of illustrations was entrusted to the strictly factual and archaeologically accurate style of Hackert and Gore.

Although there is no record of when and where the original sketches were worked up into finished watercolours, it seems very likely that they were produced in the period between July 1777 and the spring of 1778 when Hackert and Gore left Rome.[58] Certainly Hackert had finished several views of Sicilian subjects by that winter, when they were admired by the Prince of Sachsen-Gotha in his studio.[59] Inscriptions in his hand on several of Gore's watercolours in Knight's collection also testify to the close co-operation between the two artists at this time. Goethe indeed describes how Gore usually spent the evenings at Hackert's house where foreign artists gathered around a table copied Hackert's studies from nature while an Italian Abbé read aloud and expounded from Tasso and from other Italian poets.[60] Cozens would presumably have joined them, although there is no indication that he was actually taught by Hackert, as has been suggested.[61]

While the written account of the journey would have had to be consulted for the selection of illustrations, it is unlikely that it was rewritten in its present form during this period. For historical details and references to classical literature Knight would have had to make use of his library, as he confirms in the letter to Romney mentioned at the beginning: '. . . you will excuse inaccuracies and remember, that I write as a traveller without books or memorandums'.[62] It must have been after his return to England that Knight wrote the final version of his account and probably also added the concluding part on Sicilian affairs in general. He was still engaged in the project in 1782 – five years after the expedition – when he passed Hackert's and Gore's watercolours on to Thomas Hearne, presumably for further preparation for publication (see cat. no. 106). This seems to be indicated by the artist's unification of motifs, his introduction of picturesque foreground motifs and subdued, almost monochrome colouring which can also be found in Hearne's preparatory watercolours for the engravings in the *Antiquities of Great Britain*.

But this final stage was never reached. There is, in fact, no further evidence of the diary until its publication by Goethe more than thirty years later,[63] when the manuscript had been handed over to him by Charles Gore, who had probably received it as a memorial of their joint venture from Knight, when he went to settle in Weimar in 1792. The watercolours by Hackert, Gore, Hearne and Cozens remained with their owner. On 8 March 1807 Coleridge wrote to Sir George Beaumont that Knight had been 'extremely obliging' and showed them to him . . . 'from which I learnt, what I knew before, that I shall see nothing in Sicily of half the beauty of Cumberland'.[64] At Knight's death they were bequeathed to the British Museum together with his other collections.

But why did Knight abandon the project after such long and intensive preparation? It seems highly unlikely that such carefully prepared material was meant for private circulation only. The best explanation is perhaps the publication of other accounts of Sicily; in particular, in 1781 – at the very date at which they may have been preparing for publication – the Abbé de Saint-Non's lavishly illustrated folios on southern Italy began to appear. There could also have been more personal motives. In the letter to Romney, the young scholar had announced a temporary resignation from his previous inquiries into 'the faculties of the human mind' and proclaimed a change to more empirical objects of investigation, 'history and morality' or archaeology and sociology. This is exactly what he is concerned with in the diary. The first part of the text consists predominantly of archaeological observations and historical reconstructions, and this emphasis is matched by that of the illustrations. In the second, much shorter, part, his interests are sociological and his analysis more polemical than scientific. The result is an odd dichotomy between the two parts (a fact which seems to have prompted Goethe to leave out the second part altogether).[65]

Could the general observations on Sicily have been created as an afterthought when the direct confrontation with the complicated archaeological evidence was past and Hackert's and Gore's exacting presence gone and the author – back in England – had returned to more familiar idioms and topics closer to his heart? There seems to be something almost of relief at the change in the diary and the text – despite the fact, that it touches upon much that was of interest to Knight throughout his career (his scenic descriptions ranging from the beautiful to the sublime, his puristic attitude towards antiquity, his reflections on the rise and fall of civilisation) – is suggestive of someone of wide interests deliberately confining himself. This division of interest is quite characteristic of the travel literature of the eighteenth century – relics of the Catholic Church, natural curiosities, the meaning of obelisks, or the authenticity of Virgil's Tomb, are standard topics of discussion – but Knight cannot have been content with the superficiality that was characteristic of this kind of literature. Consequently there is an uncertainty of direction which is perhaps ultimately unsatisfactory in the diary – but which, nevertheless, makes it particularly fascinating.

CHAPTER THREE—*Architecture and Landscape at Downton*

Richard Payne Knight wrote to Samuel Nash, his agent and maternal uncle, from Calais on 25 September 1772 concerning the new house which he was proposing to build on the property he had recently inherited at Downton. He had meant to send plans from London but confessed that 'when I came to resolve I found so many things necessary to be re-considered, that I was obliged to defer it'. This makes it clear that he was making the plans himself and suggests that he was finding this harder than he had anticipated. Moreover, he was organizing the 'building' as well as the 'architecture' for he discussed the possibility of substituting deal for oak for some purposes. 'Let Pritchard's Bill be paid, but do not tell him that I have no design of imploying him again', he writes, and, after adding instructions concerning the planting of timber, gives an address in Florence.

A reply (but sent to Rome not Florence) tells of the bricks made and the stone being quarried for the house, and another, dated 2 November, reports that 'nothing is don to the found lations of the Hous as the plan is not fix^t upon' and that 'Mr Prich^d, has sent a bill for 10 guineas 'viz a tending 3 times at Downton to fix on a spot for the new byllding, consulting a bout muterriells and making plans'.[1] Pritchard must be Thomas Farnolls Pritchard of Shrewsbury whom Knight's relatives had recently employed at Croft Castle, to whom the Forge Bridge at Downton of 1772 is attributed,[2] and who perhaps also created the Castle Bridge which carried a new and spectacular drive across the Teme to the new house (Plates 12 and 13).

There are bills for bricks made, and for masons' and carpenters' work done at 'the New House at the Stoney Hill' in 1774. In the following year the mason's bills are more specific – the cornice of the Octagon Tower, the ashlar of the Great Tower, the cornice of the latter and a portico are mentioned; also a garden wall, the roofs of the Round and the Octagon tower, the angles of the Square Tower, the ashlar of the north and east fronts. By mid 1776, 32,500 tiles had been raised and dressed.[3] Carpenters' bills continue throughout 1777.[4] An account of the house published in Knight's lifetime says that it was begun in 1774 and inhabited in 1778.[5] This need not mean, however, that it was complete, and on 14 May 1782 Knight wrote from his house in Whitehall to Samual Nash: 'I intend finishing the great room during the course of the summer. I desire that there may be about 120 bushels of lime prepared immediately' for he was intending to be in the country early in June. A note on the letter confirms that this refers to the dining-room.[6] As has been observed elsewhere,

PLATES 12&13
Views of Downton Castle
Above: by James Sheriff
(cat. no. 76)
Below: by Thomas Hearne
(cat. no. 115.ii)

PLATE 14
Downton Castle from the
south-west

Knight began to collect ancient art in 1785. It seems sensible to suppose that he employed for this purpose the portion of his income formerly expended in building the house, decorating its interior, and on planting and clearing around about it. The house was said to have cost £60,000.[7]

The participation of amateurs in this period in the design of country houses was frequent and since Knight claimed that he designed Downton Castle (as it was soon called) and no contemporary denied the fact, there is no need to dispute it now. It is probable that Pritchard's advice concerning the foundations was followed and possible that a hint was taken from his plan, but he could not have been the consultative architect as one scholar has recently proposed. Nor is there any need to be tempted by the same scholar's idea of the young John Nash being involved in the interiors and being perhaps a relative of Samuel Nash, and thus of Knight himself.[8] Camarthen, where it seems Nash's mother was born, is a long way from Ludlow, and Nash is a common name. The James, Thomas and John Nash among the labourers employed by the carpenter John Lewis in work on the Castle[9] may well have been relatives, however. Knight's maternal grandfather had after all been a 'working carpenter'.

Placed within the Square or 'Great' Tower at Downton Castle is the circular dining-room. This room (Plate 16), conceived of in 1772, the year in which James Wyatt's imitation of the Pantheon in Rome was opened to great applause in London, is equally indebted to that great temple's interior. Its dome is of the same type – with five circles of square coffers and a similar interval before the *oculus*, but ornamented with stucco, painted and gilt. There are two types of rosette in the coffering, a double key-pattern between, and a Vitruvian scroll around the *oculus*.

The entablature, which includes an exquisite acanthus frieze, imitating that of the Temple of Venus Genetrix in the Forum of Julius Caesar, is supported by pairs of columns of porphyry scagliola in the four niches. The niches are another feature derived from the Pantheon (although they do not extend to the entablature in the Roman prototype). Each one is occupied by a life-size statue of a maiden made of artificial stone, bronzed, and stamped on the plinth COADE LAMBETH. They are recorded there in 1821[10] with sideboards in front of them and were no doubt placed there in the 1780s when the room was completed. Such statues were exhibited by Mrs Coade at the Society of Artists in 1776, 1777 and 1778 and feature in the catalogues of her artificial stone manufactory in the 1780s and 1790s.[11] One of the four is modelled on an antique statue of a vestal in the French royal collection, the others (e.g. Plate 17) are certainly classical in inspiration, but they are adapted to hold oil-lamps (subsequently replaced by electric fittings which obscure their faces). The walls were of scagliola simulating panels of serpentine set in *giallo antico*, as may be seen in old photographs, but are now painted pale blue with a white dado, to correspond with colours discovered below the scagliola.

As one would expect from an amateur with Knight's interests this room

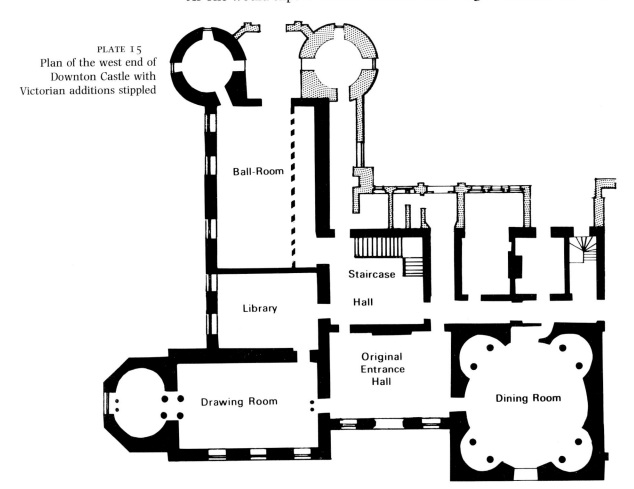

PLATE 15
Plan of the west end of Downton Castle with Victorian additions stippled

Ball-Room

Library

Staircase

Hall

Drawing Room

Original Entrance Hall

Dining Room

is first and foremost an archaeological exercise. It would have been suitable for only the most solemn feasts. A writer in 1802 and another in 1821 recorded an organ opposite the window,[12] and the organ now in the Chapel (and formerly in the Victorian ballroom) was made in 1787 by Samuel Green. However, neither it nor any organ could fit *in* this niche, which consists of looking glass mimicking a sash window and provides a concealed service entrance.

The principal entrance to the house was through a small portico next to the Square Tower. This conducted one into a square hall, with a doric entablature (without architrave) and an imposing chimney-piece. The latter is ornamented with swags pendant from lions' heads and with festoons to either side of the mask of a smiling maenad in ormolu (Plate 18) upon a ground of porphyry veneer, with a white marble cornice (into which Uvedale Price, playing blindman's buff in September 1796 with his

children and those of Lord Abercorn charged headlong with such force that a part of his eyebrow was removed). The ormolu, porphyry and the mouldings are all untypical of English sculpture in this period and the chimney-piece looks as if it was commissioned by Knight in Rome.[13] This room had been converted into a music room when Lord and Lady Northwick and their daughter Anne visited it in 1801, and a new entrance, apparently through a dismal passage, had been contrived to the north.[14] It is not improbable that it had served earlier as a music room *as well* as an entrance hall, an arrangement found at Newby Hall in this period, and the Samuel Green organ was perhaps placed here. Knight, by his own account, obtained 'sensual' and 'sentimental' but not 'intellectual' pleasure from music.[15] In any case he enjoyed it and there are accounts of musical evenings in his London house and of his enthusiasm for Angelica Catalani.[16]

This hall, as it originally was, lead to the staircase hall and also connected the dining-room to the east with the drawing-room to the west. In the drawing-room we find a highly curious chimney-piece in statuary marble (Plate 19) revealing of Knight's scholarship. The flanking columns are of the Greek Doric with the extreme taper and the exquisite collar flutings, which he had admired at Paestum when the house was nearing completion. It is among the first examples of the revival of this order in

PLATE 20
The Drawing-Room,
Downton Castle

modern Europe.[17] And it seems very likely that this chimney-piece also was made in Rome. Between the triglyphs are seven gilt brass medallions of Greek worthies suspended by ribbons and framed by garlands of the same material.

The Octagon Tower at the south-west corner of the house encloses a semi-circular room both on the ground floor and on the first floor. These are connected with the drawing-room and the principal bedroom – a screen with doubled columns framing the opening (Plates 15 and 20). The niches in this screen on the ground floor are the most likely situation for the ancient statues mentioned, in addition to a few pictures, as an ornament of the drawing-room in the account of 1797.[18] The highly restored statues recently in the garden (Plate 34) fit perfectly. The screen columns, of porphyry scagliola, are Corinthian on the ground floor and are echoed by miniature ones, of real porphyry with the capitals and a cornice of statuary marble – an unusual luxury surely acquired in Rome together with the statues and chimney pieces – which frame the doors at east and south of the double room. Upstairs the order is of a curious early form of proto-Corinthian, like that which James Stuart had found in Athens and Robert Adam at Spalato but with four acanthus leaves rising from the lower ring to support the corners of the abacus. Equally erudite and elegant is the frieze in the two rooms on the ground floor, which consists of palmettes placed sideways to create a sort of elaborated, attenuated and accelerated Greek wave. What was surely the most curious item of all upstairs, 'a very rich chintz bed in a recess, ornamented with pillars and pilasters of the Tuscan order, whose bases and capitals are of the most delicate white marble, exquisitely polished',[19] has not survived.

North of the drawing-room is the library, which retains its original mahogany cases, made for the room but by 1802 'too small to contain the books belonging to it'[20] – the fluted mouldings of the cases are continued in the dado. The chimney-piece here has a somewhat miscellaneous composition and is certainly made up of different types of white marble. The entablature, however, with a frieze of palmettes interrupted by a relief tablet of fauns with a horn and a lyre and nymphs with a thyrsus and torch is surely from a chimneypiece commissioned by Knight. The relief looks as if it is copied from a neo-attic source.

To the east of the library and north of the original hall is the staircase hall, which retains its original cornice, and the skylight was restored some years ago. In the stone treads may still be seen the slots into which an iron balustrade was once fitted. The original mahogany hand rail, irreparably rotted, was burnt within living memory. What appears to be a late eighteenth-century hall lantern now hanging in the Victorian entrance hall perhaps originally hung here.

To the north of the library there is now a large Victorian ball-room. In Knight's day this space was perhaps occupied by smaller rooms, possibly bedrooms, with a corridor, the dark corridor mentioned earlier which was adapted to connect the new north entrance with the staircase hall, the probable position of which (corresponding to the one on the first floor) is marked on the plan by a dotted line. The small room in the north-west tower served apparently as a closet[21] — its twin is a Victorian addition framing a much grander north entrance which replaced Knight's.

The stable yard and offices of the original castle, which were praised for their convenience, survive more or less unaltered to the north-east of the castle but they were only connected with the castle at the extreme east. A drawing probably of 1780 and a watercolour of 1785 (Plates 12 and 13) show that in the original east range on the south front the windows had pointed arches of the sort that survive in the stable block, but the chief reception rooms and bedrooms concentrated in the west originally had sash windows.

The view of Downton Castle engraved in J. P. Neale's *Views of Seats* in 1826 includes the detached tower to the south-east. It has been argued that this must date from after 1805, in which year Hearne's view was engraved for Britton's *Beauties of England and Wales* (vol. VI),[22] still showing this house as it was twenty years before. There was a fire at the Castle early in 1806[23] and this might well have been the pretext for some re-building and extension. In any case the great tower and the new detached tower are now boldly machicolated. The rest of the castellation was altered in the mid nineteenth century — except for that on the tower above the entrance to the stable-yard. The sash windows were also replaced with pointed ones and in some cases with gothic tracery.

Knight took some interest in the history of gothic architecture[24] and admired some gothic building — although the ornaments considered separately appeared 'crowded, capricious and unmeaning', the effect of King's College Chapel, taken as a whole, was 'more rich, grand, light and airy' than that of any other building known, either ancient or modern.[25] He even granted that the creators of Gothic cathedrals succeeded 'to a degree, which the Grecian architects, who worked by rule, never approached' in combining 'grandeur and solemnity' with 'lightness of effect'.[26] But he had no special admiration for the 'barbarous . . . rude and unskillful' military structures of that age[27] which his own house is so often supposed to imitate, and the limits of his interest in antiquarian investigation of the middle ages are clearly conveyed by a letter to Lord Aberdeen concerning the Society of Antiquaries with which, he said, he had little to do because it had become 'so thoroughly gothicized'.[28]

Knight knew that the Romans employed battlements in their military structures — probably in their domestic architecture as well, he proposed[29] — and so he found nothing incongruous in combining them with classical interiors, as had been done much earlier in the century by Vanbrugh and others. Knight's belief that the castle-style of the middle ages was derived from Roman architecture is found elsewhere in the late eighteenth century in the draft of a history of British architecture written by John Clerk of Eldin, Robert Adam's brother-in-law, and it has been plausibly argued that the castles of Adam's late period should be understood as 'Romano-British' rather than gothic.[30] In any case Knight enjoyed the mixture of ancient and medieval elements found 'in the pictures of Claude and

PLATE 21
Claude Lorrain, *View of La Crescenza* (Metropolitan Museum, New York)

Gaspard' where, he pointed out,

no critic has ever yet objected to the incongruity of it: for, as the temples, tombs, and palaces of the Greeks and Romans in Italy were fortified with towers and battlements by the Goths and Lombards in the middles ages, such combinations have been naturalized in that country; and are, therefore, perfectly in harmony with the scenery; and so far from interrupting the chain of ideas, that they lead it on and extend it, in the pleasantest manner, through different ages and successive revolutions in tastes, arts and sciences.[31]

Knight's own painting by Claude of *La Crescenza* (Plate 21) now in the Metropolitan Museum, New York, illustrates this perfectly.[32]

Despite Knight's attempt to publish his intentions[33] Downton Castle seems usually to have been regarded as a failed attempt at imitating the gothic. Thus the *Gentleman's Magazine* in 1797 complained of its inaccuracy . . . 'the very battlements want copings'. The same critic also found it disappointingly 'long and flat' where a more broken and vertical skyline and animated surface would have been more picturesque.[34] Here Knight would probably have agreed, for the ideal picturesque house contrasted with a plain Palladian one in *The Landscape* of 1794 (Plates 22 and 23) appears far busier than Downton Castle, with tall chimneys and gables and with projecting bays with large Tudor windows and very little

PLATES 22 & 23
Benjamin Pouncy after
Thomas Hearne,
contrasting plates from
The Landscape (cat. no. 80)

uninterrupted wall-surface. And in 1805 Knight wrote that his house was 'less perfect' than it would have been had he executed it 'at a maturer age';[35] although he was evidently still pleased with it, and fully aware of its originality.

It would seem that Downton is the first country house of any import- ance erected in Europe since the Renaissance which was designed from the outset with an irregular plan. Sir Nikolaus Pevsner, who was the first to appreciate this, cited two important precedents: Vanbrugh's house at Blackheath known as 'Vanbrugh's Castle' and Horace Walpole's Strawberry Hill.[36] Both are suburban villas where a certain playful disregard for the solemn laws of architectural propriety is less surprising than in a country seat and in both cases, moreover, the irregularity was the consequence of additions made for convenience to an earlier, regular, structure — additions which were, however, flaunted, instead of being concealed as they usually were.

Walpole, expressing his pleasure in the way Strawberry Hill had spread, related its 'want of symmetry' to that of 'grounds and gardens'.[37] Indeed the artificial ruins which were built in the mid eighteenth century as landscape ornaments were usually irregular. And there can be little doubt that Knight would have been fully aware of these, for his cousin, Edward Knight of Wolverley, encouraged by his friend and neighbour William Shenstone of the Leasowes, was keenly interested in the subject. One of his notebooks (compiled between 1759 and 1761) is crowded with notes on all the garden architecture he had seen on extensive tours around Britain and he was, in common with his brother-in-law Coplestone Warre Bampfylde, the amateur artist, a friend of Henry Hoare of Stourhead. Edward Knight was also a keen collector of landscape paintings and prints.[38] It was surely by thinking of the landscape, and in particular the effect of irregular buildings in the landscape paintings of Claude or Gaspard that Richard Payne Knight felt able to design as he did. An irregular house blended best with irregular scenery, provided more variety of view *from* the landscape and better views *of* the landscape. It meant that an added wing no longer needed to be disguised by shrubbery or matched by a dummy wing on the other side. It also meant that houses could be more easily extended when need required. Knight's friend and rival Uvedale Price was the first to develop these ideas in print in his *Essay on the Picturesque* in 1794: he expanded on them further in his *Three Essays on the Picturesque* in 1810, by which date Knight had supported many of them in his *Principles of Taste*.

It is striking that some of the classical country houses erected during the period that Knight and Price made their case for free planning and varied elevations were uncompromising exercises in elementary geometry. The best example is Belsay Hall, Northumberland (Plate 25), built between 1807 and 1817 by Sir Charles Monck, advised by Knight's friend Sir William Gell and with the assistance of John Dobson, which has a plan, 100 foot square, sheer ashlar walls, Doric columns with razor sharp fluting, immaculate proportions and precise Greek detailing. Knight was also a friend of 'Athenian' Aberdeen, whose protégé, William Wilkins, had erected at The Grange, in Hampshire between 1805 and 1809 a replica of the great portico of the Thesion in Athens, not simply as a garden ornament — for which purposes Greek temples had long been imitated — but as the front of a country house.[39] The interiors at Downton reveal Knight's archaeological sympathies, but he was severely critical of attempts to disguise English country houses as Greek temples. He thought that ancient domestic architecture was not regular — a point over which Lord Aberdeen politely disagreed[40] — and he was sure that such architecture was not suited to the English landscape. For this reason he even censored the common eighteenth-century practice of placing classical memorials in the landscape park to contribute to its elegiac mood, and railed against those who would 'With urns and cenotaphs our vallies fill / And bristle o'er with obelisks the hill'.[41] He is attacking here the very gardens, such as Stourhead, which his cousin so admired. The top-lit cavern and the so-called Roman Bath (Plate 24) which Knight created or at least adapted in the grounds at Downton were not at all classical. In the city Knight had no objection to regularity of plan, nor to the imitation of classical temples at least for sacred purposes. He favoured, as an idea for a national monument after the Napoleonic Wars, a church 'upon a simple plan something like the Pantheon in Rome'.[42] He added that to execute it 'we should be allowed a million of money, and ten years to expend it'.

Knight complained strongly of the 'poverty' and 'meanness' of modern imitations of classical architecture,[43] and although he admired the Greek Doric he seems to have conceived of it as a much less austere style than did most of his contemporaries — this is suggested by the Doric chimney-piece at Downton — and he was not attracted by the aesthetic purism of enthusiasts like Monck for whom Greek architecture provided rules of universal validity. He admitted that rules may have helped preserve under the 'Macedonian Kings and first Roman emperors' that 'elegance and purity of taste, which distinguishes all the works of those periods', but he believed they also 'restrained genius' and prevented 'grandeur of effect'.[44]

PLATE 24
William Owen, The 'Roman Bath' near Downton Castle (cat. no. 117)

PLATE 25 *Left*
Belsay Hall,
Northumberland

PLATE 26 *Right*
East Cowes Castle, Isle of
Wight (destroyed)

Knight greatly admired the English architect who broke most rules — Vanbrugh, who had been praised so eloquently by Price, Reynolds and the Adam brothers, despite his 'extravagancies' and 'absurdities'.[45] In general Knight deplored rules in art. He congratulated Shakespeare on ignoring them and pointed out that the decline of Latin eloquence coincided with the establishment of schools of rhetoric and that the progress of French painting was halted by the foundation of systematic art education.[46]

It was not only Knight's fellow hellenists who resisted the case which Knight and Price made for irregularity in rural architecture. Most of the new country houses erected in imitation of medieval abbeys or castles in the same period were symmetrical — Eastnor Castle in Herefordshire built by Smirke for Lord Somers between 1812 and 1820, for instance, or, near Chester, Eaton Hall, built by Porden for Lord Grosvenor, between 1804 and 1812. A good idea of the resistance that was felt to the idea of irregularity may be obtained from Richard Elsam's *Essay on Rural Architecture*.[47] Elsam attacks another author, James Malton, for recommending in his *Essay upon British Cottage Architecture* 'the adoption of whatever appears to be the result of chance, the want of contrivance, and also of all regularity', and yet Malton had only dared to be irregular at the very bottom of the hierarchy of buildings — his villas are as regular as Palladio's.[48]

The architect in this period who designed country houses with irregular plans most frequently and with most confidence was, without question, John Nash. And the best of these was East Cowes Castle (Plate 26), the house on the Isle of Wight which he began to build for himself in 1798 and modified and extended over the next two decades.[49] Here the octagonal,

round and square towers used by Knight at Downton were combined with turrets, varied in height and far more boldly grouped, with their massive walls contrasted with Tudor bay and oriel windows which caught spectacular views of the Solent. The combination of the baronial stronghold with Tudor elements and with an arcaded loggia and a conservatory and with interiors in a classical taste offended some as incongruous, but Knight approved such combinations[50] and would probably have liked the house, recognizing it as a child of Downton.

Nash had come into Knight's orbit when he was establishing a modest reputation in Wales in the early 1790s. He was employed by Knight's cousin Thomas Johnes to modify his gothic revival house at Hafod, Cardiganshire, and for Knight's friend, Price, he built a stucco residence — a 'whimsical castellated mansion' — on the coast near the ruins of Aberystwyth Castle.[51] He had planned a 'square' house, but Price explained to him that he wanted one of a form better designed both to merge with the setting and to catch views of the cliffs and the sea on the one hand and the mountains on the other.[52] Hafod had a regular plan and so too did Price's villa, although of an unorthodox, triangular, form. But Nash would surely have seen Downton, perhaps when visiting Price's seat at Foxley or when employed in the mid 1790s in Worcestershire.[53] Ironically, it was when he entered into partnership with Humphry Repton, the landscape gardener who had quarrelled with both Knight and Price, that Nash put the ideas he had obtained from these men into practice. Repton indeed was prepared in his Red Book of 1803 for 'Stanedge' (Stanage) Park, a seat not far from Downton and formerly belonging to the Knight family, to declare his admiration for his antagonist's irregular castle, 'where the inside was first consulted, and the outside made to conform'.

PLATE 27 *Left*
Stonebrook Cottage, near Downton Castle

PLATE 28 *Right*
Thomas Hearne, *The 'Alpine Bridge'* (cat. no. 115.x)

Nash's castellated and gothic country houses were not his only irregular buildings — for some of his smaller ones built for agents or dowagers or parsons he devised a free style consisting of loggias, round towers, a few classical details and distinctive deep eaves. Lower down the hierarchy but probably the most admired of all his works were his cottages with creepers around the porches, dovecotes, gable windows, tall chimneys and quaint lean-tos inspired no doubt as much by the cottages in paintings by Dutch masters such as Van Ostade as by his study of English rural building. Here Nash was clearly indebted to Price rather than Knight who wrote about such buildings only in order to express his distaste for contrived rusticity.[54] Knight's own cottage was of plain stone masonry without any 'affectation either of rudeness or ornament' and out of the ordinary only in that the projecting windows of the sitting room and bedroom above were not of wood.[55] The lower of these windows still survives in a building which has otherwise been extensively rebuilt (Plate 27) and on the lintel we may still make out a motto (adapted from a maxim of Plato's)[56] which Knight had cut there. Among the affectations ridiculed by Knight in his *Principles of Taste* were 'pastoral seats, gates and gateways, made of unknown branches and stems of trees'[57] but he included 'a common rustic bridge' supported by stilts of rough branches in the middle distance of the view of the picturesque house in *The Landscape* a decade earlier (Plate 23), and there was one such bridge at Downton itself, illustrated in Hearne's watercolours of the landscape there (Plate 28), and noted by Lipscomb as the 'Alpine bridge'.[58]

The watercolours of Downton made by Hearne between 1784 and 1786 celebrating Knight's improvements represent what is one of the earliest and most beautiful of all such series to have survived. The hill opposite the house 'clad with rich wood in a variety of shapes to its very summit, and opening at parts into rude sheep walks', the steep drop of the hill upon which the house itself stood where, upstream the Teme was most narrow and impetuous, and the walks on either bank which Knight created were generally agreed to be enchanting — 'the most wild, rich, and solitary path I ever trod', wrote one visitor; 'the walk through the wood', conceded another, 'surpasses anything I have ever seen of the kind.'[59]

The reform of English parks — the beginnings of the 'English landscape garden' — occurred about fifty years before Knight inherited Downton. The level parterres and straight canals, enclosed formal gardens, the fountains and topiary derived from Dutch, French and Italian examples were replaced by meandering streams and walks and by the illusion of fields sweeping up to the front of the house (devices in fact kept the cattle in the middle distance) and clumps of mixed trees irregularly scattered over gently undulating ground. The house would appear as a surprise glimpsed obliquely between clumps, across a serpentine lake instead of serving as before as the imposing climax of a long avenue. Price and Knight were at the vanguard of a campaign against such 'improvements'. They found the work of Lancelot Brown and his followers tame, and their curves just as artificial as the straight lines they replaced. And although the originators of this reform in taste — William Kent especially — saw themselves as imitating landscape paintings by Claude and Gaspard, Knight considered that these painters and the Dutch masters he loved as keenly, encouraged an admiration for effects far richer and more intricate than those embodied in the fashionable English park with its 'unvaried round' —

> One even round, that ever gently flows,
> Nor forms abrupt, nor broken colours knows;
> But wrapt all o'er in everlasting green,
> Makes one dull, vapid, smooth, unvaried scene.[60]

We have Knight's views on the landscape of several parts of Britain: he admired Loch Tay and the Falls of the Clyde,[61] and the waterfalls at the Devil's Bridge near Aberystwyth;[62] the confluence of streams at Betws y Coed and a waterfall nearby 'with a hard Welsh name'.[63] This is the wild scenery of the sort which the English upper classes were in the last two decades of the eighteenth century keenly discovering — scenery described in numerous travel works, the subject of countless watercolours by many professional, by still more amateur, artists.

Knight professed to admire, although with some qualifications, 'the late Mr Southgate's farm near Weybridge' — the 'Ferme Ornée', Woburn Park — and recommended for the guidance of those who wished to make 'tame flat country' attractive humble ornaments found in 'Hobbima, Waterloe and Adrian Vandervelde',[64] but the estates that impressed him most were those in which wild natural scenery was to be found — his cousin's seat at Hafod, for instance, or Hawkstone in Shropshire, with its ruined castle, its precipices and rocks 'more fantastically broken into a greater variety of fine forms than any I ever saw, and enriched with a greater variety of vigorous vegetation'. And of course his own Downton where, he conceded, the rocks were 'very inferior in Form, Colour and Intricacy' to those at Hawkstone but where there was clear running water — 'a Beauty for which nothing can compensate'.[65]

Both Knight and Price were involved in the mid 1790s in controversy with Humphry Repton, a professional improver whom they had both befriended but who had in many of his works abandoned their principles, because, he claimed, his friends were too preoccupied with wild scenery suited to pictures but impractical in reality, but also no doubt because it was prudent for him to comply at times with the conservative views of his clients. Repton had to gratify the self-importance of his potential employers as well as the 'eye of taste'. Knight held up for special ridicule his recommendation for promoting visible evidence of the status of the Egertons of Tatton Park in Cheshire 'by placing the family arms upon the neighbouring milestones'.[66] Despite their quarrels Repton in fact put many of the ideas of his critics into practice, as did his partner, Nash. By the end of the century Repton consistently avoided the isolated clump and bald lawn and mechanically serpentine line. He also increasingly revived formal elements — terraces, walled gardens, even avenues in the areas close to the house — claiming priority for this change of taste over both Knight and Price.[67]

Although Knight and Price were allies in opposition to Repton and the defenders of Brown, Knight was naturally quarrelsome and in the second edition of *The Landscape* he expressed reservations over the philosophical basis of his friend's notion of the picturesque.[68] These he developed in the *Principles of Taste*.[69] In the debate between them Price showed more common sense and far more agreeable polemical manners but Knight a profounder grasp of aesthetics and psychology. Relations were strained and were probably not helped by a quarrel which almost ended in litigation, between Knight's brother and Price over some fences.[70] Lady Oxford is said to have patched things up between the two men[71] and certainly they were on good terms again by 1818, when they were visiting each other. Price by now was working on the pronunciation of the ancient languages, and Knight, in his patronizing way, commended these endeavours, and even toyed with the idea of printing them together with his Homer.[72] One of Knight's last improvements at Downton was to create a walk where his friend had recommended — despite his earlier dismissal of the idea.[73] By then the taste which these two men had pioneered in landscape grounds was orthodox. Within a decade the revolution in the planning of country houses which they had begun would be complete.

CHAPTER FOUR — *The Symbolical Language of Antiquity*

On 17 July 1781 Sir William Hamilton wrote to his friend Sir Joseph Banks confirming the remarkable rumour that he had 'actually discovered the cult of Priapus in full vigour as in the days of the Greeks and Romans at Isernia in Abruzzo'.[1] An engineer, he explained in a subsequent letter, working on a new road, had chanced to witness the celebration of a feast in honour of the Saints Cosmus and Damianus in this remote town. In the course of this ceremony waxen ex-voti representing 'the male organs of generation, of various dimensions, some even the length of a palm' were 'publickly offered for sale' and then taken to the church dedicated to the Saints and presented, 'chiefly by the female sex'[2] who kissed them as they placed them in a bowl in the vestibule, offering such dedications as 'St Cosimo, I thank you', 'Blessed St Cosimo let it be like this'.[3] Hamilton had visited Isernia hoping to see this for himself and, although he found it had been suppressed in meantime, he was able to salvage some of the 'Great Toes' as the local inhabitants quaintly called the ex-voti. These fragile trophies he carried personally to London in 1784 and deposited in the British Museum with strict instructions to 'keep hands off'.[4]

A couple of weeks earlier the Society of Dilettanti, of which Hamilton

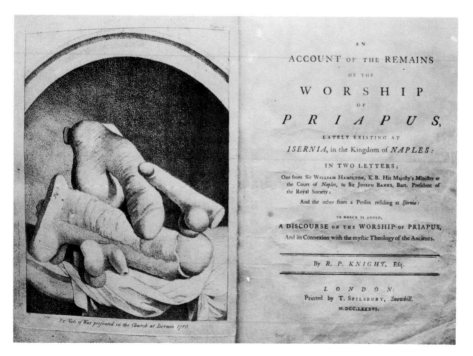

Ex-Voti of Wax presented in the Church at Isernia 1780.

AN

ACCOUNT OF THE REMAINS

OF THE

WORSHIP

OF

PRIAPUS,

LATELY EXISTING AT

ISERNIA, in the Kingdom of NAPLES:

IN TWO LETTERS;

One from Sir WILLIAM HAMILTON, K.B. His Majefty's Minifter at the Court of Naples, to Sir JOSEPH BANKS, Bart. Prefident of the Royal Society;

And the other from a Perfon refiding at Ifernia;

TO WHICH IS ADDED,

A DISCOURSE ON THE WORSHIP OF PRIAPUS,

And its Connexion with the myftic Theology of the Ancients.

By R. P. KNIGHT, Efq.

LONDON:

Printed by T. SPILSBURY, Snowhill,

M.DCC.LXXXVI.

PLATE 29
Frontispiece and title-page of the *Account of the Worship of Priapus* (cat. no. 79)

PLATE 30 *facing*
Johan Zoffany, *Charles Townley and his Collection* (cat no. 210)

was a prominent member and Banks the Secretary, had voted to print his account. It eventually appeared in 1786 with an engraving of the 'Great Toes' serving as its bizarre frontispiece (Plate 29), followed by a far longer *Discourse on the Worship of Priapus* . . . written by the member of the society who supervised the publication, Richard Payne Knight. Hamilton's 'communication' provided the pretext for Knight's *Discourse*, but the *Discourse* is far more than a mere commentary on the ceremonies at Isernia, and in fact owes far more to the ideas of Hamilton's old friend and protégé the eccentric French antiquarian and adventurer Pierre François Hugues, self-styled 'Baron' d'Hancarville.

It was about the same time that Hamilton first sent news of the feast at Isernia that d'Hancarville seems to have arrived in England to stay in the London house of the great collector Charles Townley[5] — he was painted there, looking very much at home, by Zoffany (Plate 30). While there he wrote the greater part of his *Recherches sur l'Origine, l'Espirit et les Progrès des Arts de la Grèce*, which was published in 1785. In this extraordinary book d'Hancarville attempted to describe an ancient and universal theological system from which all subsequent religions had derived, and which was revealed by the symbols to be found in ancient remains — he cited those in Townley's collection in particular — and also in the remains of eastern nations. Townley himself, as is clear from the manuscript catalogues which he made of his collection, was much impressed with these ideas and Knight, a close friend of Townley, who had contributed at least in a small way to the production of the *Recherches*, reiterated in his *Discourse* d'Hancarville's account of the ancient theology, discovering the same symbols, sometimes by reference to the same sculptures and coins.

In the opinion of d'Hancarville and his friends, previous efforts to explain the ancient mythology had failed because attention had been paid more to the evidence provided by literature than to that provided by artefacts — engraved gems, painted vases, coins and sculpture. The more primitive of these, when compared with the imagery found in oriental art, revealed that, beneath all the elaborate diversity of mythology associated with all the different religions of the world, there lay concealed — deliberately concealed — the evidence of a common monotheistic theology, which d'Hancarville, with immense erudition and seemingly inexhaustible energy, was able to reveal. He was not alone in making such speculations at that date. Among comparable works the short treatise *On the Gods of Greece, Italy and India* by Sir William Jones should be mentioned and, the best known of all such books, published a little later, the *Origine des tous les Cultes* by Charles Dupuis.

The discoveries at Herculaneum appear to have directed the attention of antiquarians to the phallic nature of much Greek and Roman worship and, as Partha Mitter has shown,[6] engravings and descriptions in contemporary voyage literature revealed a similar element in the practices of Asian, and in particular, Indian cults. Comparing the evidence before them these syncretist mythographers postulated that the ancient theology must also have been of an intensely sexual character, expressive of ideas of generation and creation. At the heart of it they discovered a variety of cosmogonical accounts. Thus for d'Hancarville the Creation was first expressed by the extraordinary image of a bull striking a huge egg with its horns. Such an image, he explains, worshipped by the Japanese in a form related to the images found on the coins of ancient Mediterranean nations (which he illustrated together – Plate 31), represents the 'Être Générateur', symbolised by the bull, in the action of vivifying the primordial 'Chaos', or matter in its first state, signified by the egg.[7] Elsewhere the 'Être Générateur' is found to have been represented by the phallus and the lingam, and was later personified as the god Dionysus of the Greeks, Bacchus of the Romans and Brahma of the Hindus. Numerous other

PLATE 31
Illustration to
d'Hancarville's *Recherches*

deities of many world religions are likewise found to be personifications of such abstract principles as the active and passive or male and female forces operating in the universe. In addition, the ancient theology encompassed the subsidiary processes of creation and generation operating in the natural world. Indeed d'Hancarville declares this religion to be 'celle de la loi de la nature'[8] – not the product of a blind superstition but an attempt to explain and epitomise the elemental forces in nature. Both Townley and Knight place particular emphasis on this aspect of the ancient system so that some of Townley's catalogue entries read more like the propositions of a natural philosopher and there are moments when the language employed by Knight in his *Discourse* is redolent of eighteenth-century French materialism.

When discussing specific symbols in detail emphasis is placed on the relatively sophisticated understanding of the natural object which is entailed. Both d'Hancarville and Knight for instance provide detailed botanical accounts of the lotus, with acknowledgements to Banks,[9] in order to show that it was chosen to symbolize the productive powers of nature because of its remarkable fecundity. Since the symbols of the ancient theology were the product of reasoned observation, the modern interpreter may legitimately refer to contemporary scientific knowledge or to his own experience. Thus Knight also records his own observations of the adder to illustrate why the snake served as a symbol of the vivifying powers of nature.[10] Moreover, as Knight was later to point out – and here he differs from d'Hancarville – the occurrence of similar symbols in the art of different parts of the world need not be explained by recourse to elaborate and cumbersome theories of diffusion, if we recognize that this early pictorial language was simply the product of what all men would commonly observe.[11]

Tracing the progress of ancient art from the first crude productions of early man to the perfect works of Classical Greece, d'Hancarville discovers that at every point formal considerations were subordinate to symbolic meaning. The artists of Classical Greece, he explains, recalled the principles of the ancient system either by formal references to their original symbols or by sophisticated allegories of great complexity which in turn lead d'Hancarville to advance the most minute and intricate interpretations. Thus after devoting some thirty pages to expounding the meaning of the ancient glass vessel (the 'Portland Vase' now in the British Museum) which Hamilton had brought to England together with the 'Great Toes', he reflected with not a little satisfaction 'qu'il n'est pas une *forme* dans ces figures, pas une *attitude*, pas un *caractère* qui ne serve a développer l'intention de l'artiste. Il n'y existe pas un seul *accessoir* qui ne contribue a développer le sujet'.[12]

For d'Hancarville symbol and emblem were incorporated in the very fabric of ancient works of art, and he detects meaning even in abstract shapes. Thus of the 'Townley Vase' – it is placed on the bookcase in Zoffany's painting – and other marble vases with bacchic decoration he argued that the 'forme ovalaire' had been chosen to represent 'l'Oeuf de la Création'.[13] Townley was able to think in this way as well and his protégé, the dealer James Christie, even proposed that Greek vases were fashioned upon the shapes of the seed vessels of the lotus and associated plants and might be classified by reference to the Linnaean classification of the Nelumbium genus.[14] In like manner Knight could speculate on the relationship of the Corinthian column with those of the Egyptians which were modelled for sacred reasons upon the stem and seed vessel of the lotus. Knight, however, is concerned to trace how forms evolved and does not emphasize the conscious recollection of primitive forms as d'Hancarville does.

Convinced of the general truth of his argument d'Hancarville finds confirmation in every fact, every sculpture, coin or gem which he brings into this great repository of recondite learning. The absurdity and implausibility which this frequently lends to the content of his work is only compounded by the extraordinary manner in which it is presented. After the first chapter, which is ordered into numbered sections, the book becomes increasingly chaotic, the later chapters not only swollen in length but supplemented by footnotes which can extend over as many as twenty pages. The material was not of course easy to organize and, besides, as we know from Townley, d'Hancarville was in a hurry.[15]

The book's idiosyncrasies naturally laid it open to ridicule. In his literary journal, the *New Review*, Henry Maty gave an abstract of the *Recherches* in a manner that makes even d'Hancarville's more convincing arguments seem implausible; he took every opportunity to pass a derisive comment, or to point up an absurdity and concluded that he could have wished for 'less tautology, more order, more clearness, less mixture of old and known things with the new, and a smaller torrent of erudition'.[16] D'Hancarville, infuriated, replied point by point, issuing a further torrent in so doing, although Townley pleaded with him not to do so in his own interest – 'Si vous entrez en lice avec ce Maty vous lui donnerai l'occasion d'exposer les méprises et les erreurs qui sans votre réponse seront bientôt oubliés par le mérite général de l'ouvrage . . .'.[17] It is clear from this letter that, although a 'zealous advocate'[18] of d'Hancarville (as his friend Thomas Whitaker recalled), Townley was not an indiscriminate admirer of the *Recherches*, and this is plainer still in a note to John Wilkes which he enclosed with a copy of the book. Wilkes will find 'many real discoveries and useful observations which amply compensate for the conjectures, chimaeras and absurdities that may be found in them in common with all works of this kind'.[19]

With the exception of Maty's review the critical reception of the *Recherches* was surprisingly favourable – far more so than most commentators have supposed – but it is unlikely that d'Hancarville's ideas were ever widely followed. This was not only because of their complexity and obscurity but because they differed so much from conventional English antiquarianism; from the attitude of Addison or of Spence for whom it was a 'laudable amusement'[20] to seek in coins and sculpture for illustrations to the poets, and also from the attitude of historians who looked at coins to confirm the dates of Roman campaigns, the genealogy of Hellenistic tyrants and the names of Greek cities. John Pinkerton, who in his *Essay on Medals* remarked of the *Recherches* that it was a 'fanciful work',[21] considered that the bull, when it appears on an ancient coin, indicated nothing more than its place of manufacture.[22] For d'Hancarville, it indicated, as we have seen, very much more, and even the ugliest or oddest curiosities, the smallest and apparently most trivial works of art, could serve as vital evidence of an entire theological system. Thus Townley could write to Charles Greville with great excitement that a small gem he had received from Rome 'comprises the whole ancient mysteries viz. that from the unison and proper temperature of heat and fluid emanates the spirit of all productions'.[23]

Visitors to Townley's collection would have found that his catalogue eschewed all 'elogies and amplifications' on the beauty of the marbles, and concentrated principally on their symbolic meaning. Thus of the most admired sculpture in his possession, the female bust (Plate 32) beside which d'Hancarville sits in Zoffany's painting, we are not offered the usual superlatives and a snippet from Ovid but instead an explanation that it represents Isis, a personification of the 'passive means' of generation, placed in the centre of the lotus flower, the earlier symbol of the same. Nollekens, who copied the bust, is supposed to have considered it to be merely a portrait of the sculptor's model. The more common view amongst connoisseurs was that it was Clytie, as emerges from a rather embarrassed correspondence concerning the correct description of the miniature copy of the bust engraved by Marchant on a gem for Knight's friend, Cracherode.[24]

Townley's activities as an interpreter of ancient art were not confined to his own collection. He appears to have answered the queries of fellow collectors less well versed in ancient symbolism than himself. Thus, for instance, we find him writing on 16 May 1791 to George Cumberland,

PLATE 32
Roman portrait bust known as Clytie (British Museum)

forwarding d'Hancarville's explanation of an intaglio in Cumberland's possession.[25] But, in this respect, by far the most interesting of Townley's associations was with another member of an old Lancashire Catholic family, Henry Blundell of Ince.

Blundell had been encouraged to form his collection by Townley and always deferred to his friend in matters concerning the antique, describing himself as a 'dabbler' in this field.[26] Townley is reported to have thought only five or six marbles in Blundell's massive collection to be of any real worth[27] — however, he certainly advised on acquisitions and, in the early nineteenth century, even bid on his behalf at London sales. He also supervised the drawing and engraving of the collection though a correspondence between the two men concerning the business reveals that their friendship was not always harmonious.[28] Townley wrote when the job was done that he would have been pleased to do it for anyone 'but such an irresolute, capricious, and unintelligent head as that belonging to our friend of Ince'.[29]

Blundell was requesting from Townley explanations of the meanings of his statues at least as early as 2 January 1787. In the same year he confessed to his friend that he did not find such satisfactory explanations as he could wish in 'D'Ankerville's work': 'He seems to refine a good deal and often to wrest things to his own ideas of être generateur. But I am so little versed in ancient coins, medals etc. that it appears to me difficult to understand ye many oddities of ye ancients'.[30] By 1803, however, Blundell felt sufficiently confident to publish a catalogue of his collection though, characteristically, he went to great length to excuse its mistakes and to point out that it was not meant for the eyes of the 'learned antiquarian'.[31] Townley's interpretations — of the lotus and of Bacchus and so on — abound but are prefixed with 'it is said' and 'antiquarians pretend' and other qualifications. By 1809, four years after Townley's death and a year before his own, Blundell's reservations had hardened into outright rejection. In his revised catalogue he ridicules 'the fertile imagination of a D'Ankerville',[32] quoting from Christie and from a letter of a friend — doubtless Townley — with contempt, and asserting that they were labouring to interpret what were 'mere ornaments sculptured according to the taste and fancy of the artist'.[33] He makes no reference to Knight, who was by then the leading exponent of such ideas in England.

The debt which Knight owed to d'Hancarville in composing his *Discourse* has already been mentioned and is indeed acknowledged in its opening pages, although Knight remarks rather pointedly that he will describe the ancient system 'as concisely and as clearly as possible'.[34] Like Townley, he was surely well aware of the excesses and idiosyncrasies of the *Recherches*. Moreover, whilst the *Discourse* must be seen primarily as a contribution to this sort of speculation, it is most remarkable because of its full and open discussion of ancient phallic rituals illustrated with engravings which would raise an eyebrow even today, and still more remarkable because it contended that it was from these cults that Christianity itself derived. As we shall see the poet William Mason was not alone in condemning the book for conveying both 'Shame to each eye, profaneness to each ear'.[35] Sexual symbolism had of course been vital to d'Hancarville's thesis (as it was to other writers of this period) and the connection between phallic cults and Christianity is implicit in his view of the history of religions. But Knight makes the first his principal subject and the second his central theme and develops material of a purely antiquarian interest into a polemic against orthodox morality and the Christian Church.

It is hardly surprising that Knight, in a letter to Banks of 18 June 1785 should have expressed certain misgivings about the publication of his *Discourse*. 'I fear that it will be impossible to make the work fit for any but very prophane persons', Knight writes, but goes on to suggest certain changes of expression which might 'give less offence to the Godly'. Thus for instance 'holy spirit may be changed into Divine Spirit' and the word 'Trinity' replaced by 'Triade'; but it is clear from Knight's tone that he found these trivial alterations something of a nuisance, and he returns to his point that it would be impossible to make the work generally acceptable: 'I meant my discourse only for the Society and a few real dilettanti'.[36] Accordingly when the 'Priapeia' was announced as ready for distribution to members of the Society of Dilettanti on 3 March 1787 the stipulation was added that the Secretary should not 'on any pretence whatever part with any other copy without an order made at a regular meeting'. Each member was however allowed 'once and no more' to recommend by name a friend to whom he wished the Society to send a copy.[37] The list of recipients included such distinguished names as Walpole, Gibbon, Boswell, Malone, Wilkes and the Duke of Portland; and a specially bound copy was presented to the Prince of Wales.

Assured that circulation of the book would be limited Knight made none of the alterations he had previously entertained. Moreover, its 'private' character seems to have lent something to the tone of his *Discourse*, for breaking through the erudite scholarship we sense a somewhat raffish delight in the indecency of its subject, and the occasional private joke or allusion of strictly local interest give it an informality which we would not expect of a work intended for wider readership. It addresses instead a circle of young, like-minded intellectuals centred around Knight and Townley who came to dominate the activities of the Dilettanti at this time – men such as Charles Greville, Hamilton's nephew; and Roger Wilbraham, a keen supporter of Fox, possessing 'a great deal of classical knowledge', according to Farington but 'a debauchee & much given to loose conversation on such subjects, to which he finds Knight equally inclined'.[38]

D'Hancarville had been congratulated by one of his reviewers for showing by his allegorical approach that the 'licentious representations' of the ancients were rather 'expressions of piety'.[39] Likewise Knight argues that phallic remains should not be considered 'in their direct and obvious sense' but rather as 'symbolical representations of some hidden meaning'.[40] Thus, for instance, he urges us to regard the ithyphallic hands worn as amulets by the ancients as representing 'the act of generation, which was considered as a solemn sacrament, in honour of the Creator'[41] and the group of a satyr enjoying a goat (the illustration of which Knight mentioned to Banks as quite unsuitable for the general reading public) he explains as 'the incarnation of the Deity and the communication of its creative spirit to man'.[42] There seems no reason to doubt that for the most part Knight was perfectly serious in advancing such explanations and yet he knew that however convinced we are by his high-minded interpretations the 'direct and obvious sense' of these objects cannot be effaced.

They are then ambiguous, but far from ignoring this ambiguity, Knight actively exploits it. The disjunction between symbolic meaning and actual appearance is a source of ironic effect which contributes greatly to the character of the *Discourse* and perhaps serves to forestall ridicule. But, most important, it is upon this ambiguity that the polemics of the *Discourse* turn. Tracing the connection between pagan cults and Christianity, Knight identifies certain iconographical correspondences. Some, like that of the dove, or the ringing of bells, are relatively innocuous, but others are considerably less so. By far the most outrageous is that concerning the Cross. The Cross, Knight coolly asserts, was used by the ancients as 'the least explicit representation of the male organs of generation',[43] which, in this refined form, 'served as the emblem of creation and generation, before the Church adopted it as a sign of salvation; a lucky coincidence of ideas which, without doubt, facilitated the reception of it among the faithful'.[44] Considered allegorically the notion of such an emblematic borrowing, ludicrous as it is, need not be so offensive, but, as Knight well knew, it is impossible for us to conceive of it solely in these terms.

Knight opens the *Discourse* with the observation that although all men are constitutionally the same their moral sentiments and ethical standards are conditioned by external circumstances. If we divest ourselves of the 'prejudices of education and fashion'[45] we should acknowledge that there is 'no impurity or licentiousness in the moderate and regular gratification of any natural appetite . . . . Neither are organs of one species of enjoyment naturally to be considered as subjects of shame and concealment more than those of another'.[46] Thus in an age without our artificial prejudices what more natural image could men find 'by which to express their idea of the beneficient power of the great creator'[47] than the phallus? That modern standards of decency are the product of acquired habit not only helps to explain the adoption of such symbols but is itself confirmed as historical fact by the prevalence of such cults in antiquity. Knight is keen to emphasise that these were public rituals of great solemnity, although again he cannot resist playing up what seems to us so ludicrously in-congruous in the idea of the 'pious matrons of antiquity',[48] or for that matter those of Isernia, cherishing the image of the phallus. Nevertheless the case which Knight presents had a serious and more pressing applica-tion. For his arguments apply not only to the phallic rituals of antiquity but also to those of oriental peoples described by many eighteenth-century travellers and embodied in remains such as the fragment of a relief from Elephanta acquired by Townley in 1785 and published by Knight in the

'Priapeia' (Plate 33). Thus the greatest contemporary advocate for enlightened toleration towards Hinduism, Sir William Jones, explaining to his readers the worship of the 'lingam', makes a point very similar to Knight's: 'it never seems to have entered the heads of legislators or people, that anything natural could be offensively obscene; a singularity which pervades all their writings, but is no proof of depravity of morals'.[49]

The subject of religious toleration becomes Knight's chief concern in the closing pages of his *Discourse*. Although sceptical of all forms of religious belief he is concerned here, as in other works, not with the validity of such beliefs but with their influence upon manners and society. Here, tracing the disintegration of the ancient system, Knight compares the two parallel religious traditions which, he believes, derived from it: the polytheistic cults of the Greeks and Romans and the monotheistic religions of the Jews and Christians. The former, though not in themselves particularly laudable, were at least free from 'two of the greatest curses that ever afflicted the human race, dogmatical theology, and its consequent, religious persecution'.[50] Believing that the 'divine spirit' made its appearance in innumerable forms, Knight explains, the ancient polytheists naturally respected the objects of devotion of their neighbours. It was also a joyous religion, whereas the hierarchies of the Jewish and Christian faiths encouraged 'awful and venerable'[51] practices and transformed 'the Creator and Generator Bacchus' into a 'jealous and irascible God'.[52]

The practices and imagery of phallic worship which lingered on, stripped of their original symbolic significance, in the popular religions of the Greeks and Romans could hardly be defended. Accordingly Knight writes that they were 'foully prostituted to promiscuous vice';[53] but the exaggerated severity of this appears almost to mock the sentiment, and in the catalogue of the phallic rites of later antiquity which follows there is no hint of such censure. The feeling is, that however absurd or offensive these activities may now seem, they at least caused no harm, a view again echoed by other works of the period though never better expressed than by Sylvain Marèchal writing of the priapic remains of Herculaneum: 'le spectacle d'un peuple voluptueux qui sanctifie l'acte de la génération . . . est plus doux que le spectacle d'un champ de bataille où des milliers d'hommes expirent de la main de leurs semblables'.[54] The spectacle of 'un peuple voluptueux' perhaps never fully emerges in Knight's *Discourse* but the idea of an innocent and playful people enjoying a form of worship 'of the festive kind'[55] is strong and is further highlighted by the bleak and sombre picture he paints of Judaism and Christianity. Knight had said at the beginning of his work that of all the pagan rites none was 'more furiously inveighed against by the zealous propagators of the Christian faith'[56] than the ritual worship of the phallus. Now, in the closing pages of the *Discourse*, examples of its occasional re-emergence are made to appear as instances of liberation from a rigorous and oppressive régime.

Although distribution of the *Priapeia* was restricted, a total of about eighty copies appear to have been presented to various non-members and learned societies and it seems inevitable that it should eventually have fallen into the wrong hands. Indeed the very 'secrecy' of the work seems to have contributed to suspicions of Knight's motives and was exploited in the attacks made upon it – attacks however which seem not to have been made before the early 1790s although by this time the book must have seemed far more dangerously subversive than when it originally appeared. Of these attacks the best known is that of T. J. Mathias who, in the footnotes of his popular satire *Literary Pursuits . . .*, declared that the book was clearly intended for no other purpose than the 'obscene revellings of Greek scholars in their private studies'[57] for it contained 'all the ordure and filth, all the antique pictures and all the representations of generative organs in their most odious and degrading protrusion'.[58] 'The Dilettanti Society', he concludes 'best know what emblem modelled in wax, is laid upon the table at their solemn meetings.'[59]

Far more formidable opposition to Knight's *Discourse* appeared in the October 1794 number of the literary review *The British Critic*, which had been started in the previous year at the instigation of a group of Anglican Clergymen styling themselves the 'Society for the Reformation of Principles', and had the declared intention of preventing 'the corruption which prevails among scholars and persons of the higher orders of life'.[60] Enjoying considerable success (it quickly equalled the circulation of *the Monthly*), *The British Critic* became a major outlet for reactionary opinion in the 1790s. Knight was clearly a suitable target and nearly everything he published was subjected to the most hostile criticism in its pages, its editors Robert Nares and William Beloe becoming two of his greatest antagonists. 'These two insolent blockheads have without any provocation, and merely to court favour with some high church prelates, attempted to injure me in so many ways',[61] Knight complained in 1805, 'they cannot traduce and calumniate me more than they have done already.'[62]

The attack on Knight's *Discourse*, which began this long confrontation, appeared in a review of a 'Narrative' of an expedition into India by a detachment of the British army, written by a young officer, Lieutenant Edward Moor. Moor's 'Narrative' included a disgusted survey of the 'monstrous delineations' and 'heating exhibitions'[63] on the walls of Hindu Temples, but also an impartial account of the sympathetic explanations of Jones and (in a long note at the end)[64] a paraphrase of Knight's *Discourse* which is so unprejudiced that one wonders whether his condemnation of Hindu cults in the text is sincere (certainly he approaches the subject far more mildly in a later work, *The Hindu Pantheon*). In any case the *British Critic* thanked Moor for taking the side of the argument that he had, clearly seeing an opportunity to pronounce more widely on the issues he had raised, and to attack not just Knight but all allegorical interpretations of, and indeed all apologies for, phallic worship. It argued that the profound meanings which modern interpreters had discovered in phallic rituals were inventions of later times. 'The popular corruption is prior, and the mysteries of later date',[65] it contended, the mysteries being no more than the imposture of 'Brahmins, Hierophants and Philosophers'[66] who attempted to palliate and excuse a religion of the 'most depraved idolatory'.[67] The position is the exact reverse of that adopted by d'Hancarville, Knight and Jones, and the question ultimately rests, like so many in eighteenth-century mythography, upon a matter of juggling with the chronology of ancient religions.

Direct treatment of Knight's *Discourse* is reserved until the end of the review. It is abused as a 'Clandestine work'[68] and indeed it appears from the quotations given that the anonymous reviewer may have worked solely from Moor's paraphrase. This however was sufficient for him to hope that the work would 'never burst from the awful and Eleusinian darkness in which it is at present reserved for the sight of the initiated alone'.[69]

Knight, who, as his admirer Thomas Love Peacock observed, was 'fond of paper war',[70] defended the *Discourse* in the Preface to his *Progress of Civil Society*, though characteristically his defence seems intended more to inflame the hostility of his critics rather than to appease it. He declares that he has never written anything which was not consistent with the duties of 'a good subject, a good citizen, and a good man; I might perhaps add of a good Christian did I understand the meaning of the term'.[71] However he also presents a brief but remarkable examination of the nature of our ideas of obscenity. If we take the obscene to mean that which 'tends to promote lewdness and debauchery'[72] or 'criminal obscenity'[73] then the *Discourse* was free of it and anyone who found otherwise must have 'appetites and desires of a very extraordinary kind'.[74] It was 'obscene' only in the sense that engravings in books of anatomy might be so described. The distinction is an important one upon which discussions of pornography are argued even today.

It is difficult to assess how much harm, if any, the *Discourse* caused Knight. That he had written such a work was clearly common knowledge when he was at the height of his reputation, but if he was censured for it, it was surely by those who would have attacked him in any case. Thus, for instance, when he was considered for the Professorship of Ancient Literature at the Royal Academy in 1818 it was used against him by his opponents, but was clearly not the source of their opposition. The idea that Knight would have been particularly bothered by attacks on this early work seems completely out of character. The story has been recounted, in practically everything that has been written about him, that he was so alarmed by its reception that he attempted to withdraw from circulation as many copies as he possibly could and (in the more picturesque versions) destroyed them. No reference is ever given for this and the minutes of the Society of Dilettanti plainly show that copies of the book were being distributed as late as 1797[75] with no apparent disturbance in the meantime. Moreover Knight himself declared in 1796 in the preface to the *Progress of Civil Society* that should he ever resume his studies on the subject of the *Discourse* he would 'without fear or hesitation repeat and submit to the public any opinion or expression'[76] which it might contain.

Knight did return to the subject, many years later, in his *Inquiry into the Symbolical Language of Ancient Art and Mythology*, a work intended for the second volume of the *Specimens of Antient Sculpture* as a complement to his essay on the style and manufacture of ancient art in the first volume. Since publication of the second volume was delayed he arranged to have a small edition privately printed in 1818 and it also appeared, in serial form, over nine consecutive numbers of *The Classical Journal* between 1821 and 1823. In a note attached to both of these printings he solicited supplementary information and suggestions from fellow scholars, which suggests that he recognized that a work of this kind was a cumulative project; that more examples of a certain symbol could be revealed which might support his arguments or slightly alter his interpretations.[77]

This is the principal difference between the *Inquiry* and the *Discourse*. His description of the ancient theological system, and of the symbols by which it was expressed, remains by and large the same, and even some of the phraseology in the *Inquiry* is borrowed from the earlier work. But he is now able to furnish more proofs and far more examples, which makes it a work of sounder scholarship, if less enjoyable to read. As we would expect, the range of religious traditions considered is much broader, for much had been published since the 1780s. On Egyptian antiquities for instance, he makes use of the 'extensive and accurate survey'[78] of Vivant Denon, and he is able to introduce much on Scandinavian and Celtic mythologies and much more than formerly on Hindu worship. In this field especially, the literature had been greatly augmented — by the 'Asiatic Researches' of Jones and others and by the publications of Thomas Maurice in particular — and Knight was most enthusiastic about the subject (we find Samuel Parr tempting a friend to dinner with the prospect of the conversation of 'Mr. K. — about the mysteries of oriental mythology, theology and theogony').[79]

The great variety of faiths which Knight considers in the *Inquiry* made the distinctions between theology, mythology and now folklore even more important than in the *Discourse* and there is perhaps even a hint that a more pluralist approach to ancient beliefs and practices might be necessary. The ancient system is still found to be fundamental to all religious traditions, but Knight seems particularly interested here in the character and origins of popular superstitions. To explain their development, he adduces his own observations on human nature, but also considers the euhemerist explanations and the theory that primitive man's superstitions derived from his fear of the universe which had been advanced by his eighteenth-century predecessors.

It has been suggested that the *Inquiry* indicates that there had been a great change in Knight's opinions since he wrote the *Discourse* — a substantial moderation of his anti-clericalism and of his view on sex. Certainly some of the irony of the earlier work is omitted but he is still quite candid in his treatment of phallic remains, repeating the arguments that they should not be regarded as obscene. His pleas for religious toleration are just as forceful, only now, following the general tendency of his work, they are taken from the mouth of a Roman orator and put into that of the King of Siam. If the *Inquiry* is less polemical then that is because it is more of an 'official' and 'scientific' work, as was the *Specimens* which it was designed to accompany. The preface to his verse romance *Alfred* fully confirms that Knight was no less keen a controversialist in his seventies than he had been in his thirties — here he expresses his detestation of the Christian conception of everlasting damnation.[80]

CHAPTER FIVE—*Collecting, Interpreting and Imitating Ancient Art*

By the 1770s the English had become the principal buyers of the most valuable class of art – ancient marble sculpture – in the chief market, Rome, which they visited as young men on the Grand Tour. The leading dealer there was the banker Thomas Jenkins, who chiefly supplied highly restored pieces which could serve as imposing and glamorous furniture for grand houses. Knight's first acquisitions were probably of this character[1] – the very patched up Bacchus and his female companion (Plate 34) still at Downton – and, as was suggested in Chapter Three, he probably bought porphyry columns and chimney-pieces in Rome at the same date. By his own account, however, Knight's collection began after Downton

PLATE 34
Highly restored antique
statue, Downton Castle

Castle was complete, in 1785 when Jenkins sent a superb bronze head from Rome (Plate 35).[2] He concentrated on collecting coins and gems and bronzes, kept not at Downton but in his London home, as a private museum. He eventually possessed nine marble heads, but it seems likely that he did not wish to compete as a collector of ancient marbles with his friend Charles Townley. (One of the heads was certainly purchased before Townley died[3] but the others probably, and four of them certainly, later.[4])

Among the greatest cabinets of coins in England were those of the Earl of Pembroke and the Duke of Devonshire, but the majority of important collectors were professional men with antiquarian interests and the most important of them all in the eighteenth century was the anatomist William

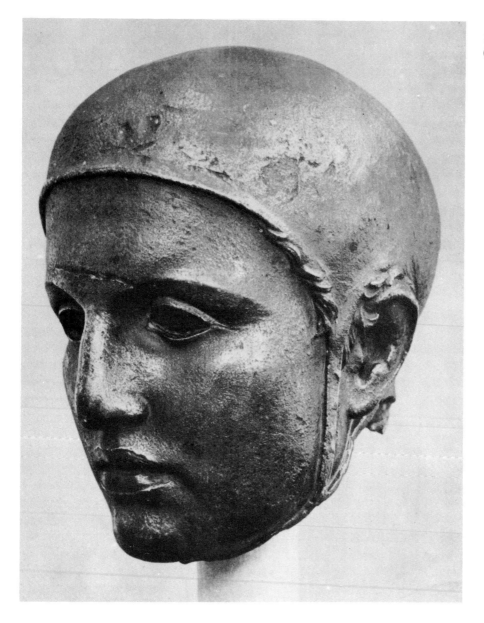

PLATE 35
Bronze Head of a Wrestler
(cat no. 31)

Hunter. Like the great collecting doctors of the early part of the century – Sloane, Mead or Woodward – he accumulated shells, minerals and manuscripts as well as antiquities. When Hunter died in 1783 his cabinet was 'the greatest in Europe if we only except that of the French King'. Into it had 'sunk' many other English collections such as that of the lawyer Philip Carteret and that 'most complete series of Syrian, Phoenician, Grecian, Roman and other Coins' assembled by another lawyer, Matthew Duane, 'for the Illustration and Confirmation of History'.[5] Hunter did not obtain all of these however for it was at the sale of Duane's collection in 1785 that Knight began his own. Hunter's decision to donate his collection to the nation (Knight tried to divert it to the British Museum[6] but it went to Glasgow University) must also have influenced Knight.

The immediate stimulus for Knight's collection of coins may have been his contact with d'Hancarville, whose *Recherches* published in 1784 showed how much evidence coins could provide – or could be made to provide – on the origins of ancient religion and language. Winckelmann too had shown how important coins could be in tracing the stylistic development of ancient art, and Knight may also have been encouraged by the example of his cousin Edward, who seems to have begun collecting coins and medals (Greek, Roman and modern) at the end of 1772.[7]

Unlike most earlier collectors of coins Knight greatly valued them for their beauty as well as for their historical interest. His enthusiasm, which is not conveyed by his concise Latin catalogue, bursts forth in English in the great opening sentence of the paper which, as an old man, he read to the Society of Antiquaries:

> Among the wrecks and fragments of ancient art and magnificence, which have resisted the waste of time, or escaped the more destructive ravages of barbarism and bigotry, none are so universally allowed to approach so near to abstract perfection, both in design and execution; or so far to surpass all subsequent efforts of imitation, as those large silver coins of Syracuse . . . commonly called Syracusan Medaglions.[8]

Until about 1760 these most beautiful examples of Greek art were rare (Colour Plate II) – although examples were to be seen in the Farnese collection and in that of Baron Stosch. Then over six hundred of them suddenly came to light in a single tomb and other tombs yielded more.[9] Knight was not the only collector to benefit; he had a rival in his friend Sir John Rushout (later 2nd Lord Northwick) whose series of the coins of Greek Sicily was as fine as his own and included the collection of the Prince of Torremuzza – its most splendid specimens were superbly published at the suggestion of Canova.[10]

Knight's collection at the time of his death comprised 5,205 coins. His cabinet of gems was much smaller, but was also filled with an eye to quality rather than quantity. In size it resembled that of his friend Cracherode – containing 111 pieces whereas Cracherode's contained 83 – rather than those of Charles Townley or the first collection of Sir William Hamilton (of 511 and 647 pieces respectively)[11] or the even larger collection of the

Duke of Marlborough.[12] The taste for antique cameos and gems was then at its height. Unlike coins they had always been relished above all for their beauty — as stones, of course, as well as carvings. A good idea of the reputation enjoyed by Knight's collection may be obtained from the fact that Mary Berry, having studied the cabinet of the Grand Duke of Tuscany, could declare Knight's to be 'quite as good'.[13] An unusual feature of Knight's collection was the high percentage of cameos (Colour Plate III) which it included, and these were certainly easier than intaglios for the amateur like Miss Berry to appreciate — some were unusually large (Plate 36).

PLATE 36
Cameo *Head of Jupiter* (cat. no. 18)

There were in Knight's collection when he died about 800 works in bronze — not only statuettes of great beauty, but charms, kitchen-ware and armour, chiefly of anthropological or historical importance, and many pieces of sculpture which he considered as of inferior style but valued for comparative purposes. Kept with his bronzes, or at least catalogued with them, were a number of curiosities which Knight believed to be ancient — the oddest of these was a ball of millofiori glass (cat. no. 71) — and some pieces which he knew to be modern, such as a Renaissance boar spear (cat. no. 69), a silver cup which he attributed to Cellini (cat. no. 47), a Renaissance ivory relief (cat. no. 70) and a hone stone carving by Georg Schweigger after a Dürer print, which he considered to be by Dürer himself.[14] There were also a few items of bone and coral, some stone age weapons which Knight brilliantly identified as ancient axe heads,[15] and some ancient work in gold and in silver (cat. nos. 42–6).

The sources of Knight's collection are not easy to trace. He does not always supply a provenance in his catalogue of bronzes, rarely in his catalogue of gems, and never in his catalogue of coins, and such small works of art whatever their fame or value travelled swiftly and unnoticed to and fro across frontiers. For the collecting of antiquities in general Rome was of course the centre. Among the resident dealers there who supplied Knight with bronzes were the banker Thomas Jenkins,[16] who has already been mentioned, the architect and cicerone James Byres[17] and the gem-engraver Nathaniel Marchant.[18] Jenkins and Marchant certainly also sold gems and we know that Knight had a cameo from Byres.[19] He purchased at least one bronze from the Abbate Filippo Aurelio Visconti, brother of the leading antiquarian in Rome – Ennio Quirino Visconti, cataloguer of the Museo Pio-Clementino[20] – and he acquired some which had belonged to earlier scholars and antiquarians such as Gori[21] and Bellori.[22] He also had gems which had belonged to the princely collections of the Strozzi,[23] the Albani[24] and Borghese.[25] His chief rival in this field, Sir Richard Worsley, secured pieces from the Farnese, the Colonna, the Prince of Conti and the Duke of Mantua.[26] Knight, like Worsley, was not only supplied from Rome. He obtained bronzes from the Gaddi family in Florence[27] and, most interesting of all, he obtained the collection of erotic ancient bronzes which had embarrassed visitors to the curious Villa of the philosophical Venetian Senator Angelo Quirini at Alticchiero near Padua, presumably soon after Quirini's death in 1796[28] when political turmoil in Italy drove so much onto the market.

Knight of course acquired much of his collection at auction and privately from other collectors or from dealers in London. He even found some important bronzes in a broker's shop there.[29] It is also notable how many smaller pieces in bronze were given to him by English friends – Charles Townley, for instance, with whom he also made exchanges,[30] Samuel Rogers,[31] Taylor Combe,[32] Lord Northwick,[33] Lord Lansdowne,[34] and the Duke of Buccleuch.[35] He acquired some very valuable pieces in this way as well, such as the Capheaton silver treasure presented by Sir John Swinburne.[36] Other collectors, for instance Sir Richard Worsley who was so proud of his Greek marbles and his gems, gave him small bronzes[37] in recognition of the specialist character of his collection. Knight's refusal to traffic in art, his dedication to the integral preservation of his collection, and his determination to present it to the nation were surely also acknowledged.

Despite the importance of gifts from English friends, Knight's acquisitions in France were more spectacular. Whatever his views of the French Revolution as a political occurrence, he can only have welcomed its effect on the art market. He was in Paris in 1791 buying from Le Brun, the leading dealer there,[38] and securing, after tricky negotiations, some important pieces from the collection of the learned traveller the Duc de Chaulnes, which had been bought as a speculation by a sharp dealer in oriental bric-à-brac.[39] From the dissolved Jesuit College at Lyons a fellow member of the Society of Dilettanti, Roger Wilbraham, purchased several pieces including an important bacchic mask[40] which found its way into Knight's collection along with the silver plate found at Caubiac (cat. no.

42) and the statuettes found at Mâcon (Colour Plate IV and cat. nos. 44–6). In making these acquisitions Knight was assisted by one of the leading French collectors of coins and antiquities (and also 'curiosités de la Chine, de l'Inde, de la Gaule'), the Abbé Charles Philippe de Tersan (sometimes spelt Tersant) who himself – 'upon the dangers which threatened all the French clergy in 1792' – sold Knight a highly important bronze Mercury found near Huis in 1732 which he had inherited from the Abbé Chalat[41] and some pieces which he had himself excavated or purchased.[42] Knight's contact with Tersan dated back to 1788 if not earlier. In that year, as also in 1791, he bought coins from him – and he also bought very heavily (spending nearly £500) at the sale of the great numismatist Michelet d'Ennery (1709–86), whose collection Tersan catalogued.[43]

Looking through Knight's catalogue of bronzes it is clear that one source was of greater importance even than Tersan. Sir William Hamilton, Envoy Extraordinary and Minister Plenipotentiary at the Court of the Two Sicilies in Naples is now chiefly remembered for his mistress, later his wife, the beautiful and accomplished Emma Hart (cat. no. 61), for his researches on volcanoes and for his great collections of Greek vases – of which the first, sumptuously published by d'Hancarville, was bought by the British Museum in 1772 and the second (published by Tischbein) was partly lost at sea in 1798 (divers recently have recovered the scraps) and partly sold to Thomas Hope. Knight admired Greek vases and he eventually owned about fifty of them.[44] Together with keener collectors such as Thomas Hope and Sir Harry Englefield he was a bidder at the important sales of the early nineteenth century and he even paid over £30 for a few examples, but he said that he was concerned to secure suitable ornaments for the tops of his cases, which hardly suggests that it was a serious interest,[45] and it is noteworthy that he hardly ever refers to vases in his writing on ancient art.

As well as vases, Hamilton's first collection contained gems and coins and bronzes.[46] It is perhaps no coincidence that it was in 1785, soon after Hamilton had revisited London, that Knight commenced collecting these very items. Of a little over a hundred bronzes in his catalogue Knight notes 'from Sir William Hamilton' or 'sent by Sir William Hamilton'. One or two pieces might have been gifts and one piece, an ass's head, was a present – perhaps not an entirely kind one – from Lady Hamilton, whom Knight greatly admired.[47] Many of the bronzes must have been supplied by dealers because they were cleaned or restored in ways that Hamilton must have known that Knight deplored. Little, however, is recorded of their provenance, although we do know that one bronze face had served as the head of a walking stick 'in which employment Sir W. Hamilton found it in the hands of a Calabrian peasant'.[48] Some of the bronzes were Etruscan, others from the ancient Greek colonies of southern Italy, and some may have come, despite the security supposed to prevent this, from the buried cities of Herculaneum and Pompeii. Goethe was sure that some bronze candelabra he glimpsed in Hamilton's cellars must have 'strayed' from the Royal collection of Herculaneum antiquities (then kept at Portici).[49]

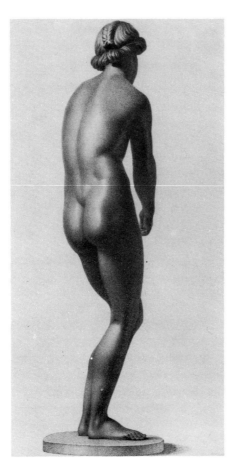
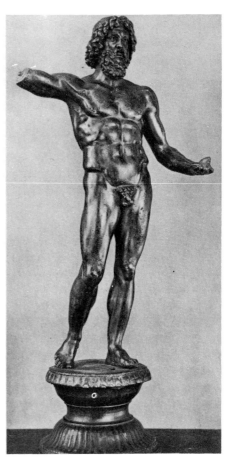

These must be the candelabra in Knight's collection catalogued as 'duplicates' from Portici.[50]

Hamilton may have been the chief source of Knight's bronzes (Knight also in 1791 bought coins from him to the value of £48 16s 0d),[51] but the most important sculpture (Plates 37 and 38) in Knight's collection came from a hoard which some peasants uncovered at a site near Paramythia in north-west Greece in 1791 or 1792, the years when Knight was busiest buying in France. A coppersmith in the local town gave some pieces away, and sold some, principally to a dealer who took them to Saint Petersburg where the Empress Catharine died before he had concluded the sale with her. Six of the statuettes were acquired by Count Golowkin and have disappeared. Ten were acquired by 'a learned and respectable Polish traveller', Christopher von Wiessiolowski (also spelt Wierislowsky) and taken to Warsaw. Knight, who had acquired a stray statuette from the group which had been purchased at Janina and taken to England by a dragoman at the Turkish Embassy, succeeded in acquiring Wiessiolowski's examples, which seem to have been taken to London where they were valued by Townley at £585. Later from his friend Lord Aberdeen, who travelled to Greece in 1803, Knight received another fragment from the same hoard.[52]

Aberdeen was not the only traveller who supplied Knight's collection. Sir William Gell, who was more interested in topography than art, and whose voyage to Greece and Asia Minor (commenced in 1811) was sponsored by the 'Dillys' as he called them, seems to have kept Knight's interests in mind, as did Dr E. D. Clarke.[53] Gell, Aberdeen and Clarke all deplored the depredations made on the Parthenon by the agents of Lord Elgin[54] – a much less learned man but one who as British Ambassador to the Porte had far greater influence. However, they picked up what they could. And wherever they went baskets of ancient coins were sold to them by peasants. (Albanian women used the silver ones as ornaments in their head-dresses but were prepared to swap these for new ones.)[55]

These men were travelling in the eastern Mediterranean at a time when Napoleon had closed Italy to the English. Knight, however, had contacts there. Among these was James Millingen, failed banker, successful dealer and considerable scholar, of Dutch extraction but with an English education, who was Resident first in France and then in Rome and Naples. In addition to coins he supplied Knight with some of the repoussé bronze and silver ornaments from ancient chariots found near Perugia in 1812.[56] There was also – perhaps above all – an Italian dealer, Angelo Bonelli, who had made 'a very large sum by importing pictures from Rome' and who is first mentioned in London when he sold thirty-five paintings at Philipe's on 8 May 1806. He had 'an agent or partner in Sicily, employed to buy medals and antiquities to any amount'. As well as coins, and at least one bronze,[57] he supplied Knight with gems – as we shall see.

Gell also settled in Italy after the Napoleonic wars and was an important figure in expatriate society in both Rome and Naples. In a letter from Rome of 25 June 1818 sandwiched between a discussion of the topography of Troy and an account of the excavations in the Forum, he mentions that he has sent home

> by Lord Craven a very curious & perfect Bronze Vase . . . It was found some-where near Metapontum in Magna Graecia & belonged to the Ex-Queen to some of whose people to whom she owed their wages she gave it or they stole it at the return of the old Government. I am so apt to give away my goods, that now in my old age & infirmities I am resolved to sell it, & as I know it is well worth 100£ being I believe quite unique I have desired Mr Gandy to destroy it if I cannot get at least 50 for it as I will not be cheated because I was born a gentleman any more. So if your know of any persons who purchase such articles . . .[58]

Another important contact was probably Sir William Drummond, friend of Lord Aberdeen and a fellow member of the Society of Dilettanti, who as Ambassador to the Porte had done his best to frustrate the activities of his predecessor, Lord Elgin.[59] He also served as Hamilton's successor in Naples. In both positions he doubtless took advantage of the opportunities pres-ented to all diplomats at that date to acquire and traffic in works of art.[60] Among his and Elgin's predecessors as Ambassador to the Porte was Sir Robert Ainslie, who resided in Constantinople between 1776 and 1792.

The rare coins of the 'collezione Ainsleana' were the subject of four volumes published between 1789 and 1790 by the numismatist Domenico Sestini, who in 1790 devoted a separate volume to the 'monete Armene dei Principi Rupinensi' in the same collection.[61] Sestini paid obsequious tribute to Ainslie in these works but abused him as a crook in a later publication.[62] Ainslie was a member of the Society of Dilettanti and evidently well known to Knight, to whom he presented a bronze Egyptian cat[63] and from whom Knight acquired two gems[64] — another, which, as we will see, was to prove the most controversial item in Knight's entire collection, the fragment of a cameo of Flora, was said to have come from Ainslie. In 1801 Knight expended the enormous sum of £1,258 6s 0d on a 'moiety' of his collection of coins.[65]

The most obvious characteristics of Knight's taste as reflected in his collection are his special interest in objects of metal (he was, we must remember, the grandson and the nephew of ironmasters) and his preference for objects of a small scale. This second characteristic has been advanced as an explanation for Knight's failure to appreciate the merits of the Parthenon sculpture. However it must be conceded that Knight showed plenty of enthusiasm for life-size sculpture in the text he supplied for the *Specimens of Antient Sculpture* and he even enjoyed envisaging the colossal cryselephantine cult effigies of the Greeks — which, had they survived, would have been sufficient 'to reconcile even a Jew or a Mahometan to idolatory'.[66] However, he did have some resistance to the idea that the great sculptors of antiquity were personally engaged in architectural sculpture and he knew that in antiquity such works had never been as highly regarded as free-standing statues. Such work he seems to have felt must have been of subordinate importance, even 'decorative' as distinct from 'fine' art. Thus he likened the Parthenon frieze to grisaille painting.[67] As such it was 'extremely light and elegant'. In a private letter he wrote that the difference between the best pieces of marble sculpture in Townley's collection and the Parthenon frieze was like that between the altarpieces of Titian and the decorations (produced for houses by Adam and Wyatt) of the minor artist Biagio Rebecca![68] As if in belated recognition of this error in judgement he warmly welcomed the acquisition of the frieze of the Temple of Apollo at Bassae.[69] Also he was eventually prepared to give more praise to the frieze and to the metopes of the Parthenon, although he consistently (and quite rightly) emphasized the uneven quality to be found in the latter.[70]

Whatever his view of large marble sculpture, it is true that Knight did not like large mural paintings. He held that there was 'more real grandeur and sublimity' in Raphael's *Vision of Ezekiel* or in Rosa's *Saul and the Witch of Endor* 'than in all the vast and turgid compositions of the Sistine Chapel'.[71] He could rationalize the preference ably:

When the whole of a picture does not come within the field of vision, from the point of distance best adapted to show the beauties of particular expression and detail in the parts, it is too large; since its effect on the mind must necessarily be weakened by being divided, and the apt relation of the parts to each other and to the whole, in which the merit of all composition consists, be less striking when gradually discovered than when seen at once.[72]

This is not easily refuted, and we might also agree that Raphael would have been better employed painting his 'designs of Cupid and Psyche' in oil rather than in supervising the decoration of the 'corridors of the Vatican',[73] but a moment's reflection as to what would be lost if the *School of Athens* was executed on a smaller scale makes one realize that this preference for cabinet pictures was a serious limitation in Knight's taste.

Knight's enemies were certain that his taste had been corrupted by his pleasure in miniature art. How could the fastidious admirer of coins and gems appreciate the grand forms of the *Theseus*? And, in any case, unfortunately for Knight, a story was circulated at the time of his controversial evidence to the Select Committee concerned with the purchase of Lord Elgin's marbles, that cast doubt on his connoisseurship even in this area of art. It was broadcast thus by Croker in a deadly footnote to his abuse of Knight in the *Quarterly Review*:

> Mr Knight some years since bought an antique cameo of FLORA for 250L. and as long as our intercourse with the continent was restricted, his FLORA was undoubted; but lo! Sig. PETRUCCI [*sic*], an ingenious Italian, comes to England, and discovers the supposed antique to be a modern gem: this, of course, Mr Knight denies – Petrucci insists, and at last Petrucci, in his own defence, is obliged to confess, what he has since sworn before a magistrate, that *he* is *himself* the author of the *modern antique*, which he was employed to engrave by Sig. BONELLI, who paid him *twenty Scudi* for it, and of whom Mr Payne Knight was fortunate enough to repurchase it, as an undoubted antique.[74]

In a pamphlet replying to Croker Knight stated his version of the facts. About three years before – that is in about 1812 – he had bought gems from 'Mr Bonelli of Golden Square', among them the cameo of Flora (Plate 39), valued at £100 (not £250), and 'paid for partly in money, and partly in duplicate medals'. The cameo was not sold as certainly an antique but

> not only the purchaser, but the late Mr Marchant, whom he consulted as usual, and other experienced judges, held it to be so; nor was it doubted till about four months ago, when Mr Pistrucci proclaimed it at Sir Joseph Banks's to be his own work, executed for Mr Bonelli for twenty Roman Crowns, exclusive of the stone which his employer supplied. Mr Knight however, so far from persisting and blustering, as the Reviewer states, expressed his satisfaction in Italian, and in the presence of Sir Joseph Banks, at there being a living artist of so much merit; and from thence went to Mr Bonelli and urged him to tell the truth, assuring him at the same time that, admitting the work to be Pistrucci's, he had no charge to make against him; the unique beauty of the stone being a sufficient reason for the price. Bonelli persisted that he had bought it among a parcel of others, said to have belonged to the late Sir Robert Ainsley, covered with a calcarious incrustation, which he employed

PLATE 39
Probably Benedetto Pistrucci, Cameo *Head of Flora* (cat no. 19)

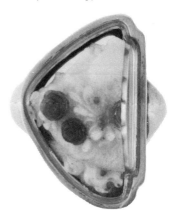

Pistrucci to remove, and paid him twenty Roman Crowns for the work, and the expence of having it set in a ring. As the readiest means of judging between them, Mr Knight commissioned Mr Pistrucci to make a fac-simile, which he accordingly did, and at the end of three months brought it, of the same form indeed, but in style and execution as different as possible to his eye, and demanded for it, not as the reviewer states, *ten*, but *fifty pounds sterling*; and in addition that the purchaser should formally acknowledge both to be by the same hand. This impudent proposal, repeated the next day in writing, Mr Knight civilly, yet peremptorily declined; but so far from blustering or persisting obstinately, proposed that both works should be submitted together to the most able and experienced judges, to decide between the two contrary asserters, being himself quite indifferent in it, the article remaining the same, whoever made it; and its pecuniary value being no consideration, he never having sold, or attempted to sell, otherwise than at public auction without reserve, any work of art, at any other price than that which he paid.[75]

Knight certainly was not unduly flustered. His friendship with and kindness to Sir Joseph Banks did not 'abate a single atom' during the contest between Knight and Bonelli and Banks's protégé Pistrucci. Or so Banks claimed in July 1816 when reporting to Thomas Andrew Knight that Pistrucci was employed at the mint . . . 'his reputation increases daily while Bonelli has left town and gone to Paris to answer some questions which your brother has occasion to put to him'.[76] (Bonelli had a large sale at Phillips' in March 1818 at which he perhaps sold his stock.) Pistrucci, although certainly not someone whose word it would be wise to trust on all occasions, seems unlikely to have dared to invent his story and to the eyes of modern experts the carving does not look ancient. On the other hand, the secret mark which he claimed to have made on the stone has not been found[77] and the facsimiles he made have not, it seems, been compared with the work in the British Museum.

In any case the story provides no evidence that Knight was easily duped – nor does the fact that about a third of his gems are now regarded (but have not of course been proved) to be modern, for the percentage of supposed forgeries in most collections of this period is considerably higher. Only one item in his catalogue of gems is described as modern and that, curiously, was a head of Augustus by Pistrucci which Knight praised in the highest terms.[78]

That Knight was a very keen observer could not be disputed by anyone familiar with his writing. He was unusual then (and would be now) for always thinking about the artist's technique. The geometric designs on the reverses of early Greek coins were in Knight's day generally considered as marks of the anvil by which the metal blank was held steady whilst the obverse was struck by a punch die, but Knight recognized that the process must have been the reverse: and these marks made by the die of a punch which drove the metal into the main anvil die.[79] Again, Knight was constantly speculating as to the extent to which bronze (or brass as he called it) was chiselled. He was distinguished among writers on sculpture in this period by his awareness of how frequently antique marble sculptures reproduced a style of work more proper to the casting and chiselling of bronze – and were, thus, copies.[80] Also – and again this was most unusual – Knight drew attention to the varied texture and evident 'tooling' in marble sculpture. No one would now ridicule him for this as the ignorant Croker did,[81] but some modern historians, eager to discredit Knight, have suggested that the marks of the chisel which Knight admired in the *Laocoon* – and which 'express, when seen at the proper distance, the trembling elasticity and palpitation of the flesh, and even the grain and texture of the skin' – were made by a Renaissance restorer.[82] If so, then it is quite unlike the usual practice of restorers at that date. Knight's voice was also one of the first to be raised in criticism of the practice increasingly common in the early nineteenth century of sculptors not carving or casting their own works – in antiquity, by contrast, 'the last finish was by the chisel, wielded by the hand that had modelled, and directed by the mind that had conceived the whole'.[83]

It has sometimes been suggested that Knight's failure to appreciate the fragmentary sculpture of the Parthenon was due to an eighteenth-century prejudice in favour of antique art which had a uniform polished finish and which was highly restored.[84] But not only were Knight's views on finish quite different from those of most eighteenth- and nineteenth-century connoisseurs; he also made serious criticisms of the practice of restoration. None of his own bronzes was restored for him and when they had been at an earlier date he recorded it with regret, as he also did excessive cleaning.[85] He deplored the clumsy restoration of one of the marble heads in his collection. He pleaded for the removal of a beautiful marble head at Petworth from its modern bust and arranged for it to be so emancipated in the illustration of it in *Specimens* (cat. no. 93). In that publication Knight carefully described restorations and ensured that the engravers indicated them by dotted lines – even apologizing in a note for Townley's failure in one case to do so as well. Both he and Townley were also careful to exclude from this anthology statues whose character was substantially the invention of the restorer, such as Lord Lansdowne's *Diomedes with the Paladium* which was in fact originally a *Discobolus*. Knight was even apologetic about including Townley's own copy of the *Discobolus* because the head did not belong.[86]

Knight's attitudes may most effectively be thrown into relief by contrast with those of one of the most avid but less discriminating collectors of ancient marbles in England in this period – Henry Blundell, whose attitude to the symbolic content of ancient art was discussed in Chapter Four. Jenkins supplied him with his first piece in 1777[87] and thereafter he had never looked back. He had a number of fragments in his collection – including the rump of a Venus formerly the property of Stosch,[88] and bits of legs and heads,[89] and indeed Cavaceppi, the leading restorer in Rome in the late eighteenth century who supplied Blundell with a number of pieces, including some forgeries, sold him separate antique hands specially mounted on coloured marble plinths – spare parts which he hadn't been able to transplant (cat. no. 57). This shows that Blundell wasn't simply interested in 'furniture'. However he not only preferred restored marbles but took a very cavalier attitude to the process of restoration. He published a set of prints of his collection in 1809 – the same year that *Specimens* appeared – in which he illustrated a reclining statue which he had acquired from the Bessborough collection. This was a sleeping Hermaphrodite with children at its breast and as such had excited the curiosity of d'Hancarville years before.⁹⁰ Blundell found it 'unnatural and very disgusting to the sight'. But 'by means of a little castration and cutting away the brats', he continued breezily, 'it became a sleeping Venus and as pleasing a figure as any in this collection'.⁹¹

The awareness of restoration which one finds in Knight was encouraged by the writings of Winckelmann and his circle and successors. It was Winckelmann's friend Mengs who was chiefly responsible for suggesting that many of the most admired antique statues – indeed even the *Apollo Belvedere* – were copies made for the Romans of earlier, lost Greek or Hellenistic originals, often of bronze.⁹² Whilst many of the leading authorities on the continent were denying this theory or qualifying it, Knight (acknowledging no debts, needless to say) accepted it entirely. In 1791 he had suggested that both the *Farnese Hercules* and the *Belvedere Torso* were probably copies made in the second century AD.⁹³ By 1809 he was prepared to entertain the idea that the *Belvedere Antinous*, the *Apollo Belvedere*, the *Dying Gladiator*, the *Fighting Gladiators* and the *Niobe Group* were copies.⁹⁴ By then he had more complicated ideas concerning the *Torso*. The lettering of the signature could not date from before 100 BC, but inscriptions were sometimes added to earlier works and the execution here was earlier, because better, than was possible after 100 BC. However the execution was inferior to the composition. Perhaps, therefore, it was a free copy of a famous colossal bronze by Lysippus.⁹⁵ This reads like a parody of the sort of hypothesis in which modern archaeologists delight. Some of Knight's speculations concerning the status of famous statues in Italy were prompted by his recognition of the merits of duplicates of them in English collections, such as the head of Niobe at Brocklesby (Plate 40) and the head of Venus at Petworth (cat. no. 68). His original supposition that the sculpture of the Parthenon dated from the Emperor Hadrian's restoration of Athens was based on the misunderstandings in outdated travel literature but his persistent suspicion that parts of the pedimental sculpture were Roman⁹⁶ was conditioned by 'advanced' rather than out-dated ideas.

Even more important then the awareness of restoration and of copies in the new archaeological writing of the late eighteenth century was the keen interest in tracing the chronological development of ancient art, through successive stylistic phases, with the purpose of discriminating the 'fairest relics of the purest times'. This meant of course a stronger distinction between Greek and Roman art than had formerly been usual. Knight's collection included no Roman coins. 'The coins of Mithridates are the last which display any of that greatness of style, which distinguishes those of the Greek republics and Macedonian kings', he wrote and con-

PLATE 40 *Left
Head of Niobe* (cat. no. 55)

PLATE 41 *Right
Bronze Figure of a Ram-
Headed Deity* (cat. no. 38)

sidered that to compare the coin portraits of Alexander and his successors with those of Augustus and his was like comparing the paintings of Titian and Rubens with those of Denner and Vanderwerf.[97] He despised the grotesque decoration discovered at Pompeii and Herculaneum as a 'miserable style of daubing popular among a people who had no principles of true taste'.[98] For Roman architecture he had more admiration – indeed he imitated the Pantheon at Downton – and the powers of imitation and execution possessed by sculptors under the Emperors, especially in the age of the Antonines and Hadrian, were praised by him, although not their powers of invention.[99]

These are the values to which all Winckelmann's readers paid lip-service, but in practice taste changed slowly. Thus we find Goethe greeting the sarcophagus in the church of Agrigento in 1787 as the most glorious relief he had ever seen and a specimen of the finest Greek taste,[100] Knight, a decade earlier, had noted its resemblance to that of Julia Mammea and Alexander Severus at Rome, observing,

> The Sculpture is much in the same stile, perhaps not so good, tho' the Grigen-tines, who never saw any thing better, esteem it as a prodigy of art, and have persuaded some travellers who judge more by the Ears than by their Eyes, to

be of the same opinion. It appears to me to be Roman, and probably contained the ashes of some Consul or Praetor under the Emperors.[101]

To the austere early phases of Greek art, on the other hand, Knight was unfailingly sympathetic. Of the Doric order of the ruined temples at Paestum and at various sites in Sicily which both Adam and Chambers, the leading architects in England in the 1760s, considered rude and 'gouty', and which William Young in his travel book published a few years earlier considered as remote from true Greek elegance as were Gothic cathedrals,[102] Knight wrote 'the general effect is grand, simple and even elegant. The rudeness appears here as an artful negligence, and the heaviness a just and noble stability'.[103] Works which he did consider to be primitive still often excited his admiration and always his interest — the earliest coins, for instance, and Etruscan (Colour Plate V) or Archaic Greek statuettes; the red jasper prism carved with cows and lions in the Minoan style which was found by Gell in the Peloponnese and published by Knight together with Gell's drawing of the gates of Mycenae;[104] Hindu and Egyptian art (Plate 41) and even the very early British art such as a beaten gold amulet from the Isle of Man[105] or a serpentine bracelet found in Cardiganshire and presented to him by his kinsman Thomas Johnes of Hafod.[106]

'The prodigious superiority of the Greeks over every other nation, in all works of real taste and genius', Knight wrote, 'is one of the most curious moral phaenomena in the history of man',[107] and throughout his life he pondered on the causes of this. The theory that climate was an important factor he strongly rejected.[108] On the other hand he believed that the rigid hierarchical society of the Hindus and Egyptians was artistically inhibiting because it rendered each craftsman 'almost as much a machine as the implement he employed' — excellent 'in works which require only methodical labour and manual dexterity' but incapable of anything 'that discovers the smallest trace or symptom of those powers of the mind, which we call taste and genius; and of which the most early and imperfect works of the Greeks always show some dawning'.[109]

As a young Whig in Sicily Knight was prompted to ponder before the ruined temples of Selinus upon the 'inestimable' blessing of liberty that 'enabled so small a state, whose dominions extended but a few miles to perform what the mighty Lords of the Earth have scarcely equalled'.[110] Similarly tinged by enlightened libertarianism is his doubt concerning the advantages of most forms of government interference in the arts (although he served on the Committee of Taste) and his attacks on academies of art established on the French principle which had produced much 'blameless mediocrity' but not a single great artist.[111] Nevertheless if Knight managed to convince himself that art owed little of value to Louis XIV he argued — with good reasons — that the most splendid coins of Greek Sicily were produced under the direct patronage of the older and younger Dionysius — tyrants of Syracuse[112] — whereas the 'attention of a popular government; such as that of Athens though interested in the merits of a great statue . . .

could not descend to the minute beauties of a piece of money'.[113] This point of view was not, however, inconsistent with Knight's belief that the Greeks were able in the early stages of their civilization to imitate nature and to innovate because they were not restricted by the rule of priests to rigid traditions.

Another factor conditioning the progress of the arts in Greece was language; for words, Knight noted, were not merely 'the signs by which we communicate ideas to each other, but the counters, by which we distinguish, arrange and subdivide them in our minds',[114] and thus effect our understanding of the visual world, and, in a society in which poetry played a vital part, effect taste in every respect. The Phoenicians who seem also to have enjoyed freedom from 'religious or political restraint' achieved, Knight believed, a degree of naturalism, at least as represented in their coinage, but no more than this because they possessed 'no Iliad or Odyssey, nor probably a language capable of such compositions'. On the other hand the 'sublime imagery' of the early Greek poets 'so exalted and expanded all around them and presented it to their heated imaginations so augmented and embellished, that imitation learned to surpass reality'.[115]

The climax of art was reached in that 'highly grand and poetical' style which 'prevailed under the first dynasties of the Macedonian Conquerors'. This was represented, Knight believed, by the *Laocoon* and the *Barberini Faun* and, rather surprisingly we must feel, in a marble head in his own collection – purchased at Burke's sale – which he believed to represent Achilles 'when retired in disgust'.[116] Knight admired nothing in literature more than the portrayal of Achilles in the *Iliad*[117] and he felt that the example of such a portrayal must have made the most profound impression upon the minds of all Greek artists.

Apart from the fact that he would have preferred the heroes to have been portrayed nude or in Classical attire rather than wearing their contemporary uniforms, the sculptors of the patriotic memorials, which Knight, as a member of the Committee of Public Taste supervised, complied with his recommendations, or rather concurred in his taste, avoiding the example of Bernini who had encouraged sculptors to attempt styles and subjects proper to the art of painting.[118] There is no evidence, however, that Knight thought highly of what was erected in St Paul's, and no one who had followed his arguments could believe that he would have been optimistic about the success of any attempt to revive in modern Britain the sculpture which had flourished in such extraordinary circumstances in ancient Greece.

It is curious that Knight's influence on the Committee of Taste was objected to not on the grounds that he was obsessively concerned with the antique but because of his taste in modern painting which was, Lawrence alleged, gratified by the 'luxurious displays of Rubens' rather than by the 'simplicity' and 'purity of Raphael'.[119] Lawrence must have read Knight's *Inquiry* hastily, for Knight declares his admiration for the purity of Raphael's designs quite clearly,[120] but it is true that Knight did enjoy the 'luxurious displays of Rubens' — as also those of Lawrence! What is more he loved Dutch painters of unelevated nature and low life and even commended Rembrandt for refusing to copy antique sculpture and preferring to seek inspiration in a wardrobe of fancy dress.[121] This may seem surprising, but it was certainly not inconsistent, for just as Knight believed that sculpture should not imitate painting so the reverse applied. In the oil painting as in the stage play 'a detailed adherence to the peculiarities of common individual nature' was often required and always admissable, whereas nature should be elevated in marble sculpture or epic poetry.[122]

And so Knight did nothing to encourage a school of English painters devoted to heroic subjects, statuesque figures, and rigidly planar compositions. The 'principles and practice' of David, he observed, 'are happily as little deserving imitation in art as in morals or politics'.[123] He had some faith in contemporary painting and in 1805 he cited as among the 'most interesting and affecting pictures that art has ever produced' West's *Death of Wolfe*, Westall's *Harvesters in a Storm* (Colour Plate VI) and Wright's *Soldiers' Tent*.[124] He approved and promoted the success of Lawrence, Wilkie and Turner. And yet at times Knight appears as an enemy of modern art, or at least profoundly convinced that modern man is fallen from aesthetic grace. The mere kitchen utensils of the ancients in metal or terracotta possessed an elegance unknown to modern manufacture,[125] he claimed, as Wedgwood's export orders steadily rose. As for the English language, it was surprisingly good for a 'corrupt dialect' but could 'never arrive at the force, majesty & precision of the Greek and Latin', or as he put it later, 'the polished languages of modern Europe, could never rival those of the Greeks and Romans in 'poetical diction and expression'.[126]

CHAPTER SIX—*'Visible Appearances'*

In the midst of correcting the proofs for the second edition of his *Analytical Inquiry Into the Principles of Taste*, Knight wrote to his friend Samuel Parr explaining how he had come to write the book. He was first induced to write it, he says, by Parr's apparent enthusiasm for the opinions of their mutual friend Uvedale Price on that vexed subject upon which both Price and Knight expended so much labour – the nature of the 'picturesque'. The two had of course crossed swords over the matter before; Knight (in the second edition of *The Landscape*) attacking Price's definition and usage of the word in his *Essay on the Picturesque*; and Price replying to this attack in his *Dialogue on the Distinct Characters of the Picturesque and Beautiful*. It was this last work in particular that had urged Knight to pursue the matter further since it had convinced him, he tells Parr, that 'the philosophy of mind had never been applied to the subject',[1] Price not being notable, he adds, for 'depth or acuteness' in this field. But he goes on to explain how the *Inquiry* had grown far beyond his initial plan of an answer to Price. Considering that a private dispute over 'the meaning of a technical term' would not be of general interest, he had resolved to give what he calls his 'whole creed upon the subject'.[2] The range of the *Inquiry*, as one of its reviewers pointed out, is indeed encyclopaedic.[3] I shall however concentrate upon Knight's arguments upon this 'technical term' since it is from his controversy with Price that Knight developed his theory of painting. But something must first be said on the nature of Knight's beliefs on the broader subject of 'Taste', and of the tradition of which his book forms an important part.

Perhaps the only work of British eighteenth-century aesthetics which is at all widely read today is Edmund Burke's *Philosophical Enquiry into the Origins of our Ideas of the Sublime and Beautiful*. Burke had proposed that there are certain qualities inherent in objects which, by a direct physiological effect upon our senses, either painful or pleasing, give rise to our ideas of sublimity or beauty. It was upon Burke's theories that Price had established his discussion of the picturesque, so Knight, in attacking Price, also sets about demolishing Burke's system. Indeed, it appears that he had formed his objections to Burke some time before he had become engaged in controversy with Price. He recounts to Parr that he had on two occasions discussed the matter with Burke who had conceded his arguments, and as far back as 1776 he had expressed certain misgivings about Burke's *Enquiry*[4] in a letter written from Rome to George Romney. Burke had, he feels, placed too much emphasis on the role of 'sensual impressions' neglecting the influence of our mental faculties on our aesthetic responses, and in a plan of a proposed work which he outlines to Romney reveals that, were he to write on the subject, he would pay much attention to the part played by memory, imagination and the passions. Nevertheless he does express his esteem for Burke's work in this letter and furthermore includes in this plan an extensive section on 'the nature of sensual pleasure and pain',[5] a section which, we may imagine, would have owed a good deal to Burke's theories. This plan approximates quite closely to that which Knight eventually adopted for his *Analytical Inquiry*, but by then he was prepared to accept virtually none of Burke's ideas, treating them with considerable contempt. The proposed section on 'sensual pleasure and pain' becomes in the *Inquiry* his first section entitled 'Of Sensation', but instead of positively establishing the role of 'sensual impressions' in forming our aesthetic responses, Knight's intention is rather to show just how very limited their influence really is. The only case where they can truly be said to play an important role, Knight concludes, is that of colour acting upon the eye.

The fundamental structure of the *Inquiry* appears to have evolved, over a long period, from Knight's response to Burke, but the arguments by which he attacks Burke are derived from the other principal current in late eighteenth-century British aesthetics – Scottish Associationism. The associationist doctrine, applied most comprehensively by Archibald Alison in his *Essays on the Nature and Principles of Taste* of 1790, denied that any of our 'emotions of taste' derived from sensation and further denied that there were any discernible qualities inherent in external objects which could be categorised as beautiful or sublime. External objects merely prompt complex trains of associations which are themselves established from previous experience. Alison attempts to account for the whole range of our aesthetic responses by association, even the pleasures we receive from colour. Thus colours only please by acting as signs expressive of other qualities which are themselves pleasing or displeasing. The colour blue for instance is universally held to be beautiful because the 'colour of the heavens in serene weather is blue'[6] while pink or rose tints are pleasing because they are associated in our minds with a young or healthy complexion.

Like Alison, Knight places a great deal of emphasis upon the influence of associations but his use of the doctrine is neither as extensive nor as methodical, and on the point of colour Alison had, Knight believed, carried his system much too far. For Knight, associationism, like Burke's sensationism, could not on its own serve as an exhaustive explanation of the nature of 'Taste', but by admitting colour to be pleasing to the eye, he laid his work open to the charge that it was self-contradictory. Francis Jeffrey, Alison's keenest advocate, condemned Knight's concession to sensation as 'a heresy inconsistent with the very first principle of Catholic philosophy'.[7] Nevertheless Knight's appeal to the Scottish tradition of aesthetics makes the *Inquiry* the most sophisticated work on the subject to be produced in England during the period.

It is by no means clear that the large number of works published on

'Taste' in Scotland during the second half of the eighteenth century were widely known in England. Certainly Alison's book was barely known at all until Jeffrey's enthusiastic article on it in the May 1811 number of the *Edinburgh Review*, after which many editions appeared throughout the nineteenth century. But in 1805, the year that Knight's *Inquiry* appeared, Francis Horner could write that Alison's *Essays* had 'only just got into Holland House . . . Nobody has heard of it before'.[8] This ignorance of Scottish writings on Taste no doubt contributed greatly to the success of Knight's book — and indeed, it was by all accounts highly successful. It went into four editions between 1805 and 1808, and such was the interest in it when it was first published that Sydney Smith wrote from London that 'Knight's book has attracted amazing attention here'.[9] But its popularity seems to have been relatively short-lived. We can only speculate on why this was so, but the rise in fortunes of Alison's more systematic work must surely have turned attention away from Knight's *Inquiry*. Likewise Price's *Essays on the Picturesque* — more generally accessible and more concerned with practical matters — continued in their popularity and were republished as late as 1852, though underpinned by an Alisonian commentary written by Sir Thomas Dick Lauder.

Price seems to have been quite unable to understand how the association of ideas could, as Alison had proposed, account for the most complex aesthetic responses. To him, as is evident from a letter he wrote to Lord Aberdeen in 1816, associationism meant only the simple and direct associations which give us pleasure when, for instance, we return to 'the school where we were educated' or the 'field where we played when boys'.[10] Considered solely in terms of such personal associations the doctrine would not only fail to provide anything like a full explanation of the nature of 'Taste', but would also militate against the possibility of establishing any fixed standard of taste. But as Alison was keen to show, in addition to associations limited to individuals or arising from local or national characteristics, certain associations would be universally held, such as that he adduces to explain the pleasing nature of the colour blue. Conversely the fact that the standard of taste was manifestly different in each country and for every individual, further served to confirm the veracity of the doctrine. Thus Knight begins his *Inquiry* by addressing this issue, showing by example the divergence of men's opinions of what is beautiful in different parts of the world, and during different ages.

The sensationalist theory which Burke advanced, however, allowed that there were certain fixed standards, since the qualities of external objects are constant, and since the 'organs of sense' in all men are physiologically the same. Accordingly, given that this was how our ideas of beauty and sublimity arose, the particular objects in the natural world may be said to be permanently and universally beautiful and sublime. This, and the general straightforwardness of the theory, must have contributed greatly to the appeal of Burke's work to Price, concerned as he primarily was simply to identify and describe the features of landscape scenery which could be categorized as 'picturesque' — something which William Gilpin had done in his short *Essay on Picturesque Beauty* of 1791.

Seeking to establish the 'picturesque' as a pleasing 'character', though distinct from beauty (he did not like Gilpin's composite 'picturesque beauty'), Price discusses certain qualities which are modifications of those Burke had proposed as qualities of beautiful objects. Thus, accepting Burke's proposition that 'smoothness' is a major source of our ideas of beauty, Price distinguishes 'ruggedness' as the principal quality of what he calls, with apologies, 'picturesqueness'. So, considering trees, for instance, he would argue that a smooth young birch may be described as beautiful while a gnarled and rugged old oak may be distinguished as 'picturesque'.

In proposing that 'smoothness' was a quality of beauty Burke appealed to a notion which received considerable attention during the eighteenth century – that of the 'harmony of the senses' or 'synaesthesia'. There was a similarity in the character of the pleasures received from each of the senses, he argued, so that if a certain quality in objects was pleasing to one sense we may expect to find it so to our other senses. Thus it will be readily agreed, Burke contends, that smooth surfaces are most pleasing to the touch, and, with a combination of extremely speculative physiology and rather fragile logic, he shows that this quality will also please our other senses, even that of sight. Price declares his conviction that 'there is, indeed, a general harmony and correspondence in all our sensations' near the beginning of his first *Essay*. He does not attempt, as Burke did, to describe how it operates, but nevertheless its importance for his arguments is as clear as it is for Burke's. For his intention in the *Essays* will be to discover 'whether there be certain qualities, which uniformly produce the same effects in all visible objects, and according to the analogy, in objects of hearing and of all the other senses'.[11] If a quality can be discerned which is so comprehensive, Price continues, then it surely deserves a distinct title and if we are to discover such it is essential that we do not 'confine our observations to one sense only'.[12]

In Knight's view Price's insistence that the senses should not be considered individually had led him into the most elementary errors. For if one was to attempt to discover the pleasures to be received directly from sensation, Knight argues, it was necessary to define the exact nature of the impressions received by each sense independently of the others. Hence his section 'Of Sensation' in the *Inquiry* is divided into five chapters in which he discusses each sense in turn. He had already outlined the elements of the argument which he presents in detail here, in his attack on Price's quality of picturesque 'ruggedness' in his note to *The Landscape*.[13] In his adoption and subsequent discussion of this quality of 'ruggedness', Knight believes, Price had failed to distinguish between a simple 'sensation' and a 'perception' acquired by the conjunction of the sense of sight and the sense of touch. There is of course, Knight says, nothing wrong in saying that we 'see' objects to be rugged or smooth. But if we are to suggest that certain qualities in objects have a direct physiological effect upon the eye, in the manner described by Burke, and accepted by Price, it is essential that these qualities are such as are apprehended by the eye alone. In suggesting otherwise both Burke and Price had, in Knight's opinion, contradicted the fundamental principles of the theory of vision.

In order to prove his point in the *Inquiry* Knight opens his chapter 'Of Sight' with a discussion of the celebrated case of a boy born blind who at the age of about fourteen years had been made to see as the result of an operation performed by William Cheselden, the eminent surgeon. Cheselden's account of the operation to remove cataracts from the boy's eyes and his observations on the boy's subsequent development, was first published in the *Philosophical Transactions* of 1728 and had received a remarkable degree of interest throughout the eighteenth century, both in Britain and abroad. Its celebrity is quite understandable for it confirmed the earlier speculations of empiricist philosophers that a man born blind given his sight would at first be unable to distinguish projection, the distances and respective magnitudes of objects before him, or any other of the perceptual features which sighted people learn to distinguish in early infancy. That we do develop this ability so soon after birth, and that we have no remembrance of the learning process in maturity, gave further interest to Cheselden's account although, as Knight points out, we may observe this process in the behaviour of very young children who 'handle and turn about all objects which they can lay hold of, now putting them to their mouths and now placing them at different distances from their eyes; by all of which they are rectifying, correcting and improving the testimony of one sense by another'.[14] Nevertheless Cheselden's case had the obvious advantage over observations made on infants that the boy was able to answer questions and describe his experiences during the short period that he was acquiring these abilities which we take for granted. But it was his initial response after the operation which is most relevant here. 'When he first saw,' Cheselden writes, 'he was so far from making any judgement about distances, that he thought all objects whatever touch'd his eyes (as he expressed it) as what he felt did his skin.'[15] Like much in the account this is rather clumsily expressed, but for contemporary theorists the significance was quite clear. As Knight says, the meaning of the boy's remark that all objects seemed to touch his eyes was that 'all the objects seen appeared only as variations of light acting upon the eye: for the colours of objects are only different rays of light variously reflected from their surfaces; and their visible projection is merely gradation and opposition of light and shadow'.[16] What the boy saw was what the eye 'naturally' sees, he continues: 'superficial dimension'[17] or a two-dimensional plane divided by areas of colour, gradated by light and shade

The nature of visible impressions independent of those of our other senses is thus exemplified by the case of 'the boy couched by Cheselden'. All that can cause pleasure or pain by a direct 'organic' effect upon the eye, then, is colour, or more strictly speaking 'light variously reflected' from the surfaces of objects. All Price's talk about 'ruggedness' is thus shown to be fallacious, but this forms only a part, though an essential part, of Knight's dispute with Price over the meaning of that 'technical term': the picturesque.

Two earlier discussions of the theory of vision are important here, that of
Adam Smith in his essay 'Of the External Senses' (published posthumously
in 1795) and, more particularly, that of Thomas Reid in his *Inquiry into the
Human Mind*. Like Knight, both Smith and Reid cite Cheselden's evidence
in order to demonstrate the distinct nature of visible impressions, but the
principal interest of their works here is that in order to convey their meaning they both use the analogy of the art of painting. For, as Smith says, the
'visible world', or what the boy first saw, 'presents to us only a plain or
surface which by certain shades and combinations of light and colour
suggests and represents to us (in the same manner as a painter does)
certain tangible objects'.[18] Reid in his short section entitled 'Of the Visible
Appearances of Objects' carries the analogy much further. Although of
course no more than an analogy it serves Reid as an extremely useful
expository device since, as he points out, whereas most of us never have to
distinguish what we see by the eye alone, the painter is constantly having
to make this distinction. As he explains, 'The painter hath occasion for an
abstraction, with regard to visible objects, somewhat similar to that which
we here require: and this indeed is the most difficult part of his art'.[19]
Difficult of course because the painter is required to represent three-
dimensional objects (or Smith's 'tangible objects') on a flat canvas and is
therefore forced, Reid continues, to 'fix in his imagination the visible
appearances of objects'.[20] Indeed it is to this end that all his skills and
techniques are directed for, Reid concludes, 'perspective shading, giving
relief, and colouring are nothing else but copying the appearance which
things make to the eye'.[21] That this was the nature of the illusion which the
painter creates was further revealed by another incident reported by
Cheselden in his account – an incident to which both Smith and Knight
refer. For the boy, shortly after the operation, when his perceptual capa-
cities were fairly well developed, was shown some paintings. Having
eventually discovered that they were meant to represent solid objects,
which by now he could distinguish by sight, he was utterly 'amaz'd when
he found those parts, which by their light and shadow appear'd now
round and uneven, felt only flat like the rest'.[22] But there are ways, other
than the effects of 'light and shadow' by which the painter creates his
illusion, and which allow Reid to shed further light upon the nature of
visible appearance. For there is a change in the appearance of objects
according to the variations of distance at which they are seen: 'There
is a certain degradation of the colour, and a certain confusion of the
minute parts which is the natural consequence of the removal of the
object to a greater distance. Those that are not painters, or critics in
painting, overlook this.'[23]

Knight acknowledges his indebtedness to Reid for much that he says in
his section 'Of Sight', but it was Reid's extensive use of the comparison
between painting and visible appearances which Knight would have
found of particular interest. Like Reid he examines the manner in which
'the imitative deceptions of this art unmask the habitual deceptions of
sight'.[24] But whilst Reid was solely concerned with what painting taught

us about the nature of vision, Knight directs his attention towards the consequent notion that painting was, in essence, the copying of purely visible appearances. It is the foundation of the theory of painting which he advances in his *Inquiry* and, as we shall see, becomes in his later art criticism the criterion by which he judges the art. As he says in his review of Northcote's *Life of Reynolds*: 'Painting is an imitation of nature, as seen by the eye, and not, as known or perceived by the aid of the other senses; and this consideration, if duly attended to, is alone sufficient to guide both the artist and the critic to the true principles of imitation.'[25] It is impossible to say whether Reid's brief passages actually prompted Knight's thinking on the subject of painting, but certain parts of Reid's discussion appear to have been at least highly suggestive. Thus his observation that there is a 'confusion of the minute parts' of objects seen at a distance, becomes for Knight the key to the historical development of the art. Early Italian artists, Knight explains, had 'pretended only to exact imitation', attempting to distinguish 'the several hairs of the head, and the pores of the skin' in representing the human figure; and 'every blade in the grass, every leaf in the trees' in painting landscape.[26] The breakthrough occurred when artists 'discovered that this was rather copying what the mind knew to be from the concurrent testimony of another sense, than what the eye saw'.[27] This realisation led artists to begin 'massing' the parts of objects on their canvases, in proportion to their situation in the field of vision. In turn this process of massing 'gave breadth to the lights and shadows, mellowed them into each other and enabled the artist to break and blend them together',[28] and thereby produced the most alluring and sophisticated effects, such as we see in the works of 'the great painters of the Venetian and Lombard schools and afterwards those of the Flemish and Dutch'.[29] For Knight the most important advance in the progress of the art of painting was not the development of linear perspective but the discovery of this principle of 'massing'. Moreover the skill with which it is effected becomes for him the mark of great painting. Thus he writes of the 'trees and trailing plants' in Titian's *St Peter Martyr* that they are — as Algarotti had claimed, in opposition to Reynolds — 'accurately discriminated' but they are also depicted 'with that breadth of massing, which leaves no trace of any drudgery of detail, but seems more like creation than imitation'.[30]

If painting is to be considered in the way Knight suggests then Price's definition of the 'picturesque' was not only founded upon philosophical misconceptions: it also arose from a misuse of the word itself. For the word Knight asserts, can mean nothing other than 'after the manner of painters', and if the art consists of the imitation of purely visible appearances then Price's quality of 'picturesque ruggedness' was surely a contradiction in terms. But there was further proof. Like Price, Knight traces the English word back to its Italian cognate and finds that it first came into the Italian language at about the same time that Giorgione and Titian were developing and perfecting this process of 'massing'. It was to this process, he concludes, that the word was originally applied, and with which, strictly speaking, it should now be associated.

As Price and Knight were keen to acknowledge, their controversy was hardly one of the greatest importance and they must surely have appreciated that to their contemporaries it must have seemed very much like splitting hairs. For, as Knight explains, the objects which his friend had enumerated were precisely those which were best suited for the painter's imitation, when the art is considered in the way he proposes. And it is rough and rugged surfaces which reflect light in such a manner as to produce the 'most harmonious and brilliant combinations of tints to the eye'.[31] Moreover it is these variations of light which are sensually pleasing because, he explains, of the nature of their 'irritations upon the optic nerves'.[32] But he completely rejects 'smoothness' as pleasing to the eye since smooth surfaces present reflections of light which are 'monotonous and feeble',[33] whilst very smooth surfaces, such as 'cut glass or polished metal'[34] cause reflections which can be positively unpleasant.

Knight fails to explain how the pleasures of sensation are communicated to the mind, and the physiology of sensual pleasure which he advances seems rather questionable. He was condemned as unphilosophical in a very hostile review in *The Literary Journal*[35] and, as has been mentioned, this concession to Burkean sensationalism was considered by Jeffrey to be a 'heresy'. As we might expect, Jeffrey's criticism of Knight on this point delighted Price since, as he wrote to Lord Aberdeen, Knight was fairly confident in his 'metaphysical skills' and had 'more than once hinted to me how wide a difference there was between us in that respect'.[36] But Price's long letters to Aberdeen on the subject of the controversy rather confirm Knight's opinion. Still convinced of his side of the argument and seeking to prove it to Aberdeen, he requires his correspondent to imagine a number of extraordinary hypothetical circumstances — such as a blind man stroking the ice on a frozen lake[37] — which prove little save his own speculative capacity.

As we have seen, Knight's observations in his letter from Rome to George Romney on how the subject of Taste should be tackled anticipates his procedure in the *Inquiry*. Likewise his comments on painting in this letter reveal attitudes towards the art which he was to hold consistently throughout his life. He is highly critical of Michelangelo and of what he calls 'the researched attitudes of the Florentine School',[38] criticisms which he later voices with increased vehemence. In the *Inquiry* he writes of the 'vast and turgid compositions of the Sistine Chapel',[39] and in his review of Northcote's *Life of Reynolds* further condemns Michelangelo for the 'pedantic display of gigantic muscles in violent action'[40] to be found in these frescoes. It is appropriate that he was writing to Romney from Rome, for Roman painting later becomes for Knight the great corrupting influence on the art of painters from Annibale Carracci to Reynolds, and the 'grand chaste and severe style'[41] which contemporary British artists carried back with them from their studies in Rome becomes the subject of a concerted attack in Knight's articles in the *Edinburgh Review*. Not only was it a style inappropriate for the circumstances which these 'students of genius'[42] would find on their return – there would be no Julius II or Leo X to support their ambitious schemes – but it was also, he believed, a style which was foreign to the nature of the art of painting itself. For as we have seen Knight believed that the true essence of painting lay in the imitation of visible appearances, and that it was to this end that the artist should direct his energies for it is 'colour, light and shade and all those harmonious and magical combinations of richness and splendour which form the charm and essence of the art'.[43] Michelangelo's English imitators, emphasizing the primacy of line and form over colour and chiaroscuro, were not only mistaking the true nature of the art of painting, but were also neglecting its chief excellences. That this was actually so is confirmed for Knight by the example of James Barry, whose condescending remarks that he will 'hold no intercourse' with Dutch and Flemish paintings prompt Knight to declare: 'With what? With the finest specimens of the greatest masters of the art considered abstractedly as the art of painting – that is the art of employing colours to imitate visible objects with the greatest possible degree of skill, judgment, taste and effect.'[44] Apparently insensible to the effects of colour, it is hardly surprising, Knight concludes, that Barry's own performances were, in this respect, 'hard, coarse, opaque, discordant and metallic'.[45]

The debate in which Knight was engaged was, of course, an old one, but the theory of painting which he had developed from his controversy with Price provides a new and original foundation for the colourist position which he adopts. The advocates of 'design', entailing not only an emphasis on line and form, but also connoting the conceptual faculties which the artist calls upon, tended to regard colour and handling as no more than the 'mechanical' parts of the art, but for Knight, as we have seen, these skills – breadth of massing, the breaking and blending of lights and shadows, and the harmonizing of tints – constitute the highest excellencies which the art could attain. For painting 'in its nature and principle' was no more than an imitative art, and the intellect plays a relatively minor rôle in the resources which the artist calls upon to effect this imitation. Indeed it was 'an eager and injudicious desire to display knowledge' that had caused Michelangelo to run into error: 'common observation'[46] would have served him better. The painter, Knight believes, should 'not confound painting with the knowledge of it'[47] and theoretical science can only mislead him or distract his attention away from familiarity with his materials, and with the technical means of the art. Moreover, academic rules, Knight says, as appears from the productions of the academies of Europe, produce nothing but insipid conformity: 'The dull, uniform, and pedantic peculiarities of a sect.'[48] That neither precept nor precedent was necessary for the creation of great painting was demonstrated by the example of Giorgione, Titian, and Correggio 'who had no models for imitation but those of nature, nor any other objects of professional study than the composition of their materials and the use of their implements'.[49] In Knight's view the painter may hope to achieve the ideal perfection of the art only from the endless pursuit of execution, and from addressing himself to the study of nature as seen by the eye, not from the rules of Academies, or from the 'dreams of inspiration and mystic lights'.[50] For Knight the great achievements of painting had been those of the artist working independently, gaining an intuitive feeling for his materials, and developing original and even idiosyncratic methods of imitation. Thus of Rembrandt's handling of paint he writes that it enabled him to imitate the 'refracted lights of transparent prismatic substances' such as 'polished gems' or 'burnished metal', 'as no other artist has ever approached and as, we believe, no other mode of execution could ever give'.[51] Rembrandt receives much of Knight's most enthusiastic praise, and he is elevated by Knight to the highest position among painters. Thus of one painting by Rembrandt Knight writes that 'in beauty and simplicity of composition, elegance of drapery, truth of expression, and grace and dignity of attitude and character it is inferior to no work of any school of Italy; and in brilliancy, richness, harmony, and unison of effect, superior to anything of any other artist of any other country'.[52] Knight's application of his colourist theories undermines the conventional hierarchy of painters. Rembrandt in particular, but also

PLATE 42
Italian, early sixteenth century, *Portrait of a Cardinal* (Minneapolis Institute of Art — before cleaning)

other Dutch and Flemish masters, are considered by him in the same terms, and on the same level, as the painters of the Italian Schools.

Knight's views were equally unconventional on the relationships between the different genres of painting. Though of course there are distinctions between flower painting, landscape painting and the painting of great historical and religious subjects, all genres of painting were, Knight believed, subject to the need for the accuracy of imitation and brilliancy of execution which he espoused. Reynolds's view that the grand and ornamental styles were incompatible, and that the colour of paintings of grave and serious episodes should be low in tone, was one which Knight could not accept. Nor, of course, could he accept the opinions of those who in 'their zeal for the grand style, affect to despise what they are pleased to call tricks of light and shade', for Titian, Rubens and Rembrandt 'without any pretensions to grandeur of form, or dignity of expression, have produced grander, and more imposing pictures, than any of those who have sought for grandeur in vast outlines and unusual postures'.[53] For Knight the style of an historical composition should be no different from that of a landscape for the style in both cases should be guided by the same criterion, that of copying visible appearances.

Moreover, Raphael, the great master invariably held up as an example by the academic teaching which Knight abhorred, was himself, Knight believed, guided by this same principle. Of the still life in his portrait of Cardinal Bibbiena Knight wrote that it was finished with 'fidelity, delicacy and transparency' such as Teniers 'might have envied'. The portrait in question (Plate 42), one of Knight's prize possessions, is not now believed to be by Raphael, but the point could be made no less fairly of Raphael's portrait of Leo X. The observation is not only significant with regard to Knight's view of the proper character of painting, but is characteristic of his rejection of the conventional hierarchies of genres and schools of painting, and indeed of his delight in the provocative reversal of received ideas in general.[54]

CHAPTER SEVEN — *Collecting Paintings and Drawings*

Any balanced appraisal of Knight's activities as a collector of paintings and drawings would rightly conclude that his greater achievement was in the latter category, although, as a critic and theorist, he wrote primarily of paintings.

The 1,144 drawings bequeathed by him to the British Museum in 1824 undoubtedly represent one of the major collections of this type formed in this country. Writing in 1838 of 'the ancient fondness of the English for drawings by the old masters', Dr Waagen understandably began his discussion with Ottley, Woodburn and Lawrence, but of other important collections he concluded, 'the best known . . . were those of Messrs Esdaile, Richard Ford, Hibbert, Payne Knight, Mordant Cratcherode, and General Sir Charles Greville'.[1] Two years earlier the English translation of J. D. Passavant's *Tour of a German Artist in England* was first published in which the author wrote the following introduction to what he considered to be the most important drawings in the British Museum:

> These drawings, which formerly existed in two separate collections, now form two sets of nine volumes each; the one bequeathed by Richard Payne Knight, Esq.; the other by the Rev. Mordaunt Cratcherode. The former bequest consists chiefly of Italian sketches; the latter, of the Flemish masters. It is to be regretted that the original possessors should not have displayed more judgment in their selection; for we find many worthless drawings intermingled with the most valuable and exquisite productions. To obviate this error in some degree, the most important have been selected, and form the first volume of each division.[2]

This passage not only reaffirms the regard in which Knight's collection was held at the time but, perhaps more importantly, it provides a clue as to what happened to his drawings subsequent to their arrival in the Museum. The only known catalogue of Knight's drawings is that produced by the Department of Prints and Drawings in 1845, in manuscript form, under the Keepership of J. T. Smith.[3] By that date, the drawings, including two albums of sketches by Gainsborough and Mortimer, had presumably been divided into sixteen volumes or portfolios (Pp. 1–5 and Oo.1–11) so, whatever the accuracy of Passavant's account, it is fair to assume that considerable re-sorting of the collection had taken place in the Museum, whose staff doubtless reattributed some of the drawings.

At least two sortings of the collection can be supposed: the first after the Bequest arrived in the Museum and prior to it being seen by Passavant, and the second subsequent to this and possibly in conjunction with the

1845 catalogue. Sections Pp. 1 and Oo. 9 of the 1845 sorting did, for the most part, contain the most important Italian and Dutch and Flemish drawings respectively, and may be indicative of some overlap between the two sortings, bearing in mind Passavant's remark at the end of the passage quoted above. His description of Knight's collection as consisting mainly of the Italian school was, however, inaccurate as it also included many important sheets by Rembrandt, Rubens, Van Dyck and others, and he could be criticised for finding 'many worthless drawings', as the quality of much of Knight's collection reveals this verdict to be unjust.

Whereas Knight's collection of drawings has remained intact, that of his paintings has, sadly, been partly dispersed[4] and works such as Mantegna's *Adoration of the Shepherds*,[5] Rembrandt's *St Bartholomew*[6] and Claude's *La Crescenza*[7] (Plate 21) have left this country. It should be borne in mind that Knight's collection of paintings, though extremely interesting and in many ways unorthodox, was outshone by those of many of his contemporaries. What follows is an attempt to trace the development of Knight's collecting activities in the two fields of paintings and drawings and to relate these to his published theories and to contemporary events.

The ambiguous nature of many of the entries in such marked sales catalogues as I have been able to examine allows only tentative conclusions to be drawn.[8] A particular problem is presented by the intriguing figure of Knight's older cousin Edward of Wolverley and Portland Place, who was a very considerable collector in his own right and whose name can easily be confused with that of Payne Knight. Thus Graves and Cronin[9] record Payne Knight as the owner of Reynolds's *Mrs Quarrington as 'St Agnes'*.[10] As a young man Knight had known Reynolds. He composed the painter's Latin epitaph and helped to organize the exhibition of his work at the British Institution. However he did not own this (or any other) painting by him, and it was, in fact, bought by Edward Knight and was Lot no. 81 in the sale of his heir, John, in 1819.[11] Edward Knight, whose importance for Payne Knight has already been stressed in earlier chapters, was certainly buying paintings in the early 1760s, and a detailed record of his numerous purchases of paintings, prints, drawings, coins, medals, furniture, furnishings, hats and breeches survives in a series of his pocket-books now in the Public Library at Kidderminster.[12] His collection of paintings, which included examples by Poussin and Claude (in whose works his collection was especially rich), Guercino, Rubens and Teniers, was undoubtedly more important than his cousin's. They frequently attended the same sales and were obviously acquainted, though there is little evidence of how close they were. Edward may, however, have purchased paintings from Payne Knight, for an entry in his pocket-book for 1 July 1785 reads: 'R.P. Knight Esq Pictures 330—15—0' which, in context, is more likely to record a purchase than a sale.

Available evidence would suggest that Payne Knight began collecting paintings, for modest prices, in either 1769 or 1770, and he was doubtless a regular visitor to the sale-rooms thereafter. This was before he inherited and before he became a serious collector of ancient art. Possibly the best

of these early acquisitions were two paintings by Wouwermans.[13] It was not until the 1790s when he bought Rembrandt's *The Cradle*[14] (Plate 43) described by Buchanan as, 'one of the most celebrated pictures of this master' from the Orleans Collection 'for 1000 guineas' that Knight could be said to have owned paintings acknowledged to be outstanding at the time. There is good reason to believe that Rembrandt was Knight's favourite artist. In addition to *The Cradle* and the *St Bartholomew*, he also owned the *Rest on the Flight into Egypt*, now generally attributed to the studio of Rembrandt[15] as well as a very considerable number of drawings by the Dutch master. Indeed, Knight referred to him as 'the great founder of the Dutch school'.[16] Of course, the late eighteenth and early nineteenth centuries were most notable in the history of English collecting for the massive importation of Old Master paintings from Italian collections in the wake of the French invasions. Knight, probably on both financial and, as will be proposed, technical grounds, stood apart from this overpriced market, his only expensive acquisition of this type being the 'Raphael' *Cardinal Bibbiena* (Plate 42). He was sensibly alert to excessive prices, as he informed Lord Aberdeen concerning Guido Reni's *Lot and his Daughters* (now in the National Gallery, London):[17]

> I believe the Falconieri Guido of Lot leading away his daughters is up for sale, and might be had at a much cheaper rate than those for which you made so magnificent an offer. It was one of the most celebrated pictures at Rome, and in my estimation worth much more than the three in Portland Place . . . [it was] at Tresham's to be sold for 1500£; but I have no doubt of much less being taken, if a little address be employ'd.[18]

This was exactly the sort of purchase which Knight was unable to make, unlike his aristocratic contemporaries.

One of Knight's earliest documented enthusiasms in the field of painting was for the work of Salvator Rosa. In his letter of 1776 to Romney, writing on what he terms the 'infinite sublime', he states, 'Salvator Rosa has excelled all other painters in this kind of sublimity', which, he continues, 'may sometimes be produced in landscape. A river winding between vast chains of mountains, such as we sometimes see in the works of Salvator Rosa, leads the mind beyond what the eye sees'.[19] Given his liking for Rosa, it is not surprising, therefore, to find that one of the first English artists he patronized was John Hamilton Mortimer (1740–79), a number of whose Salvatoresque drawings of banditti and soldiers he owned by 1780, and whose painting of *c.* 1775–7, *Banditti Fishing* (Plate 44) he may

PLATE 44
John Hamilton Mortimer,
Banditti Fishing (cat. no.
188)

have acquired in the same period. The later years of Mortimer's brief life were divided between Aylesbury and London, and it was in the capital that a curious encounter between Knight and Mortimer took place. In view of the many hostile references to Knight so eagerly picked up by Farington, the story, together with Knight's later kindnesses to the artist Richard Westall, helps to redress in part the often jaundiced view of his personality. J. T. Smith recalled:

> Sancho's visiting Mr Nolleken's studio;[20] he spake well of art, and gave the following anecdote of the late Richard Payne Knight and Mortimer the Painter, with the latter of whom he was extremely intimate. Mr Knight happening to call upon Mortimer at his house in Church-court, Covent Garden, expressed his uneasiness at the melancholy mood in which he found him. 'Why, Sir', observed Mortimer, 'I have many noble and generous friends, it is true; but of all my patrons, I don't know one whom I could now ask to purchase an hundred guineas' worth of drawings of me, and I am at this moment seriously in want of that sum.' 'Well, then,' observed Mr Knight, 'bring as many sketches as you would part with for that sum to me to-morrow, and dine with me.' This he did and enjoyed his bottle. Mr Knight gave him the two hundred guineas, which he insisted the drawings were worth; and on this splendid reception, Mortimer, who was no *starter*, took so much wine, that the next morning, he knew not how he got home. About twelve o'clock at noon, his bedside was visited by the late 'Memory Cooke',[21] who, after hearing him curse his stupidity in losing his two hundred guineas, produced the bag! 'Here, my good fellow!', cried Cooke, 'here is your money. Fortunately you knocked me up, and emptied your pockets on my table, after which I procured a coach and sent you home.'[22]

Prior to Farington's Diary, which begins in 1794, there are frustratingly few references to Knight as far as the fine arts are concerned. Commissioning the topographical watercolourist Thomas Hearne (1744–1817) to depict, in a series of views dated 1784–6 (Cat. nos. 114–16), the landscape at Downton was singularly appropriate, as Hearne's style of 'tinted drawings' and the shapes and forms of that particular terrain were well matched. There is little reason, however, to think that Knight was greatly interested in English landscape drawings for their artistic merits. The Sicilian views and those of Downton should perhaps be regarded as essentially functional topography and, whilst he did acquire a Gainsborough landscape album, a few Sandbys and was given landscape drawings by distinguished amateurs,[23] he never professed any enthusiasm in the early 1800s for the new vogue for watercolour painting that had recently sprung up. He belonged, essentially, to an earlier generation than many of the watercolour collectors and his preoccupation with the 'Picturesque' was presumably incompatible with the new 'painting' in watercolours given the latter's emancipation from the stereotyped patterns of late eighteenth-century draughtsmanship exemplified in the 'tinted' drawing. Knight may well have been apprehensive of the threat that watercolours seemed to pose to the virility of the English school of artists — and understandably so, given the part he played in the founding of the

British Institution. This fear that the supposedly grander and more intellectual aspirations of painters in oil would be distracted by the charms of the watercolour medium was certainly expressed by Knight's friends Price and Beaumont when the watercolour societies were founded in the decade 1800–10.[24] This was possibly the reason for the apparent fading of an initial enthusiasm on Knight's part for the work of John Varley, recorded in a letter of 1801 from Uvedale Price to Lady Beaumont. Lord Essex had brought Varley to Herefordshire and Knight saw his drawings at Hereford and was so pleased with them that he invited Varley to Downton to meet Sir George and Lady Beaumont. So far as is known nothing ever came of this invitation, but there may have been a clash of personalities for, according to Price, Varley was a great talker with eccentric and novel ideas of his own.[25]

Knight must have been a seasoned collector of Old Master drawings by the 1790s, for in 1791 he was buying important Italian drawings from the sale in Paris of the Abbé Tersan, from whom, as has been mentioned, Knight also acquired ancient bronzes and coins.[26] In his attitudes to drawings Knight displayed an attitude that had long been cultivated by French connoisseurs, often preferring what Ottley termed 'effusions of the moment' to 'finished drawings'. The sign of a true master, 'that masterly intelligence in the execution', Knight claimed in the *Inquiry*,

> is often more prominent and striking in a drawing or slight sketch, than in a finished production: whence persons, who have acquired this refined or artificial taste, generally value them more; since finishing often blunts or conceals this excellence: but then the drawings or sketches so valued must be the work of great painters, who knew how to finish; for, from their perfect knowledge, is derived the intelligence, which they are enabled to display in their imperfect exertions of it. The drawings of a mere draftsman are never highly esteemed, however excellently designed or brilliantly executed; a loose incorrect sketch of Rembrandt or Salvator Rosa being always preferred by persons conversant in the art, to the most elaborate productions of the light and brilliant pens of Pietro Testa and La Fage.[27]

Knight admitted that some collectors were motivated by 'a silly desire of possessing what is rare',[28] but he defended the high prices often paid for the 'slight or juvenile productions of great artists' because of the fascination in connecting these with the artist's most perfect works and hence tracing the development of his ideas or, indeed, his development as an artist. Knight's belief in the connoisseur's ability to divine an artist's genius in his drawings may be gauged from his claim in the *Edinburgh Review* for 1810 that 'an experienced and discriminating eye' would find 'as little difficulty in tracing the characteristic excellence of Titian, Claude, and Rembrandt, in a pen and bister sketch, as in the most finished of their oil pictures'.[29]

Knight's collection of drawings, although it could be said to include rather surprising items such as Watteau's *Head of a Young Woman* (cat. no. 171) or Isaac Oliver's *The Penitent Magdelen* (Pp.5–128), was especially strong in more conventional areas – the Carracci, Correggio, Parmigianino,

Raphael, Salvator Rosa, Van Dyck, the Van Ostades, Rubens and, above all others, Rembrandt. The 1845 catalogue listed five drawings by Michelangelo, an artist for whom Knight had mixed feelings, but only one has retained its attribution to the present day (cat. no. 148). He is recorded as a buyer at many of the important drawings sales in London including those of Matthew Duane, 1787, various 22–5 April 1801 (T. Philipe's), George Knapton, 1807, Earl Spencer, 1811 and Benjamin West, 1820.[30] The conclusion to be drawn from the marked-up copies I have examined would seem to be that, whereas Knight was probably selective in the sales he chose to attend, when he did so he bought heavily.[31] In a letter of 1811 to Sir George Beaumont, Uvedale Price retold an anecdote contained in a letter to him from his son Bob, of Knight's behaviour before such a sale at Philipe's (probably the Spencer sale) where both Knight and Beaumont were to be seen debating the merits of a drawing allegedly by Titian. Beaumont held one side of the drawing and Knight the other and they argued the merits and defects accordingly. Charles Long, who was also present, declined to be drawn into the argument.[32] A brief insight into how Knight's own collection was used is provided by an entry in Mary Berry's *Journal* for 12 February 1808: 'Went to dine at Mr Knight's in Soho Square. The party: Lord and Lady Oxford, Mr Lyttleton, Mr C. Moore, Mr Rogers, and Mr Lawrence, the painter, and Mrs Damer. Looked over drawings, &c. – &c. – till near eleven o'clock.'[33]

Knight was an avid collector of drawings right up until his death,[34] shortly before which he made what he probably considered his most satisfying purchase of all, an album of Claude drawings which contained at least 150 sheets.[35] Knight had enjoyed a deep appreciation of Claude from an early age. As already mentioned in the diary of his Sicilian journey he had, in describing the Bay of Naples, written of 'that pearly hue which is peculiar to this delicious climate' and appended a marginal note: 'This tint very particularly marks Claude Lorraine's coloring.'[36] He had also extolled Claude's distances in *The Landscape*:

> . . . where Claude extends his prospects wide,
> O'er Rome's Campania to the Tyrrhene tide,
> (Where towers and temples, mouldering to decay,
> In pearly air appear to die away,
> And the soft distance, melting from the eye,
> Dissolves its forms into the azure sky).[37]

Knight was especially prone, also, to pronounce on matters of connoisseurship where paintings by Claude were concerned, as Farington noted of the so-called 'Bouillon' Claudes. 'The Angerstein (Bouillon) Claudes were much the subject of conversation. – Knight says He wd. rather have Sir George [Beaumont]'s huge Claude than any of them.'[38] Curiously, there is no record of Knight's opinion of his own, admittedly much less spectacular, painting by Claude (Plate 21).

Knight bought the album of Claude drawings from Colnaghi's whose agent, Mr Binda, apparently found them at a book dealer's in a large town in Spain (or Portugal). The story of the purchase was related in the *Somerset House Gazette*.[39] The volume was described as a large album with clasps and a leather cover on to which was impressed the imperial crown. The drawings were stuck on to the leaves of the album and Knight had them cut out, 'carefully laid on coloured paper', and arranged in a large folio. According to W. H. Pyne's gossipy account in the *Gazette*, Knight beat Lawrence to the purchase of the album by offering double the sum asked. In comparing Claude's drawings 'to the studies of Turner, of Callcot, of Constable, of Ward' Pyne patriotically concluded, 'These by Claude are full of intelligence, so are those by our ingenious compeers.'[40] Constable, however, was mortified at Knight's decision to buy the Claudes and not one of his own paintings. In a letter to John Fisher (17 January 1824) he described the drawings: ' — they looked just like papers used and otherwise mauled & purloined from a Water Closet — but they were certainly old, & much rent, & dissolved, &c. but their meer charm was their age.'[41] Fisher consoled his friend by remarking, ' — "Priapus" Knight (how punishment visits a man in *Kind*) bought these drawings for the sake of seeing a set of prints, underwritten "in the possession of R. P. Knight Esqr." '[42]

Despite these unfair and untrue assertions, Knight was perhaps the greatest of all collectors of Claude's drawings and his Bequest to the British Museum included 273 'Claudes' (Colour Plate IX and cat. nos. 122–8), of which some eighty-four mixed drawings, according to Roethlisberger,[43] may have formed another album.

Until the acrimonious debate over the Elgin Marbles, Knight was regarded as one of the finest connoisseurs of his day. The inevitable perils of such claimed expertise were maliciously reported by Farington:

> He [West] told me that a Copy of the Gaspar Poussin which was brought from the Colonna Palace & brought by Beckford and now at Wests has been lately brought from Italy and is now in Oxenden Street. It has deceived *Knight*, who mentioned it to West, & that Sir Richard Worsley had offered 700 guineas for it. After seeing the Gaspar at West's, Knight wrote to him attributing his mistake to a dark room and want of Spectacles. — So uncertain is Connoisseurship.[44]

It is not hard to imagine Knight's contemporaries taking umbrage at his often abrupt, though frequently accurate, judgements. At a dinner in 1797 at Charles Townley's, 'Knight *said* Cartoons at Windsor are not original, that the Cartoon at Badminton is not original, — neither is that in the possession of Mr Hoare of Bath. — Lysons said He shd. suppose Mr Knight was mistaken, as it is possible that Mr Hoare was a very good judge, — having been 7 years in Italy under Francesco Imperiali.'[45] Such denunciation was by no means one-sided, however. In 1799 Knight had bought a portrait for 500 guineas which was then thought to be by Raphael of Cardinal Bibbiena, and which he later lent to the British Institution exhibition of Old Masters in 1816.[46] Farington noted,[47] 'Long & Hoppner spoke of the Head by Raphael which Knight had purchased.

Long said it is of no value but as having been painted by the Man who executed the Cartoons. – Graves asked 2000 guineas for it'.[48] In the same conversation Farington also reported: 'Long does not think much of Vandykes Horse which Desenfans spoke abt.' The canvas in question had been purchased by Knight from Desenfans in 1783 for 30 guineas.[49] Hoppner had earlier shown his antipathy to Knight by declaring, 'Price much superior to Knight in judgements on subjects of taste –'.[50] Despite his patronage of Lawrence and his friendship with him, Knight was also capable of the wounding public remark. According to Farington, 'He [Lawrence] told me that when his Picture of Prospero was exhibited, Knight, on the day of the dinner, said to him *loud* in the room, He was very sorry he had put in a picture which everyone condemned'. Farington commiserated with Lawrence: 'As to the herd of amateur Critics, they were likely to take the safe side in their remarks, knowing that to *object* signifies a superior taste. – while to *approve* may be hazarding something.'[51] Discussing the Committee of Taste in 1805,

> Lawrence observed . . . that Mr Knight's taste was just that which shd. not be adopted. It was founded on sensual feeling. – The simplicity of Raphael, His Purity, &c afforded no gratification to Knight, – His pleasure was derived from the luxurious displays of Rubens. – Wm Lock said he had noticed this at the Marquis of Stafford's where Knight was profuse in his admiration of a sensual picture by Rubens but did not notice pictures by Titian to which Rubens would have bowed.[52]

The connoisseur could be called upon to adjudicate in disputes concerning the value and merit of works of art. In May 1804 Knight, together with Farington, Captain Baillie and a solicitor called Graham, was called to give evidence on three pictures, allegedly by Claude, Gaspard and Ruisdael, exchanged, with a cash adjustment, by the dealer Bryant with Lord Lowther for an alleged Titian. The matter had apparently been settled by the following day.[53] Farington himself had seen the pictures the previous month, also in Knight's company, and judged them of poor quality.

Knight was later to rail at 'the successful impositions of picture-dealers, the dupery of collectors, and the quackery of both'.[54] Even Reynolds, for whom he had a very considerable admiration, was not exempt.

> We are aware, indeed, that even the best artists are not always the least fallible judges in their own art; of which Sir Joshua Reynolds was a remarkable instance. No unfledged peer or full-plumed loanjobber was more liable to be deceived, even in those branches of the art which he professed most to admire; false Corregios, false Titians, and false Michael Angelos swarming in his collection.[55]

A critical factor in determining the authenticity of a work of art was its condition, and this was a subject in which Knight expressed frequent interest. Before examining his often apposite comments concerning the restoration of Old Masters, his misguided enthusiasm for an alleged new 'process' of painting, developed in the 1790s, should be mentioned. One of the more unfortunate preoccupations of the late eighteenth century was with 'new' painting processes, the most notorious of which was claimed to enable artists to emulate the colouring of the Venetian masters and was promoted by Mary Ann Provis, based on an apparently authentic six-teenth-century Venetian manual.[56] The foremost enthusiast for the process was the President of the Royal Academy, Benjamin West, and when it appeared, early in 1797, that he might buy the monopoly of the process, speculation amongst other Academicians and interested parties increased. Knight's critical involvement may have been partly determined by his friendship for Sir George Beaumont, one of the earliest amateurs to buy the secret. Knight's suggestion that, after a subscription for Mr and Mrs Provis (to which he himself would contribute) had been gathered, the secret be made generally available,[57] was rather more honourable than other more mercenary solutions proposed. By the time the Academy exhibition opened in the Spring the process was losing popularity, yet Knight remained loyal. At the following year's exhibition, however, there were no 'Venetian' pictures on view. The critical discomfort Knight may have suffered as a result of his misplaced faith in the process could partly account for his later dogmatic views on the condition and restoration of the Old Masters, especially those of the Venetian school. It is also worth setting Knight's warnings of the deceptive qualities of many Old Masters against the dealer Buchanan's remark in a letter (3 June 1803) to James Irvine concerning the importation of pictures from Italy:

> It must . . . be taken into consideration that vanity principally prompts the English to buy — and that Vanity leads purchasers to please the prevailing taste of fashion of their friends, or to be governed by the whim and voice of artists. Of the popular Masters at present, Titian and Rubens take the lead. The former of these in his *fine* works large or small will bring any money.[58]

Knight's most important, and considered, thoughts on the matter are contained in his two articles in the *Edinburgh Review*. The state of preservation of a masterpiece was, Knight opined, a matter of public interest:

> In forming, however, and sustaining the public taste, and more especially in fortifying it against the quackery and fraud of picture-dealers, a public collection of genuine and well preserved works of the best old masters, may be of great and essential service. But, unless the colours be nearly as the artists left them, they will be more likely to deceive than instruct, by making the defects of injury or decay the criterion of excellence; to which modern artists must adapt their practice, or renounce employment.[59]

Of the Venetian pictures in the Orleans Collection Knight claimed all 'had been more or less injured — many of them utterly ruined by the French cleaners, first employed to repair, or rather destroy them, about the year 1778'.[60] Sebastiano del Piombo's *Raising of Lazarus* particularly concerned him — 'those who have only seen it since the fatal operation of cutting away the panel on which it was painted, and gluing cloth to the back of the colour in its place, can form but very imperfect notions of what it was before'.[61] Knight leaves his readers in no doubt of his disapproval of such restoration.

> This debasement and falsification, as it were, of the noblest monuments of the art, is more fatally injurious to it than their utter destruction and annihilation could be; for, if totally obliterated and extinguished, they would only leave the world in the state it was before their production; destitute, indeed of some of its choicest ornaments, yet equally ready to receive others, and applaud and reward the talents which should produce them.[62]

Despite his warnings on the impermanence of the paintings of the Venetian School, Knight was confident that 'The colours, indeed, of the Flemish and Dutch painters, Rubens, Vandyke, Rembrandt, Teniers, Ostade, &c. generally retain their freshness, so that they may be imitated without danger'.[63] This conviction may well have influenced the nature of his own collection.

As far as picture-cleaners were concerned, Knight is recorded by Farington as favouring David Seguier.

> Philip Hammond called. P. Knight had written a note to Mr Hornbury recommending *Segur* to clean His pictures objecting to Simpson who, he had heard, had committed sad scarification on *Lord Radnor's Claudes*. P Hammond says 'Knight, I suppose, wants to recommend *his own man.* & therefore objects to Simpson, but I am sure Hanbury after my report of our conversation will keep to Simpson who from what He had seen of him He likes very well'.[64]

Knight's alarums on the dangers of the deterioration or inexpert restoration of Old Masters were closely bound up with his laudable desire to encourage a vigorous and thriving national school of painting. Copying the masters was still considered an essential part of a painter's training. Knight had what might almost be called a patronising approach to the encouragement of contemporary artists. He was strongly against the training offered in European academies and the stagnation of art which he considered they engendered, but he was one of the founders and directors of the British Institution, set up in 1805 'to encourage and reward the talents of the artists of the United Kingdom, and to open an exhibition for the sale of their productions'. After Boydell's bankruptcy the lease of the Shakespeare Gallery in Pall Mall was purchased for £4500 and a further £800 was spent on fittings. Artists were provided with a real alternative to Somerset House, and the first exhibition in 1806 was a great success. After it had closed, a small but choice selection of Old Masters, lent by the directors, was exhibited and students and artists were permitted to copy from them. Knight lent *The Cradle* for this purpose. In 1813 the Directors of the Institution established a new series of special exhibitions of past masters which followed on each summer directly after the normal exhibitions. This practice did not find favour amongst living artists who, understandably, claimed that their own exhibiting time had been cut short. The first of these special exhibitions was devoted to the work of Reynolds, the second to Hogarth, Wilson, Gainsborough and Zoffany.

PLATE 45
Richard Westall, *The Sword of Damocles* (cat. no. 205)

Knight objected to the inclusion of the last named 'as He was not a *British Painter*'.[65] He was also against the exhibiting of works by Wilson in this context, as Henry Edridge informed Farington in his account of a dinner party, at which Knight was present, at Bromley Hill, the home of Knight's friend Charles Long.

> He [Edridge] spoke of the proposed Exhibition of the works of Wilson, Hogarth, and Gainsborough, & said that Mr Knight & the Revd. Holwell, two amateurs had objected to admitting the works of Wilson; they allowed them to be works of merit but not proper models for students. The pictures of Claude & Poussin should be placed before them.[66]

Knight lent one picture to this exhibition, Hogarth's *Orator Henley Christening a Child, a Sketch*.[67] At the 1816 exhibition devoted to the Italian and Spanish schools he lent five pictures,[68] only two of which can now be traced. These last pictures, together with the intriguing Hogarth, point to as yet undocumented dispersals from Knight's collection.

Knight's own patronage of contemporary artists was interesting, if unspectacular. He commissioned Thomas Lawrence to paint the portrait exhibited at the Academy in 1794 (Colour Plate VII), and before this he had also purchased Lawrence's *Homer Reciting the Iliad* (Plate 6). Farington[69] recorded that it was Knight's intention to show 'that the moderns can stand up to the Old Masters', in this instance by hanging Westall's *Moses in the Bullrushes* which he had just purchased for 150 guineas next to two of the Old Masters in his collection. In the same year Knight commissioned *The Unpaid Bill* from Turner, apparently as a pendant to *The Cradle*, which he had again lent to the Institution that year (see cat. no. 197 for a fuller discussion and alternative theory). In retrospect, though, Knight cannot be said to have pursued this aim at all consistently. Given the variety of his collecting interests and the very definite limits to the amount he was able to spend on acquisitions, this was hardly surprising, but it was a serious policy with the British Institution which invited young artists to paint pendants to Old Masters.

One of the more notable purchases of English paintings made by Knight was that of Callcott's *Morning*, bought from the artist and exhibited at the Royal Academy exhibition in 1805 (88), though, as David Brown has pointed out,[70] this action may have been prompted as much by political as by artistic motives. Callcott became a strong supporter of the Academy and his relations with Knight deteriorated to the point that in 1818 he threatened to resign his diploma if Knight were elected the Academy's Professor of Ancient Literature.

One of Callcott's companions in the 1805 censure of the Institution had been the portrait painter William Owen (1769–1825) who was born in Ludlow and whose uncle had been Knight's butler. A watercolour view (Plate 25) with a date in the 1790s of the 'Roman Bath' at Downton, testifies to Owen's early involvement with Knight, though he can hardly have been grateful to his patron for his estimation of his capabilities. Farington noted,

Owen called and I had much conversation with him. He said He was born in Shropshire and was placed for 7 years under the late *Mr. Catton*, at the recommendation of Mr. Paine Knight, who he believed proposed that inferior branch Coach Painting & Heraldry, as being most likely to be a means of obtaining a certain livelihood. — He said that He had now formed very good connexions & was doing very well.[71]

Knight's most extensive patronage of a living artist was of Richard Westall, a fact which even gave rise to ironic comment from his friend Beaumont who 'sd. He hoped Knight had enough of what He liked in Westall, in his picture of Flora; meaning the gaudiness of it'.[72] The picture was exhibited at the Royal Academy (139) in 1807 and Smirke remarked over dinner to Farington (19 June), 'Westall very unsuccessful in his Flora painted for Mr. Knight. He had taken much pains with the flowers but had not been successful.'

Knight owned a total of nine paintings by Westall, the first, *Harvesters in a Storm* (Colour Plate VI) probably purchased in about 1795. Whilst Knight was undoubtedly the artist's most extensive patron, it should not be forgotten that he was also popular with other collectors and the most instructive parallel can be found with Knight's friend Thomas Hope. Westall's appeal to both men was connected with his malleability and

PLATE 46
Richard Westall, *The Grecian Wedding* (cat no. 206)

with his ability to model his figures and compositions on Classical works of art either in their possession or in their affections. Thus in 1804 Hope commissioned two historical paintings at a cost of 450 guineas. *The Expiation of Orestes at the Shrine of Delphos*, exhibited at the Royal Academy 1805 (73), was directly inspired by works of Greek art in Hope's collection, whilst the *Reconciliation of Helen and Paris, after his Defeat by Menelaus* included a considerable amount of neo-classical furniture that, as David Watkin has remarked, was 'markedly Hopeian in character'.[73] Hope even commissioned another version of Westall's *Sword of Damocles* after having seen Knight's original version (Plate 45), exhibited at the Royal Academy in 1811.

Knight's major commission from Westall was, undoubtedly, that for *The Grecian Marriage* in 1811 (Plate 46), rightly described by the artist as 'a most liberal commission' for which Knight offered 1000 guineas. The considerable time Westall took over the picture is indicated by Farington remarking the following year (1 November), 'Westall had been in London the whole of the autumn chiefly employed on the picture of "the Grecian Marriage" ordered by Mr Payne Knight'. Knight must have been inordinately proud of the picture for in 1814 he wrote, 'We observed too, with equal satisfaction, in late exhibitions, instances of the utmost purity and dignity of heroic character and composition, embellished and not impaired by the most rich and splendid colouring, in Mr Westall's Grecian Marriage, &c.'[74]

In 1796 Westall is first recorded as a dinner guest of Knight,[75] whose subsequent treatment of the artist could almost be described as paternal. Westall, perhaps on Knight's recommendation, was one of the artists who used the 'Provis' process in 1797[76] and, for his pains, was lampooned in Gilray's brilliant cartoon, *Titianus Redivivus or the Seven Wise Men consulting the New Venetian Oracle*.[77] Paul Sandby, an opponent of the process, described Westall as 'very gaudy in his colouring and has a face like a monkey'. Westall evidently continued to receive advice from Knight. In 1807 Knight informed him he should ask 300, and not 200, guineas for a painting he had recently executed: '– Knight sd. when an Artist painted a picture on speculation He had right to ask a price different from what He made the rule for works ordered. If He made a lucky hit He had a fair claim to an extraordinary reward. –'[78] It was also Knight who, in 1814, recommended Westall to form an exhibition of his own works. In 1815 he advised Westall to visit Paris to see the works of art assembled by Napoleon before they were returned to their original owners.[79] He had also expressed his concern for Westall's situation: 'Taylor had heard that he owed £10,000.'[80] Westall's debts were undoubtedly caused by his excessive expenditure. As early as 1806 Farington had remarked, 'Westall today told me that Mr. Knight had commissioned him to paint a small picture. – He said He had commissions now for more than £1000 in pictures, and that He got more than £1400 a year. – I exhorted him to get established habits of economy.'[81]

If, today, it seems ironic that Westall should, more than any other contemporary artist, have been Knight's chosen vehicle for 'timely and liberal employment', it should at least be said that in this instance Knight was certainly true to his belief that the best encouragement for artists lay not with academies but 'employment adapted to his capabilities and acquirements, sufficient to enable him to live comfortably, by severe toil and study'.[82] Perhaps the greater irony is that the works of art so highly regarded by Knight in his own collections such as Westall's *Grecian Marriage* or Rembrandt's *The Cradle* should now, for reasons of taste and attribution respectively, be out of favour and he should be better remembered, in the field of the fine arts, for the hidden treasures of his drawings collection and for such interesting, yet at the time of the purchase perhaps little considered, acquisitions as the Sweerts *Portrait of a Girl* (Colour Plate XI) or Elsheimer's *Il Contento* (Plate 47).[83] An intriguing example of a work of art receiving a more impressive attribution subsequent to Knight acquiring it is *An Old Woman by a Spinning Wheel* (Plate 48) recently sold and exhibited as by Dou when it was, in fact, purchased by Knight in April 1806 with the attribution to a pupil and imitator of Dou, Dominicus Van Tol.[84]

Knight's inability to pay consistently large sums for his purchases,

PLATE 47
Adam Elsheimer, *Il Contento* (National Gallery of Scotland)

PLATE 48
Gerard Dou, *An Old Woman by a Spinning Wheel* (formerly at Downton Castle)

which probably gave rise to a considerable number of optimistic 'bargain' acquisitions, cannot be overstressed when assessing his collection of paintings, nor should the breadth of his collecting activities be forgotten. He was also, on theoretical grounds, opposed to large pictures, being of the opinion that the whole of a painting should be visible from the chosen viewpoint.[85] A practical consideration in his later life may have been the size of his London house at Soho Square which would have favoured smaller, 'cabinet' pictures such as formed the majority of his collection, but there is no evidence to prove that he transferred paintings from Downton to London, though it is hard to believe his acquisition of paintings ceased when he gave up the Castle in 1808, or that he would willingly have been parted from all of a collection he had built up over nearly forty years.

When considered as a whole the collection can be seen to present many curiosities symptomatic of a private taste on Knight's part and somewhat removed from his bombastic public utterances. It was not a rich man's collection but, in its greater moments – such as Ruisdael's melancholy *Silent Pool* (Cat. no. 194), the intriguing subject-matter of *Il Contento* or the exquisite charm of *La Crescenza* – one that reveals considerable originality on the part of its creator.

Notes

Notes to Chapter One

1 Page, I, p. 473n; Beesly, p. 1; Inglis-Jones, p. 240.

2 Bodleian Library, MS Eng. Misc. d 158, ff. 140, 169–71, 181.

3 Downes; Beesly, p. 2; Inglis-Jones, pp. 240–1.

4 Downton Castle Papers, T74–190; also Robinson, pp. 57, 80, 105, 114, 172f, 314.

5 Downton Castle Papers, T74–431; there were fourteen children in all – *ibid.*, T74–765.

6 *Ibid.*, T74–689.

7 Inglis-Jones, p. 242.

8 MS as cited in note 2.

9 Knight MS (Autobiography). The Wormsley registers record 1751 as 1750 according to the old style calendar and the latter date has generally been given.

10 Downton Castle Papers, T74–765; Inglis-Jones, p. 249.

11 Transcriptions in Downton Castle Papers, T74–583; see also Dawson, pp. 496–508.

12 Knight, 1794 (1795), p. 28n; 1796, p. 7n; 1805, p. 26.

13 Inglis-Jones, p. 243; *Penny Cyclopaedia*, XIII, p. 247.

14 Kidderminster MSS 283, 285–7; 294; 1361–5.

15 Knight MS (Autobiography).

16 Coleorton Papers, MA 1581–97; also, for Wales, *ibid.* –19, and, for Etna, Chapter 2.

17 Farington, 5 Sept. 1806; 1 July 1814 (reporting Westall).

18 Knight, 1796, p. 69.

19 Aberdeen Papers, 43229, f. 207 (R.P.K. to Aberdeen – the dealers cited are Arthur Champernowne and Henry Tresham), quoted Liscombe, 1980, p. 73.

20 Downton Castle Papers, T74–501.

21 *Ibid.*, T74–414a.

22 *Ibid.*, T74–724, also –190.

23 Knight, 1796, pp. 146–7n.

24 Cust, p. 119.

25 Inglis-Jones, p. 245; for his early political career see Messmann, pp. 38–40.

26 Dilettanti Papers, I, f. 20 (meeting of 10 April 1742).

27 Banks Letters, IV, ff. 143–5 (R.P.K. to Banks, 18 June 1785).

28 Knight, 1786, p. 23.

29 *Ibid.*, p. 188; see also p. 169.

30 *Ibid.*, pp. 25, 48n, 127; cf. 1791, p. 130.

31 Farington, 5 Sept. 1806 (citing Lord Oxford); 5 April 1807 (citing Westall).

32 Downton Castle Papers, T74–519.

33 Farington, 12 Jan., 4 June 1794; for Beckford see also 6 Nov. 1797.

34 Cook, p. 56.

35 Banks Letters, XVI, ff. 12–13, 19–22, 41–7, 50–2, 64, 74–6; British Library, Add. MS 36501, f. 145 (R.P.K. to Cumberland, 2 Jan. 1808).

36 *Ibid.*, f. 266 (R.P.K. to Cumberland, undated).

37 His will, dated 13 June 1814, was proved 18 June 1824 at the Consistory Court of Canterbury, Prob. 11.1687, p. 364. For the earlier will and the consequent misapprehensions of the Academy see Liscombe, 1980, p. 260, note 5.

38 For facetious anecdotes concerning him see Edwards, pp. 417–21.

39 Aberdeen Papers, 43231, f. 26 (R.P.K. to Aberdeen, 15 Oct. 1821).

40 Johnstone, VII, p. 314 (R.P.K. to Parr, 19 June 1809).

41 Berry, II, p. 345.

42 Sheppard, XXX, pp. 57, 120, Fig. 3a, giving however (like Messmann) 1808 as the date Knight moved – see, however, Johnstone, VII, p. 311 (R.P.K. to Parr, 20 June 1805). The location of his former London house is given British Library, Add. MS 36516, f. 285.

43 [Porson], p. 385.

44 Knight, 1791, pp. 111–30; cf. d'Hancarville, II, p. 225n which surely refers to Knight.

45 Knight, 1791, p. 112n. For Fourmont see Messmann, pp. 57–8.

46 Knight, 1791, pp. 23, 74, 78–9.

47 Knight, 1809, pp. xii–xiii (adapting in prose 1794 (1795), Book I, lines 197–206 and II, lines 380–90).

48 Coleorton Papers, MA 1581–63 (Price to Lady Beaumont, 9 Feb. 1805).

49 *Gentleman's Magazine*, 1809 (ii), pp. 933–5; not continued as advertised perhaps because Knight was irritated by editorial notes.

50 Aberdeen Papers, 43230, f. 332 (R.P.K. to Aberdeen, postmarked 9 Oct. 1819).

51 Gladstone, I, pp. 42, 45; M. L. Clarke, pp. 140–2, 187; Messmann, p. 131.

52 Knight, 1808 – see also 1805, pp. 275, 277, 286–90; 1809, pp. xiii, xix.

53 [Knight], 1809; also (according to Griggs, Kern and Schneider, pp. 207–8) he contributed pp. 169–77 of the article on pp. 158–87 of the *Edinburgh Review*, XVI, April 1810.

54 Knight, 1794 (1795), pp. 64–6;
Aberdeen Papers, 43230, f. 73
(R.P.K. to Aberdeen, 3 Sept.
1810).

55 [Marshall], pp. 1–31;
[Matthews], *passim*. See also
Messmann, pp. 65–70.

56 *Walpole Correspondence*, XIX,
pp. 338–40 (Walpole to Mason,
22 March 1796).

57 Farington, 17 April 1795.

58 Knight, 1796, pp. 136–7, 146–7.

59 Johnstone, VII, p. 396 (R.P.K. to
Parr, *c.* 1802).

60 British Library, Add. MS 37875,
ff. 129–30 (R.P.K. to Windham,
9 Aug. 1795); Knight, 1794
(1795), pp. 93–7.

61 Knight, 1796, pp. 55–6 and
note.

62 *Ibid.*, p. xvii (replying to
Matthias) and p. 1 (lines 9–14).

63 *British Critic*, VIII (1796), pp.
24–32; for the criticism in
general, and for Mason, see
Messmann, pp. 85–8, 94.

64 The other authors were Frere,
Gifford, Hammond and Ellis. The
parody appeared in nos. XV–
XVII and XXI in Feb., March and
April 1798. The passage
parodied here is Knight, 1796,
p. 100.

65 Knight, 1794 (1795), p. 26.

66 Knight MS (Autobiography).

67 Knight, 1796, p. 153.

68 Knight, 1806–7, p. 4.

69 *Ibid.*, pp. 11–13.

70 Coleorton Papers, MA 1581–9,
17 (Price to Beaumont, 5 Sept.
1797 and to Lady Beaumont,
7 Nov. 1798).

71 *Ibid.*, MA 1581–41 (Price to
Lady Beaumont, 31 May 1803).

72 Berry, II, p. 92.

73 Coleorton Papers, MA 1581–19
(Price to Beaumont, 11 Aug.
1800).

74 Farington, 1 April 1802; see
also 9 March 1807.

75 *Ibid.*, p. 2976, 2 April 1805 and
Minutes of the British Institution
(deposited at the Victoria and
Albert Museum), I, 1, 18, 38–40,
kindly communicated by Peter
Fullerton.

76 *British Critic*, XXIX (1807), pp.
1–21, 168–90, especially pp. 2

and 189. For the critical
reaction in general see
Messmann, pp. 105–8.

77 Romney, pp. 321–2 (R.P.K. to
Romney, Rome 1776).

78 Johnstone, VII, pp. 308–9
(R.P.K. to Parr, 20 June 1805),
but see also Farington, 10 Nov.,
1797.

79 Knight, 1805 (1808), p. 186.

80 *Ibid.*, p. 383.

81 *Ibid.*, pp. 123–4.

82 Knight, 1791, pp. 19–20; 1805
(1808), p. 147 – cf. [Knight],
1809, p. 435.

83 Haydon, 1846, pp. 215–16
(Lecture XIII, apparently
written in 1840, reporting at
second hand an event of nearly
thirty-five years before).

84 *Ibid.*, p. 243n.

85 Rothenberg, pp. 224–6.

86 Liscombe, 1980, p. 71 citing
Lord Aberdeen; Farington, 30
March 1806, 2 Feb. 1808, 25
June 1809, citing Sir Abraham
Hume, Lawrence, Beaumont and
Fox (as quoted by Rogers).

87 *Report . . . on Lord Elgin's
Marbles*; for Aberdeen and
Wilkins, see Liscombe, 1980,
pp. 104–9.

88 Haydon, 1816; [Croker], pp.
533–42.

89 [Smirke], I, pp. 19, 22–6; II,
pp. 20–5, 28.

90 Farington, 11 Feb.–1 April 1818.

91 [Knight], 1814, pp. 288–91; for
Princess Caroline see Farington
(Typescript), p. 6498, 3 and 11
May 1814.

92 Aberdeen Papers, 43230, f. 311
(R.P.K. to Aberdeen, 16 Jan.
1816).

93 *Ibid.*, ff. 88–9 (R.P.K. to
Aberdeen, 30 Nov. 1810); see
also cat. no. 96.

94 Knight, 1815.

95 Knight, 1818, pp. 14, 34–5.

96 *Ibid.*, pp. 174–5, 193.

97 Aberdeen Papers, 43230, f. 108
(R.P.K. to Aberdeen, 14 May
1812). Messmann's claim that
he gave up management of the
estate (p. 125) is perhaps based
on a misinterpretation of his
neice's statement that he was
tired of managing an

'establishment', meaning the
Castle. See also Inglis-Jones,
pp. 365ff.

98 Downton Castle Papers T74–519
(Rent Roll of 1790).

99 Aberdeen Papers, 43230, f. 30
(R.P.K. to Aberdeen, 10 Oct.
1809); quoted Liscombe, 1979,
p. 605.

100 Coleorton Papers, MA 1581–
99, 100 (Price to Beaumont,
12 Jan. 1822).

101 Aberdeen Papers, 43230, ff. 49,
72–3 (R.P.K. to Aberdeen,
undated, 1809, and 3 Sept.
1810).

102 Inglis-Jones, p. 258, citing a
memoir of Caroline, Lady Duff-
Gordon.

103 Berry, II, p. 345.

104 Aberdeen Papers, 43230, f. 59
(R.P.K. to Aberdeen, 28 Nov.
1809); cf. Knight, 1805 (1808),
p. 191.

105 Coleorton Papers, MA 1581–1
(Price to Beaumont, 28 Nov.
1794).

106 *Ibid.*, –27 (Price to Beaumont,
16 Aug. 1801).

107 Downton Castle Papers, T74–
55a, b.

108 Holland, II, pp. 79, 137.

109 See the cartoons by Gilray and
others: George, nos. 9240, 9282,
11733, 12030.

110 Will cited in note 37.

111 Aberdeen Papers, 43230, f. 315
(R.P.K. to Aberdeen, 2 Nov.
1817).

112 *Ibid.*, 43231, ff. 59–60 (R.P.K. to
Aberdeen, 26 July 1823).

113 Downton Castle Papers, T74–
619, 678; Felton, p. 178. In
1780, according to the
Downton Terrier, the 'mines and
minerals' there belonged to
Knight and to Lord Clive 'in
equal undivided moieties'.

114 Aberdeen Papers, 43230, f. 30
(R.P.K. to Aberdeen, 10 Oct.
1809), quoted Liscombe, 1979,
p. 605 with Clee Hill as 'Clare
Hill' and the holy brother as
Henry Hunt.

115 *Ibid.*, 43230, ff. 332–4 (R.P.K.
to Aberdeen, postmarked 9 Oct.
1819).

116 British Library, Add. MS 37875,

f. 130 (R.P.K. to Windham, 9 Aug. 1795); Knight, 1796, pp. 140–2n.

117 Knight, 1809, pp. liv–lxxxi; cf. 1796, p. 145n.

118 Aberdeen Papers, 43230, ff. 335–6 (R.P.K. to Aberdeen, 2 Nov. 1819), quoted Liscombe, 1980, p. 146.

119 Coleorton Papers, MA 1581–97 (Price to Beaumont, 12 Jan. 1822).

120 Aberdeen Papers, 43231, ff. 25–6 (R.P.K. to Aberdeen, 15 Oct. 1821).

121 Coleorton Papers as in note 119.

122 Knight, 1823, pp. 343ff.

123 *Ibid.*, pp. xvi–xviii.

124 *Ibid.*, pp. viii–xv (Byron); pp.

125 Coleorton Papers, MA 1581–99, 100 (Price to Beaumont, 11 March 1823).

126 Aberdeen Papers, 43231, f. 87 (R.P.K. to Aberdeen, undated but 1823).

127 Clayden, I, p. 365.

128 *Gentleman's Magazine*, 1824 (ii), p. 185.

129 *Recollections*, p. 146 – cf. Greville, IV, p. 182.

130 Downton Castle Papers, T74–525 (draft reply to Mr Gwynne of the Stamp Office concerning non-payment of legacy duty on will of R.P.K.).

131 *Ibid.*, T74–553.

132 *Ibid.*, T74–727.

133 *Ibid.*

134 T. A. Knight, 1834; Inglis-Jones, p. 377.

135 Beesly, pp. 12–13, 15; Inglis-Jones, pp. 380–6.

136 Downton Castle Papers, T74–473b (letters from R.P.K. to Samuel Nash concerning the eviction of his kinsman James Knight who was tenant at the Bringewood Forge). Samuel's son was perhaps involved in the quarrel – see Bodleian Library, MS Eng. Misc. d. 158, ff. 135–6.

137 Beesly, pp. 15f.

138 Inglis-Jones, p. 239.

139 Littlebury, p. 164.

140 Downton Castle Papers, T74.

Notes to Chapter Two

1 Knight MS (Sicilian Diary).

2 But see *ibid.*, f. 101.

3 Dryden visited the island 1701, and his *Voyage to Sicily and Malta* was published 1776; J. P. d'Orville went in 1727, his *Sicula: quibus Siciliae Veteris rudera illustrantur* was published in Amsterdam (2 vols.) 1764; Patrick Brydone went in 1770 and his *Tour through Sicily and Malta* appeared three years later.

4 Baron J. H. von Riedesel, *Reise durch Sizilien und Grossgriechenland*, Zurich 1771 (English and French editions appeared 1773).

5 The *Voyage du Mont Etna* translated from Hamilton's English by Villebois was published as an appendix to Riedesel, Lausanne 1773.

6 Stuart and Revett's *Antiquities of Athens* vol. I, appeared only in 1762 but their proposals for the publication were published in Rome in 1748.

7 Swinburne, pp. i, xvi.

8 A letter from Goethe of 15 Jan. 1810 (Weimar, Goethe–Schiller-Archiv, xlix, 3.6) is in the same hand, as is the adapted version of Knight's account of the ascent of Etna

appended to the Diary – it may well be that of one of Goethe's secretaries. The paper of the Diary, and that of the letter of 1810, is watermarked with a skirted trumpeter, and with a bear-baiter with bear, on alternate pages.

9 Goethe, 1811. Pevsner published a retranslation of parts of the Diary. Hussey, p. 124 n. 1 started the myth of the lost original's disappearance.

10 British Museum, O.o.4–(2–41).

11 Romney, pp. 331–2.

12 Goethe, 1811; Lohse.

13 Goethe, 1811, pp. 274–85 (using notes made by Gore's daughter Eliza). See also Bell and Girtin, p. 8, Fraser, and the handlist compiled in 1978 by H. Belsey.

14 Knight MS (Sicilian Diary), f. 1.

15 *Ibid.*; there is a note on Claude in the right margin.

16 *Ibid.*, f. 3.

17 McCarthy, p. 760; *Italienische Reise*, 23 March 1787.

18 Knight MS (Sicilian Diary), f.8.

19 *Ibid.*, f. 16.

20 *Ibid.*, f. 18.

21 *Ibid.*, ff. 17–18.

22 Hackert had worked for the Bourbons in Naples since 1770 although he was only appointed

court painter in 1786.

23 Lang, 1959, p. 56.

24 Knight MS (Sicilian Diary), f. 25.

25 *Ibid.*

26 *Ibid.*, ff. 23, 26.

27 *Ibid.*, f. 29.

28 *Ibid.*, f. 32.

29 *Ibid.*

30 *Ibid.*

31 *Ibid.*, f. 36.

32 *Ibid.*, f. 41.

33 *Ibid.*, f. 44.

34 *Ibid.*, f. 46.

35 *Ibid.*, f. 47.

36 *Ibid.*, f. 53.

37 *Ibid.*, f. 56.

38 *Ibid.*, f. 57.

39 *Ibid.*, f. 60.

40 *Ibid.*, f. 61.

41 *Ibid.*, f. 75.

42 *Ibid.*, f. 76.

43 *Ibid.*, f. 78.

44 *Ibid.* (quoting from Tasso's *La Gerusalemme liberata* 14, X– cf. Hoole's translation of 1792: 'Survey yon sea, the mighty and the vast! / Which here can no such glorious titles claim, / A pool unnoted and a worthless name').

45 Knight MS, ff. 82–3.

46 Gore carefully annotated the Sicilian views in his collection (Weimar, Goethe-Nationalmuseum, Th.Scr.2.2.³–.

This is quoted from the drawing of the 'Grotta del Capro' (no. 93).

47 Knight MS (Sicilian Diary), ff. 88–90.
48 *Ibid.*, ff. 72, 103.
49 *Ibid.*, f. 66.
50 *Ibid.*, f. 95.
51 *Ibid.*, ff. 95–7.
52 *Ibid.*, ff. 116–17.
53 *Ibid.*, f. 119.
54 Besides the watercolours in Knight's bequest (see note 10), there are Sicilian views by Hackert in various German collections (Krönig, 1979). One hundred and twelve watercolours and sketches by Gore are preserved in Weimar (see note 46). Cozens repeated at least one of his copies after Gore (cf. B. M. Knight Bequest, O.o.4–6 and B. M. Cracherode Bequest, G.g.3–394), and see also Bell and Girtin, no. 106, I and II.

55 Oppé, p. 112 suggested a quarrel – cf. Bell and Girtin, p. 11 and Messmann, p. 29 note 75 who assume Cozens remained behind for financial reasons.
56 It was Hackert who obtained royal permission and perhaps initiated the whole idea and he certainly made most use of the material collected there – many of his views were engraved (e.g. in Francesco Morelli's *Vedute della Sicilia*).
57 The diary concludes with the entry for 6 June '. . . we embarked for Naples' (f. 94). The 1845 catalogue of Knight's Bequest cites an inscription on the original mount of a view of Monte Carrino by Hearne (O.o.4–4) 'On the Road back from Naples. July 1777'.
58 Goethe, 1811, p. 215. As mentioned in Chapter One

Knight was in Paris in the winter of 1777 so the watercolours were finished by then if he carried them back with him, but they may have been brought back by Gore in 1779.
59 MS Italienisches Reisetagebuch of Prince August von Sachsen-Gotha und Altenburg, f. 80 (6 Dec. 1777) – to be published by Dr G. Eckardt.
60 Goethe, 1811, p. 278.
61 Bell and Girtin, p. 24.
62 Romney, p. 332.
63 Ehrlich.
64 W. A. Knight, p. 57.
65 Goethe omitted the general observations but a translation of several pages of them exist in his hand attached to the manuscript in Weimar (MS 25/XUV) so he perhaps considered publishing the entire text.

Notes to Chapter Three

1 Downton Castle Papers, T74–414, quoted Inglis-Jones, p. 247, with minor variations.
2 Pevsner, 1963, p. 118.
3 Downton Castle Papers, T74–413.
4 *Ibid.*, –414a.
5 Felton, p. 158.
6 Downton Castle Papers, T74–473b, quoted Inglis-Jones, p. 251.
7 Lipscomb, p. 265.
8 Rowan.
9 Downton Castle Papers, T74–413, 414a.
10 Felton, p. 161.
11 1776 (no. 194); 1777 (no. 183); 1778 (no. 287).
12 Lipscomb, p. 269; Felton, p. 161.
13 Coleorton Papers, MA 1581–5.
14 Inglis-Jones, p. 252.
15 Knight, 1805 (1808), pp. 48–9.
16 Berry, II, p. 378; Inglis-Jones, p. 258, quoting a memoir by Caroline, Lady Duff-Gordon.
17 Pevsner, p. 208.
18 *Gentleman's Magazine*, 1797 (i), p. 473.
19 Lipscomb, p. 269.

20 *Ibid.*
21 *Ibid.*, p. 268.
22 Rowan.
23 *Gentleman's Magazine*, 1806 (i), p. 132.
24 Knight, 1805 (1808), pp. 163–6.
25 *Ibid.*, p. 167.
26 *Ibid.*, p. 176.
27 *Ibid.*, p. 222.
28 Aberdeen Papers, 43230, f. 88 (R.P.K. to Aberdeen, 30 Nov. ?1811).
29 Knight, 1805 (1808), pp. 163–5.
30 Fleming.
31 Knight, 1805 (1808), p. 160.
32 Kitson, pp. 126–7.
33 Knight, 1805 (1808), p. 223; Felton, p. 159.
34 *Gentleman's Magazine*, 1797 (i), p. 473; cf. Lipscomb, p. 268.
35 Knight, 1805 (1808), p. 223.
36 Pevsner, 1968, p. 111.
37 *Walpole Correspondence*, XX, p. 127.
38 Kidderminster MSS 102–7, 122, 125, 294, 1428.
39 Colvin, pp. 554, 894.
40 Knight, 1805 (1808), pp. 164–9; Lord Aberdeen in Wilkins, p. xii

(for other disagreements see pp. xi, xli–ii, lxiv).
41 Knight, 1794 (1795), p. 54.
42 Aberdeen Papers, 43230, ff. 310–11 (R.P.K. to Aberdeen, 16 Jan. 1816), quoted Liscombe, 1980, p. 110.
43 Knight, 1805 (1808), p. 179.
44 *Ibid.*, p. 175.
45 *Ibid.*, pp. 180, 227.
46 *Ibid.*, pp. 215, 234, 241, 245, 251, 254n.
47 Elsam included the passage on pages 2–4 of his 2nd Edition (London 1805).
48 Malton's *Essay* appeared in 1798. Even his grander cottages, c.g. Plates 16, 18 and 20, are, or rather appear, regular.
49 Summerson, p. 84; Davis, p. 60.
50 Knight, 1805 (1808), p. 223.
51 Lipscomb, pp. 162–3.
52 Coleorton Papers, MA 1581–16 (Price to Beaumont, 18 March 1798), cited Allentuck, p. 69.
53 Davis, p. 21.
54 Knight, 1805 (1808), p. 224.
55 Aberdeen Papers, 43230, ff. 49–50.

56 *Ibid.*, ff. 58–9.
57 Knight, 1805 (1808), p. 224.
58 Lipscomb, p. 267.
59 *Gentleman's Magazine*, 1797 (i), p. 473; Greville, IV, p. 182.
60 Knight, 1794 (1795), p. 24.
61 Aberdeen Papers, 43230, f. 133.
62 *Ibid.*, f. 71; also Coleorton Papers, MA 1581–19, cited Allentuck, p. 67.
63 Aberdeen Papers, 43230, f. 71; also Coleorton Papers, MA

1581–19.
64 Knight, 1794 (1795), p. 45n.
65 Aberdeen Papers, 43230, f. 70.
66 Knight, 1794 (1795), p. 12n – also p. iv.
67 Pevsner, pp. 145–6, seems to support Repton here – but when exactly did Knight intervene to save the terrace at Powis Castle, mentioned by Price, III, pp. 87–8?
68 Knight, 1794 (1795), pp. 17–24.

See Farington, 8 Sept. 1794.
69 Knight, 1805 (1808), p. 196 especially.
70 Downton Castle Papers T74–534 (letters of 1811 and 1812).
71 Smirke, cited by Farington.
72 Aberdeen Papers, 43230, ff. 318–19, 332–4, quoted Liscombe, 1979, p. 609.
73 Coleorton Papers, MA 1581–99 (Price to Beaumont, 11 March 1823).

Notes to Chapter Four

1 British Library, Add. MS 34048, f. 14.
2 Hamilton, p. 9.
3 *Ibid.*, p. 10.
4 British Library, Add. MS 34048, f. 17. The waxes were M560–4 in the MS Catalogue of the Museum Secretum. Several fragments survive.
5 Exactly when is unknown – see Webster.
6 Mitter, Chapter 2.
7 D'Hancarville, I, pp. 67ff.
8 *Ibid.*, p. xix.
9 *Ibid.*, p. 5; Knight, 1786, p. 92.
10 *Ibid.*, p. 35.
11 Knight, 1818, section 230.
12 D'Hancarville, II, p. 155.
13 *Ibid.*, I, p. 199.
14 Christie, Appendix Section I.
15 Towneley Hall Papers, DDTo Box 13.
16 Maty, p. 24.
17 Towneley Hall Papers, DDTo Box 13.
18 Whitaker, p. 327.
19 British Library, Add. MS 30873, f. 25.
20 Pinkerton, 1789, I, p. xxvi.
21 *Ibid.*, I, p. 168.
22 *Ibid.*, I, p. 194.
23 British Library, Add. MS 40714, f. 237.
24 British Museum, Dept. of Greek and Roman Antiquities 64a.

25 British Library, Add. MS 36496, f. 326.
26 Towneley Hall Papers, DDTo Box 2.
27 Spiker, p. 316.
28 Towneley Hall Papers, DDTo Box 2.
29 *Ibid.*, Box 13.
30 *Ibid.*, Box 2.
31 Blundell, 1803.
32 Blundell, 1809, II, advertisement.
33 *Ibid.*
34 Knight, 1786, p. 25.
35 Mason, III, p. 74.
36 Banks Letters, IV, ff. 143–5.
37 Dilettanti Papers, Minutes IV.
38 Farington, 22 July 1798.
39 Gillies, p. 326.
40 Knight, 1786, p. 24.
41 *Ibid.*, p. 47.
42 *Ibid.*, p. 55.
43 *Ibid.*, p. 116.
44 *Ibid.*, p. 48.
45 *Ibid.*, p. 27.
46 *Ibid.*, p. 28.
47 *Ibid.*
48 *Ibid.*, p. 46.
49 Jones, p. 255.
50 Knight, 1786, p. 188.
51 *Ibid.*, p. 183.
52 *Ibid.*, p. 193.
53 *Ibid.*, p. 176.
54 Maréchal, VII, p. 89.
55 Knight, 1786, p. 182.

56 *Ibid.*, p. 23.
57 Mathias, p. 19.
58 *Ibid.*
59 *Ibid.* – but in later editions only.
60 Broadsheet entitled 'A Proposal for a Reformation of Principles', 1 Jan. 1792.
61 Johnstone, VII, p. 308.
62 *Ibid.*, p. 310
63 Moor, pp. 56ff.
64 *Ibid.*, pp. 392–402.
65 *British Critic*, 1794, p. 388.
66 *Ibid.*, p. 385.
67 *Ibid.*, p. 388
68 *Ibid.*, p. 390.
69 *Ibid.*, p. 388. They returned with added vehemence to the subject when reviewing *The Progress of Civil Society*.
70 Peacock, VIII, p. 188.
71 Knight, 1796, p. xvii.
72 *Ibid.*, p. xviii.
73 *Ibid.*, p. xix.
74 *Ibid.*
75 Dilettanti Papers, Minutes IV (4 June 1797).
76 Knight, 1796, p. xxi.
77 A copy of the 'Symbolical Language' with annotations in Knight's hand is in the British Library – C.60.l.3.
78 Knight, 1818, p. 154.
79 Field, II, p. 137.
80 Knight, 1823, p. viii.

Notes to Chapter Five

1 *Gentleman's Magazine*, 1797 (i), p. 473.
2 Michaelis, pp. 75–84, for

Jenkins – see also Cat. no. 180 here.
3 Dallaway, p. 314; A. H. Smith,

III pp. 138–9 ('Aratus').
4 At Burke's sale (Christie's) 5 June 1812 busts of Hercules

(28), Flora (29), and a
'Gladiator' (64) for 15, 19 and
36 guineas; at Nollekens's sale
(Christie's), day 3, 5 July 1823,
a bust of Pertinax (84) for 20
guineas.

5 Nichols, II, p. 280n; III, p. 498n;
IV, p. 607; V, pp. 450–1;
Pinkerton, I, p. 13.

6 British Library, Add. MS 36501,
f. 145 (R.P.K. to Cumberland,
2 Jan. 1808).

7 Kidderminster MS 288.

8 Knight, 1821, p. 369.

9 D'Hancarville, II, p. 175n.

10 Noehden. Nos. 3, 6, 8, 9, 11
and 22 are from Torremuzza's
collection.

11 Walters, 1926, p. x.

12 Story-Maskeline.

13 Berry, III, p. 231.

14 Knight MS (Bronzes), p. 141,
unnumbered but after xlix.

15 Knight, 1814.

16 Knight MS (Bronzes), xxiii. 16.

17 *Ibid.*, x. 10; xix; lxx. 6.

18 *Ibid.*, xxiii.12.

19 Aberdeen Papers, 43230, f. 124
(R.P.K. to Aberdeen, 18 July
1812).

20 Knight MS (Bronzes), lxx.4.

21 *Ibid.*, lxvi.1.

22 *Ibid.*, xxxi. 3; xli. 1.

23 MS (Gems), 90.

24 *Ibid.*, 80.

25 *Ibid.*, 13, 48, 62, 79

26 *Museum Worsleyanum*, II, pp.
3–37.

27 Knight MS (Bronzes), v.1; lii.5.

28 *Ibid.*, xxxii.2; xlvi.1, 8; lx.9, 17;
lxv.6, 7; lxxi.4; lxxvii.7. For
Quirini see Haskell, pp. 368–72.

29 Knight, 1809, plates iv and
lxxiv.

30 Knight MS (Bronzes), xlvi.3.

31 *Ibid.*, xxx.5.

32 *Ibid.*, xlvi.17, xxiii. 18.

33 *Ibid.*, xcvii.13.

34 *Ibid.*, vii.11.

35 *Ibid.*, xv.3.

36 *Ibid.*; see Cat. no. 43.

37 *Ibid.*, lx.11; lxxxix.73; xcvii.12.

38 *Ibid.*, l–1.

39 *Ibid.*, iii.1; xlix.1; lii.1; lix.1;
lxv.3, 4, 5; lxxxv.1.

40 *Ibid.*, xi.2; *Specimens*, II, plate
xxv. For Wilbraham's collection
(which is not mentioned by
Michaelis) see also d'Hancarville,
I, pp. 134n, 314n, 369; III,
p. 87.

41 Knight MS (Bronzes), lx.4;
Knight, 1809, plates xxxiii–
xxxiv.

42 Knight MS (Bronzes), lx.5,
lxxxvi.4.

43 Knight MS (Notebook of Coins).

44 Michael Downing reckons there
were 51 (but possibly 53). They
are predominantly dionysiac in
theme and consist of 7 black-
figure (Attic), 33 red-figure, 2
Corinthian and 9 black-glazed
(Attic and south Italian).

45 He bought at the Chinnery sale
(3–4 June 1812, Christie's) and
the Coghill sale (18–19 June
1819, Christie's). For his
attitude see Aberdeen Papers
43230, f. 117 (R.P.K. to
Aberdeen, 13 June 1812),
quoted Liscombe, 1979, p. 606.

46 Michaelis, pp. 106, 109–11.

47 Knight MS (Bronzes), viii.1;
Holland, II, p. 79.

48 Knight MS (Bronzes), lxix.2.

49 Goethe, *Italienische Reise*, 27
May 1787.

50 Knight MS (Bronzes), xvii.2, 8.

51 Knight MS (Notebook of Coins).

52 Towneley Hall Papers, DDTo
'Antiq.' (in folder headed 'Dealing
with Classical subjects . . .').
Specimens, II, pp. lxv–lxvi gives a
garbled account stating that
Aberdeen presented Knight with
two items.

53 Knight MS (Bronzes), xiv.3
(Gell); xviii.6; lxxiii.3; xcv.1
(Clarke) – and see E. D. Clarke,
Part 2, III, p. 197n for coins.

54 *Ibid.*, Part 2, II, p. 483
especially – he was echoed by
other authors, e.g. Dodwell and
Eustace.

55 E. D. Clarke, part 2, II, pp.
728–9 and III, p. 400.

56 Knight MS (Bronzes), xx.1, 2, 3,
4; Walters, 1921, pp. 1–3. For
Millingen as a dealer in medals
see also Aberdeen Papers,
43229, ff. 91–2. For
Millingen's high opinion of
Knight see Millingen, p. 24.

57 Aberdeen Papers, 43229, ff.
125–6; Knight MS (Bronzes),
xc.8. For Bonelli see also
Farington, 5 June 1816.

58 Quoted with kind permission of
the Pierpont Morgan Library.

59 A. H. Smith, 1916, p. 257;
Rothenberg, pp. 200–2.

60 Aberdeen Papers, 43229, f. 121.

61 The four volumes were the first
of a series of nine – the *Lettere e
Dissertazione numismatiche* –
published in Livorno
(subsequently Rome and Berlin).

62 Preface to *Descriptio Numorum
veterum . . .*, Lipsiae 1796.

63 Knight MS (Bronzes), xviii.1.

64 Knight MS (Gems), 4 and 86.

65 Knight MS (Notebook of Coins).

66 Knight, 1805 (1808), p. 109.

67 Knight, 1809, p. xxxix and plate
xiv.

68 Aberdeen Papers, 43229, f. 237
(to Aberdeen, undated, probably
1807), quoted Liscombe, 1979,
p. 605 and 1980, p. 108, who
reads Ribera for Rebecca.

69 *Ibid.*, 43230, ff. 310–11 (R.P.K.
to Aberdeen, 16 Jan. 1816),
quoted by Liscombe, 1979, p.
607 and 1980, p. 109.

70 Knight, 1809, p. xxxix; *Report
. . . on Lord Elgin's Marbles*.

71 Knight, 1805, p. 308.

72 [Knight], 1810, pp. 308–9; cf
[Knight], 1814, p. 276.

73 [Knight], 1810, p. 309.

74 [Croker], p. 539n.

75 [Knight], p. 2; see also Banks
Letters, XIX, ff. 275–81 (Banks
to R.P.K. and vice versa, 16 and
19 June 1816).

76 Downton Castle Papers, T74–
583, no. 32 (transcription of
letter from Banks to T.A. K.,
6 July 1816).

77 Dalton, p. lv.

78 Knight MS (Gems), 110. He had
however earlier possessed a gem
engraved by Marchant, which is
listed in his *Catalogue of
Impressions*, 1792.

79 Knight, 1818, pp. 71–2.

80 Knight, 1809, pp. xxiii, xxv,
and text accompanying plates
v–viii.

81 [Croker], p. 534.

82 Knight, 1809. p. l;
Rothenberg, p. 400.

83 Knight, 1805 (1808), p. 245.

84 Implied by Rothenberg, pp. 214–15.
85 Knight, 1809, plate lxx; Knight MS (Bronzes), lx.16; lx.1; lxx.5. 6.
86 Knight, 1809, plate xxix.
87 Blundell, 1809, I, plate 29.
88 *Ibid.*, II, plate 145; Ashmole, no. 63.
89 E.g. Ashmole, nos. 83g, h; 142.
90 D'Hancarville, I, p. 397n.
91 Blundell, 1809, I, plate 41 (no. 531).
92 Haskell and Penny, pp. 105–6.
93 Knight, 1791, p. 20.
94 Knight, 1809, pp. xliii–xlvii, lii and text accompanying plates xxxv–xxxvii, xlv–xlvi.
95 *Ibid.*, pp. xlvii and li–liii.
96 Knight was relying on Wheler, Spon and Pockocke.
97 Knight, 1794 (1795), p. 61n.
98 *Ibid.*, p. 65n.
99 Knight, 1809.
100 Goethe, *Italienische Reise*, 24 April 1787.
101 Knight MS (Sicilian Diary), ff. 49–50.

102 Pevsner, pp. 200–7.
103 Knight MS (Sicilian Diary), f. 3.
104 Knight, 1809, I, p. xviii and endpiece of Dissertation; Walters, 1926, no. 89 – cf. the Babylonian signet in the Englefield sale, Christie's, 6–8 March 1823, day 3 (21).
105 Knight, 1818, p. 144.
106 Knight MS (Bronzes), xvi.2, 3.
107 Knight, 1809, p. x.
108 Knight MS (Sicilian Diary), f. 112; [Knight], 1810, p. 303.
109 Knight, 1796, pp. 90–2; 1809, pp. v–vii; 1818, pp. 192–3; 1822, p. 8.
110 Knight MS (Sicilian Diary), f. 37.
111 Knight, 1808, p. 241n; [Knight], 1810, pp. 311, 323–5; [Knight], 1814, pp. 268, 279–80.
112 Knight, 1821, p. 374. The view was, however, controversial – see Noehden, p. 44.
113 Knight, 1809, p. xxvi.
114 *Ibid.*, p. xi. Cf. Knight, 1794, p. 59.

115 Knight, 1794 (1795), p. 59; 1796, p. 106; 1805, p. 59; 1809, pp. vii–xiii; 1822, p. 8.
116 Knight MS (Bronzes), I–1. It is the 'Gladiator' mentioned in note 4 as from Burke's collection which was formed in Italy by William Lloyd, advised by Cavaceppi.
117 Knight, 1805 (1808), pp. 283–4, 310, 344, 360, 375.
118 *Ibid.*, p. 312 (costume), pp. 192–3 (sculpturesque).
119 Farington (Typescript), pp. 3057–8, 24 Aug. 1805.
120 Knight, 1805 (1808), pp. 184, 434–5.
121 Knight, 1805 (1808), pp. 109–10.
122 *Ibid.*, pp. 311–12.
123 [Knight], 1810, p. 313; cf. [Knight], 1814, p. 268.
124 Knight, 1805, pp. 311–12.
125 Knight, 1794, p. 56 and plate iii.
126 Knight MS (Sicilian Diary), f. 119; 1795, p. 70; 1805, p. 129; 1809, p. 430.

Notes to Chapter Six

1 Johnstone, VII, p. 308.
2 *Ibid.*, p. 309.
3 *The Critical Review*, Nov. 1805, pp. 225–37.
4 Johnstone, VII, p. 309.
5 Romney, p. 331.
6 Alison, p. 296.
7 Jeffrey, I, p. 27.
8 Horner, I, p. 320.
9 S. Smith, I, p. 112.
10 Aberdeen Papers, 43228, f. 56.
11 Price, I, p. 47.
12 *Ibid.*, p. 46.
13 Knight, 1794, (1795), p. 19.
14 *Ibid.*, 1805 (1808), p. 95.
15 Cheselden, p. 448.
16 Knight, 1805 (1808), p. 58.
17 *Ibid.*
18 A. Smith, p. 299.

19 Reid, p. 183.
20 *Ibid.*
21 *Ibid.*, p. 184.
22 Cheselden, p. 449.
23 Reid, p. 185.
24 Knight, 1805 (1808), p. 69.
25 [Knight], 1814, p. 285.
26 Knight, 1805 (1808), p. 149.
27 *Ibid.*
28 *Ibid.*, p. 150.
29 *Ibid.*
30 [Knight], 1814, p. 285 – cf. 1810, p. 300.
31 Knight, 1805 (1808), p. 70.
32 *Ibid.*, p. 57.
33 *Ibid.*, p. 64.
34 *Ibid.*, p. 65.
35 *The Literary Journal*, Feb. 1806, pp. 113–28.

36 Aberdeen Papers, 43228, f. 64.
37 *Ibid.*, f. 35.
38 Romney, p. 325.
39 Knight, 1805 (1808), p. 308.
40 [Knight], 1814, p. 286.
41 *Ibid.*, p. 282.
42 *Ibid.*, p. 264.
43 *Ibid.*, p. 273.
44 [Knight], 1810, p. 299.
45 *Ibid.*
46 [Knight], 1814, p. 286.
47 *Ibid.*, 1810, p. 316.
48 *Ibid.*, 1814, p. 279.
49 *Ibid.*, 1810, p. 314.
50 *Ibid.*, 1814, p. 270.
51 *Ibid.*, 1810, p. 317.
52 *Ibid.*, p. 300.
53 Knight, 1805 (1808), p. 309.
54 [Knight], 1810, pp. 300–1.

Notes to Chapter Seven

1 Waagen, I, p. 59
2 Passavant, pp. 91–2.
3 British Museum, Dept. of Prints and Drawings, shelf mark REG.A.60.
4 See, for example, the following sales catalogues: Sotheby's, 26 June 1957 (24–6); Sotheby's, 27 June 1962 (8–10); Christie's,

4 May 1979 (77–107);
Sotheby's, 17 June 1981 (81–8);
Sotheby's, 8 July 1981 (61–9).

5 Now in the Metropolitan Museum, New York, acquired 1932. Transferred from wood to canvas, 40×55.5, see E. Tietze-Conrat, *Mantegna*, London 1955, pp. 190–1 (where attributed to Mantegna School *c.* 1460, though others place it 1449–50). As with a number of paintings in this essay, first mentioned by other sources as being in Boughton Knight's collection, I have assumed they were, in fact, purchased by Payne Knight himself as none of the subsequent owners of Downton is known to have acquired outstanding works of art. Knight also owned a magnificent drawing by Mantegna, *Allegory of Vice and Virtue* (Popham and Pouncey 157, Pp. 1–23).

6 Now in the Getty Museum, California, purchased by Mr Getty at the Kincaid Lennox sale, Sotheby's, 27 June 1962 (10) and presented to the Museum, 1971. Canvas, 86.5× 75.5, signed and dated 1661. Bredius, no. 615. Probably acquired by Knight in the early nineteenth century (see *Catalogue of the Paintings in the J. Paul Getty Museum*, 1972, no. 117 for the correct provenance).

7 Now in the Metropolitan Museum, New York, acquired 1978. Canvas, 39.5×59.0; *c.* 1649 (see M. Roethlisberger in *Paragone*, no. 233, 1969, pp. 54ff.); acquired by Knight in 1806 according to Kitson, p. 127.

8 It is extremely difficult to be precise on the matter of Knight's early purchases. A possible, though by no means certain, candidate for the earliest is lot 23, *Unknown, Our Saviour in the Garden*, Christie's, Anon. sale, 15 July 1769 (16s 6d to 'Mr Night'), recently Christie's, 4 May 1979 (89) as L. Carraci, *Christ in the Garden of*

Gethsemane, copper, 40×30. For other possible early purchases by Knight mentioned in the latter sale, see lot nos. 82, 86, 91, 103–5.

9 Graves and Cronin, II, p. 777.
10 Waterhouse, 1941, p. 62.
11 Phillips, 23–4 March.
12 Kidderminster, MSS. 285–92. Before 1776 Edward Knight very rarely spent more than £15 on a work of art – the largest sum was £65 for a Gaspard – but thereafter, and especially after his father's death in 1780, he was prepared to pay between £200 and £500, often several times per annum.
13 Baron Alt Sale, Christie's, 25 April 1770 (39 and 40), recently Christie's, 4 May 1797 (104–5).
14 Buchanan, p. 196. Together with Westall's *Grecian Marriage* and his album of Claude drawings, this would have been amongst Knight's most expensive purchases. Bredius, no. 568 (now described by Gerson and others as a studio work of the early 1640s), Rijksmuseum, Amsterdam.
15 Panel 76.5×64.0, sold Christie's, 4 May 1979 (106). Bredius no. 540.
16 [Knight] 1810, p. 317.
17 M. Levey, *National Gallery Catalogues: the Seventeenth and Eighteenth Century Italian Schools*, London 1971, no. 193. In fact the picture came from the Palazzo Lancellotti, not the Palazzo Falconieri.
18 Aberdeen Papers, 43229, f. 207 (undated).
19 *Op. cit.*, pp. 324–5.
20 Ignatius Sancho (1729–80), a negro befriended by Sterne and others, painted by Gainsborough, probably 1768 (Waterhouse 598), his *Letters* published 1782.
21 Possibly Goldsmith's neighbour and protégé, William 'Memory' Cooke (d. 1824).
22 J.T. Smith, I, pp. 29–30.
23 Beaumont also presented him with a landscape of *Stratford Mill, near Dedham*, oil on paper

laid on panel, 30.0×39.5, inscribed verso: *G. H. Beaumont amico suo R. P. Knight pinxit et D.d. 1821*; Sotheby's 17 June 1981 (87).
24 Coleorton Papers, MA 1581–79.
25 *Ibid.*, MA 1581–28.
26 28 April 1791, for example Gozzoli's *Entombment* (cat. no. 140), see also Popham and Pouncey 20 and 179. Knight probably bought extensively on a 1791 visit to Paris as Pouncey and Gere 86 has on the verso, possibly in Knight's hand, *Bt at the sale of the Marq: de la Mure at Paris for 260 Liv: April 22, 1791*. The Abbé Tersan, whom Knight sometimes spelt *Tersaint*, is often misread in published provenances of British Museum drawings as *Gersaint* (see p. 70).
27 Knight, 1805 (1808), pp. 103–4.
28 *Ibid*.
29 *Op. cit.*, pp. 297–8.
30 My observations are based on marked-up copies of these catalogues in the Dept. of Prints and Drawings, British Museum, respective shelf marks A.6.16–20; B.1.22/1; A.6.14; A.1.30/22. The Knapton sale catalogue is at Colnaghi's.
31 At the Spencer sale, for example, Knight bought twenty-three lots for a total of £83.
32 Coleorton Papers, MA 1581–70.
33 Berry, II, pp. 339–40.
34 The last reference in Farington to Knight in this respect occurs in the entry for 7 June 1820, 'Messrs. West's I went to before breakfast & Looked at some Lots of drawings R. & B. West and Henderson were there also R. P. Knight & Ward.'
35 Roethlisberger, I, pp. 56–7, 453; *Somerset House Gazette*, 1824, I, p. 346, II, p. 189.
36 *Op. cit.*, p. 1.
37 Knight, 1794 (1795), p. 16.
38 Farington, 17 April 1803. The Bouillon Claudes were purchased from Angerstein in 1824 for the newly founded National Gallery – *The Marriage of Isaac and Rebeccah* and *The Embarkation of the Queen of Sheba*. Beaumont's

'large Claude' would have been the *Landscape with Narcissus* which later formed part of his gift to the National Gallery 1823–8. See also Farington, 7 May 1803, for Fuseli's favourable comments on the Bouillon Claudes.

39 *Op. cit.*, I, p. 346.

40 *Ibid.*, II, p. 189.

41 Beckett, VI, p. 150.

42 *Ibid.*, p. 151.

43 Roethlisberger, I, p. 453.

44 Farington, 30 July 1803.

45 *Ibid.*, 5 March 1797.

46 Sold Sotheby's, 26 June 1957 (24) as Lorenzo Costa *Portrait of a Cardinal*, oil on panel, 82.0× 77.0, where said to have been acquired by Knight from a brother of Admiral Graves who purchased it in Rome from the heirs of the niece of Cardinal Bibbiena. Acquired 1969 by the Minneapolis Institute of Arts, see their *Bulletin*, LIX, 1970, where attributed to Correggio by Everett Fahy.

47 Farington, 17 February 1799.

48 See also Farington, 13 February 1799, 'Knight has bought a portrait by Raphael from Graves for 500 guineas. Graves had asked 2000 for it.'

49 *Ibid.* Canvas, about 114.0× 114.0. Collection D. P. H. Lennox, Esq.

50 Farington, 10 November 1797.

15 *Ibid.*, 18 November 1797.

52 *Ibid.*, 24 August 1805.

53 *Ibid.*, 14 and 15 March 1804.

54 [Knight], 1810, p. 310.

55 *Ibid.*, pp. 310–11. On Reynolds

as a collector see M. Royalton-Kisch in *Gainsborough and Reynolds in the British Museum*, London 1978, pp. 61–75.

56 Gage, pp. 38–41.

57 Farington, 11 March 1797.

58 Brigstocke, pp. 76–84.

59 [Knight], 1810, p. 315.

60 *Ibid.*

61 [Knight], 1814, p. 283, see also C. Gould, *National Gallery: Catalogue of the Sixteenth-Century Italian Schools*, London 1975, pp. 242, 245 n. 1, 2.

62 [Knight], 1814, p. 284.

63 [Knight], 1810, p. 315.

64 Farington, 23 May 1814.

65 *Ibid.*, 23 April 1814.

66 *Ibid.*, 13 July 1813. In addition to his Claude, Knight owned a 'Poussin', *The Woman taken in Adultery*, sold Sotheby's, 26 June 1957 (25), now German art market, tentatively attributed by Anthony Blunt to Colombel but by Richard Verdi to an earlier hand.

67 The main version of this painting was exhibited at the Tate Gallery, London, *Hogarth*, 1971–2 (26).

68 (17) *Portrait of the Cardinal Bibbiena*, 'Raphael', see n. 46; (24) *Portrait of Maria Raffalino*, Parmigianino; (77) *The Magdelene, from the Aldobrandini Palace*, A. Carracci (presumably a lost version or copy of the painting now in the Galleria Doria-Pamphili Rome – see D. Posner, *Annibale Carracci*, London 1971, II, no. 125); (79) *St Francis with the Angel*, L.

Carracci (untraced); (86) *Portrait of a Lady and Her Son*, Giorgione (Christie's, 4 May 1978 (78) as P. Bordone, *Portrait of a Lady*, half length, with her child beside her, in a niche – previously exhibited Royal Academy, winter 1882 (151) as Giorgione, 'a lady of the *Malipieri* [*sic*] family').

69 Farington, 11 February 1808.

70 Brown, p. 24.

71 Farington, 3 July 1802.

72 *Ibid.*, 8 May 1807.

73 Watkin, p. 43.

74 [Knight], 1814, p. 287.

75 Farington, 4 May 1796.

76 Westall was apparently still using the process for his exhibition pictures in 1799; see Farington, 27 March 1799.

77 George, VII, no. 9085.

78 Farington, 5 April 1807.

79 *Ibid.*, 19 July 1815.

80 *Ibid.*, 22 May 1815.

81 *Ibid.*, 23 May 1806.

82 [Knight], 1810, pp. 324–5.

83 Now in the National Gallery of Scotland, Edinburgh, acquired 1970. Copper, 30.1×42.0. See K. Andrews, *Adam Elsheimer*, Oxford 1977, no. 19. Two other Downton paintings, the Fetti and the Wtewael (cat. nos. 176, 209), formerly bore incorrect attributions to Elsheimer, as Waterhouse noted in 1953.

84 Christie's, 4 May 1979 (107); exhibited *Gerard Dou Artemis*, 1981 (4); see Gaskell – also Nauman in *Burl. Mag.* 1981, pp. 617–18.

85 [Knight], 1810, pp. 308–9.

1 Charles Gore and Thomas Hearne, *Mount Etna from the Convent of Nicolosi* (cat. no. 111)

IV *Silver Statuette of Tyche* (cat. no. 44)

II   *Two Syracusan Tetradrachms*
      (cat. nos. 25 and 26)

III   *Three Ancient Cameos* (cat. nos. 3, 7 and 9)

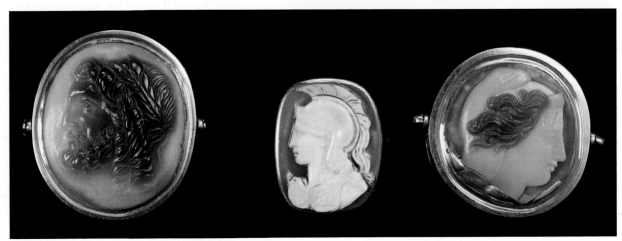

*Bronze figure of an Etruscan
Warrior* (cat. no. 41)

VI Richard Westall, *Harvesters in a Storm* (cat. no. 200)

VII Sir Thomas Lawrence, *Richard Payne Knight* (cat. no. 184)

VIII Thomas Hearne, *View of the River Teme at Downton* (cat. no. 115.ix)

ix Claude Lorrain, *Wooded View* (cat. no. 126)

XI Michael Sweerts, *Head of a Girl*
(cat. no. 196)

X Pier Francesco Mola, *Head of a Bearded Man wearing a Hat*
(cat. no. 149)

Bibliography

Published works by Richard Payne Knight

We have not listed the catalogue of the summer exhibitions held at the British Institution in 1813, 1814 and 1815 in which Knight's participation was suspected by his contemporaries, for even if he could be proven to be sole author, he was not writing as an individual. Also an MS notebook in which Knight described his collection of paintings and a book of letters to him recorded at Downton Castle earlier this century have not been traced.

An Account of the Remains of the Worship of Priapus lately existing at Isernia, in the Kingdom of Naples: in two letters; one from Sir William Hamilton, K.B., His Majesty's Minister at the Court of Naples, to Sir Joseph Banks, Bart., President of the Royal Society; and the other from a Person residing at Isernia: to which is added, A Discourse on the worship of Priapus, and its connexion with the Mystic Theology of the Antients by R. P. Knight. London 1786 (but 1787).

An Analytical Essay on the Greek Alphabet. London 1791.

The Landscape, a Didactic Poem. London 1794. (The 2nd ed. of 1795 with an Advertisement and Postscript and some additions to but no subtractions from the verse which was reprinted in facsimile in 1971 is generally referred to. The 1st ed. appeared before end of April 1794 – Farington, I, p. 184 – the 2nd ed. before 11 May 1795 – *ibid.*, II, p. 342.)

The Progress of Civil Society. London 1796.

An Analytical Inquiry into the Principles of Taste. London 1805. (This passed through three editions in one year. The fourth of 1808 which has many corrections and additional notes was reprinted in facsimile in 1972 and is generally referred to.)

Monody on the Death of the Right Honourable Charles James Fox. London 1806–7.

Carmina Homerica Ilias et Odyssea, a rapsodorum interpolationibus repurgata, et in pristinam formam . . . redacta; cum notis ac prolegomenis . . . studio et opera R. P. Knight. London 1808. (A limited edition comprising only the Prolegomena; the same with additional notes was printed in the *Classical Journal* for 1813 – VII, pp. 321–54; VIII, pp. 33–79, 289–328; the edition proper appeared in 1820.)

Specimens of Antient Sculpture, I, London 1809. (The second volume of this is not by Knight. He was assisted in preparing this first volume by Charles Townley – the text is however his. The work was described in minutes of the Society of Dilettanti which sponsored it as 'about to be published in March 1808' – Cust, p. 128 – but 1809 appears on the title-page and on many of the plates, and 1810 on the cover.)

Anonymous review of 'The Works of James Barry Esq. Historical Painter', *Edinburgh Review*, XVI, 1810, pp. 293–326.

'Inscription on a helmet and cauldron found in the Alpheus, near Olympia' – a letter to the editor of *The Classical Journal*, I, no. 2, 1810, pp. 328–30. (The letter is unsigned but the works were all in Knight's collection and the theories typical.)

'Conjectures concerning the Instruments called Celts', a paper read to the Society of Antiquaries, 29 April 1813, *Archaeologia*, XVII, 1814, pp. 220–3.

Anonymous review of Northcote's *Life of Reynolds*, *Edinburgh Review*, XXIII, 1814, pp. 263–92.

Explanation of Part of the Evidence of Richard Payne Knight Concerning the Elgin Marbles. London 1816. (A reply to Croker written in the third person but hardly anonymous.)

Anonymous paragraph commencing 'The interesting Grecian Sculpture discovered in the Temple of Apollo, in Phigalia . . .', *Morning Chronicle*, 27 Jan. 1816.

An Inquiry into the Symbolical Language of Ancient Art and Mythology. London 1818. (Projected as the preliminary dissertation of the second volume of *Specimens of Antient Sculpture* in which it was eventually published as an appendix; it was also published in the *Classical Journal*, XLIV–LIII.)

Carmina Homerica . . . London 1820 (see Knight, 1808).

'On the Large Silver Coins of Syracuse', a paper read to the Society of Antiquaries, 15 Feb. 1821, *Archaeologia*, XIX, 1821, pp. 369–78.

'Observations on the Coins found by Colonel Caldwell in the Tumuli described in the proceeding letter from Sir Anthony Carlisle, Knt.', a paper read to the Society of Antiquaries, 18 April 1822, *Archaeologia*, XXI, 1822, pp. 5–10.

Alfred; a Romance in Rhyme. London 1823.

Nummi Veteres Civitatum, Regum, Gentilium, et Provinciarum, Londini in Museo Richardi Payne Knight, ab ipso Ordine Geographico Descripti. London 1830. (Published by the Trustees of the British Museum using Knight's manuscript material.)

Manuscript material referred to

Aberdeen Papers: Volumes of letters to the Earl of Aberdeen. British Library, Add. MSS 43228–31.

Banks Letters: The collection of copies of the correspondence of Sir Joseph Banks made for Dawson Turner. 20 vols., Department of Botany, Natural History Museum.

Coleorton Papers: Letters from Uvedale Price to Sir George and Lady Beaumont. Pierpont Morgan Library MA 1581.

Dilettanti Papers: Volumes of miscellaneous manuscript material relating to the Society of Dilettanti; and the Society's Minutes. Deposited in the library of the Society of Antiquaries.

Downton Castle Papers: Bundles of miscellaneous material, mostly manuscript, from Downton Castle. The Property of D. P. H. Lennox, Esq. deposited in Herefordshire County Record Office.

Kidderminster MSS: Accounts, notebooks and letters relating to the Knights of Wolverley and Lea Castle in Kidderminster Public Library.

Knight MS (Autobiography): A brief outline of his own life dated 9 Feb. 1811 and addressed to Messrs. Cadell and Davies, Booksellers of the Strand. Bodleian Library, Montagu MS d. 3. ff.124–6.

Knight MS (Bronzes): A catalogue of his bronzes including some works in marble and in various other materials. Department of Greek and Roman Antiquities, British Museum.

Knight MS (Gems): A catalogue of his gems. Department of Greek and Roman Antiquities, British Museum.

Knight MS (Notebook of Coins): A notebook recording purchases of coins (see cat. no. 84).

Knight MS (Sicilian Diary): A copy of a manuscript diary by Knight entitled on the first page 'An Expedition into Sicily. 1777'. Weimar, Goethe–Schiller-Archiv, MS 25/xliv, 7.

Towneley Hall Papers: Boxes of miscellaneous material, mostly manuscript, from Towneley Hall. The property of Lord O'Hagan, on deposit in Lancashire County Record Office.

Bibliography of publications not by R. P. Knight

Alison, A. *Essays on the Nature and Principles of Taste.* 4th ed., London 1815.

Allentuck, M. 'Sir Uvedale Price and the Picturesque Garden: the evidence of the Coleorton Papers', in *The Picturesque Garden and its influence outside the British Isles,* edited by Pevsner (Dumbarton Oaks Colloquium on the History of Landscape Architecture, II), Washington 1974.

Andrews, K. *Adam Elsheimer.* Oxford 1977.

Ashmole, B. *A Catalogue of the Ancient Marbles at Ince Blundell Hall.* Oxford 1929.

Askew, P. 'The parable paintings of Domenico Fetti', *Art Bulletin,* XLIII, 1961.

Barbier, C. W. *William Gilpin,* Oxford 1963.

Beckett, R. B. *John Constable's Correspondence.* 6 vols., London and Ipswich 1962–8.

Beesly, P. *A Brief History of the Knight Family* (mimeograph 1958).

Bell, C. F. and Girtin, T. 'The drawings and sketches of John Robert Cozens', *Walpole Society,* XXIII, 1934–5.

Benesch, O. *The Drawings of Rembrandt.* 6 vols., London 1954–7.

Blundell, H. *An Account of the Statues, Busts, Bass-Relieves, Cinerary Urns, and other Ancient Marbles and Paintings, at Ince, collected by H. B.* Liverpool 1803.

— *Engravings and Etchings of Sepulchral Monuments, Cinerary Urns, Gems, Bronzes, Prints, Greek Inscriptions, Fragments, &c in the Collection of Henry Blundell, Esq., at Ince.* 2 vols., [?Liverpool] 1809.

Bredius, A. *Rembrandt, the Complete Edition of the Paintings,* revised by H. Gerson. 4th ed., London 1971.

Brigstocke, H. 'William Buchanan: his friends and rivals', *Apollo,* August 1981.

Brown, D. B. *Augustus Wall Callcott.* Catalogue of exhibition at the Tate Gallery, London 1981.

Buchanan, W. *Memoirs of Painting.* 2 vols., London 1824.

Butlin, M. and Joll, E. *The Paintings of J. M. W. Turner.* London and New Haven 1977.

Castellus, G. (Prince of Torremuzza) *Siciliae Veteres Nummi.* Palermo 1781. (There are appendices of 1789 and 1791.)

Caylus, Comte de *Recueil d'antiquités égyptiennes, étrusques, grecques et romaines.* 7 vols., Paris 1752–67.

Cheselden, William 'Account of some observations made by a young gentleman born blind', *Philosophical Transactions of the Royal Society,* XXXV, 1727–8, pp. 447–50.

Christie, J. *A Disquisition upon Etruscan Vases.* London 1825.

Clarke, E. D. *Travels in Various Countries of Europe.* 3 parts (part 2 of 3 vols., part 3 of 2), London 1810–19.

Clay, E. and Fredericksen, M. *Sir William Gell in Italy: Letters to the Society of Dilettanti 1831–35.* London 1976.

Clayden, P. W. *Rogers and his Contemporaries.* London 1889.

Colvin, H. M. *A Biographical Dictionary of British Architects.* London 1978.

Cook, B. 'The Townley marbles in Westminster and Bloomsbury', *British Museum Yearbook,* II, 1977, pp. 34–77.

Cornforth, J. 'Hampton Court, Herefordshire', Part II, *Country Life,* 1 March 1973.

[Croker, J. W.] 'Lord Elgin's collection of sculptural marbles', *Quarterly Review,* 1815–16, XIV, pp. 513–47.

Cunningham, A. *Life of Sir David Wilkie.* 3 vols., London 1843.

Cust, L. *History of the Society of Dilettanti,* edited by Sidney Colvin. London 1914.

Dallaway, T. *Anecdotes of the Arts in England.* London 1800.

Davis, T. *John Nash.* London 1966.

Dawson, W. R. (ed.) *The Banks Letters: a Calendar of the Manuscript Correspondence of Sir Joseph Banks*. London 1958.

Downes, R. L. 'The Stour partnership, 1726–36', *Economic History Review*, III, 1950, pp. 90–6.

Edwards, E. *Lives of the Founders of the British Museum*. London 1870.

Ehrlich, W. '. . . wegen Kunstverwandtschaft und freundlicher Lebensteilnahme', *Goethe-Jahrbuch*, XCI, 1974, pp. 117–29.

Farington, J. *Diary*. In course of publication: 6 vols. edited by Garlick and Macintyre, New Haven and London 1978, have now appeared. A typescript of the original is in the Department of Prints and Drawings, British Museum.

'Felton'. *A New Guide to the Town of Ludlow . . . published by Felton*. Ludlow [1821].

Field, W. *Memoirs of the Life, Writing and Opinions of the Rev. Samuel Parr*. 2 vols., London 1828.

Fleming, J. 'A "Retrospective View" by John Clerk of Eldin, with some comments on Adam's castle style', in *Concerning Architecture: Essays on Architectural Writers and Writing presented to Nikolaus Pevsner*, edited by Summerson. London 1968.

Fraser, P. D. 'Charles Gore and the Van de Veldes', *Master Drawings*, XV, 1977, pp. 375–89.

French, A. *Gaspard Dughet*, Catalogue of exhibition at Kenwood House, London 1980.

Friedlaender, W. and Blunt, A. *The Drawings of Nicolas Poussin*. 4 vols., London 1963.

Furtwängler, A. *Masterpieces of Greek Sculpture*. London 1895.

– *Antike Gemmen*. Leipzig 1900.

Gage, J. 'Magilphs and mysteries', *Apollo*, July 1964.

– 'Turner and the picturesque: part II', *Burlington Magazine*, 1965, pp. 75–81.

Garlick, K. *Sir Thomas Lawrence*. London 1954.

Gaskell, I. 'Gerrit Dou and *trompe l'oeil*', *Burlington Magazine*, 1981, p. 164.

George, M. D. *Catalogue of Political and Personal Satires*. Vols. VII–IX, London 1942–9.

Gerson, H. *Philips Koninck*. Berlin 1936.

[Gillies, J.] Review of d'Hancarville's *Recherches*, *Monthly Review*, Nov. 1785.

Gladstone, W. E. *Studies on Homer and the Homeric Age*. 3 vols., Oxford 1858.

Goethe, J. W. von. *Philipp Hackert: Biographische Skizze, meist nach dessen eigenen Aufsätzen entworfen, von Goethe*. Tübingen 1811.

Granville, Lord. *Private Correspondence*, edited by Castalia, Countess Granville. 2 vols., London 1916–17.

Graves, A. and Cronin, W. V. *A History of the Works of Sir Joshua Reynolds P.R.A.* 4 vols., London 1899–1901.

Greville, C. *The Greville Memoirs, 1814–1860*, edited by Strachey and Fulford. 8 vols., London 1938.

Griggs, I., Kern, J. D. and Schneider, E. 'Early Edinburgh Reviewers: a new list', *Modern Philology*, XLIII, 1945–6, pp. 192–210.

[Hallam, H.]. Review of Knight's *Inquiry*, *The Edinburgh Review*, VII, 1806, pp. 295–328.

Hamburg. *Goya: Das Zeitalter der Revolution*, Catalogue of exhibition at the Kunsthalle, Hamburg, 1980–1.

Hamilton, Sir W. *See* Knight 1786.

d'Hancarville, P. H. 'Baron'. *Recherches sur l'Origine, l'Esprit et les Progrès des Arts*. 3 vols., London 1785. (The third volume appeared later, apparently in 1786, despite the title page.)

Harcourt-Smith, Sir C. *The Society of Dilettanti: its Regalia and Pictures*. London 1932.

Haskell, F. *Patrons and Painters*. 2nd ed., New Haven and London 1980.

Haskell, F. and Penny, N. *Taste and the Antique*. London and New Haven 1981.

Hawcroft, F. W. *Watercolours by John Robert Cozens*, Catalogue of exhibition at the Whitworth Art Gallery, Manchester 1971.

–. 'Grand Tour sketchbooks of John Robert Cozens, 1782–1783', *Gazette des Beaux Arts*, March 1976.

[Haydon, B. R.]. 'To the critic on Barry's works', *The Examiner*, 26 Jan., 2 Feb., 9 Feb., 1812.

Haydon, B. R. 'On the judgment of connoisseurs', *The Examiner*, 17 March 1816.

–. *Lectures on Painting*. 2 vols. (but not so numbered), London 1844 and 1846.

–. *The Life of B. R. Haydon*. 2nd ed., 3 vols., London 1853.

–. *The Diary*, edited by W. B. Pope. Cambridge (Mass.) 1960–3.

Hayes, J. *The Drawings of Thomas Gainsborough*. 2 vols., London 1970.

Haynes, S. *Etruscan Sculpture*. London 1971.

Head, B. V. (with others). *A Guide to the Principal Coins of the Greeks*. London 1932.

Held, J. *Rubens – Selected Drawings*. 2 vols., London 1959.

Holland, E., Lady. *Journal*, edited by the Earl of Ilchester. 2 vols., London 1908.

Horner, F. *Memoirs and Correspondence*. 2 vols., London 1843.

Hussey, C. *The Picturesque*. London 1927.

Inglis-Jones, E. 'The Knights of Downton Castle', *The National Library of Wales Journal*, XV, 1968, pp. 237–88.

Jaffé, P. *Lady Hamilton in Relation to the Art of her Time*, Catalogue of exhibition at Kenwood House, London 1972.

Jeffrey, F. *Contributions to the Edinburgh Review*. 2nd ed., 3 vols., London 1846.

Johnstone, J. *The Works of Samuel Parr*. 7 vols., London 1828.

Jones, T. 'Memoirs', *Walpole Society*, XXXII, 1946–8.

Kitson, M. *Claude Lorrain: Liber Veritatis*. London 1978.

Knight, T. A. *To the Occupiers of the Estates of the late R. P. Knight Esq*. Ludlow 1834. (A pamphlet dated 1 Dec. 1833.)

–. *A Selection from the Physiological Papers*. London 1841.

Knight, W. A. *Memorials of Coleorton*. Edinburgh 1837.

Krönig, W. 'Kehrtwendung der Blickrichtung in Vedutenpaaren von Philipp Hackert', *Wallraff-Richartz-Museum-*

Jahrbuch, XXX, 1968, pp. 255–74.

—. 'Philipp Hackerts Ansichten Griechischer Tempel in Sizilien (1777)', Supplement to the Catalogue of the exhibition *Berlin und die Antike*, Berlin 1979.

Lane, E. N. *Corpus Monumentorum Religionis Dei Menis*. Leiden 1975.

Lang, S. 'The early publications of the temples at Paestum', *Journal of the Warburg and Courtauld Institutes*, XIII, 1959, pp. 48–64.

Layard, G. S. *Sir Thomas Lawrence's Letter-Bag*. London 1906.

Levey, M. *Sir Thomas Lawrence*, Catalogue of exhibition at the National Portrait Gallery, London 1979–80.

Life and Landscape in Britain 1670–1870. Catalogue of exhibition held at Thomas Agnew and Sons Ltd. London 1981.

Lindeman, P. *Joachim Anthonisz. Wtewael*. Utrecht 1929.

Lipscomb, G. *A Journey into South Wales*. London 1802.

Lipscombe, R. W. 'Richard Payne Knight: some unpublished correspondence', *Art Bulletin*, LXI, 1979, pp. 604–10.

—. *William Wilkins 1778–1839*. Cambridge 1980.

Littlebury's Directory and Gazetteer of Herefordshire. 1876–7.

Lohse, B. *Jakob Philipp Hackert, Leben und Anfänge seiner Kunst*. Emsdetten (Westf.) 1936.

Lugt, F. *Les Marques de Collections*. Amsterdam 1921.

McCarthy, M. 'Documents on the Greek Revival in architecture', *Burlington Magazine*, 1972, pp. 760–5.

Mahon, D. *I Disegni del Guercino della Collezione Mahon*. Bologna 1967.

Mahoney, M. *The Drawings of Salvator Rosa*. 2 vols., New York and London 1977.

Manners, Lady V. and Williamson, G. *Angelica Kauffman R.A.* New York 1924.

Marchant, N. *A Catalogue of One Hundred Impressions of Gems*. London 1792.

Maréchal, P. S. *Les Antiquités d'Herculanum avec leurs explications*. Paris 1780.

Mariette, P. J. *Traité des pierres gravées*. 2 vols., Paris 1750.

[Marshall, W.]. *A Review of the Landscape, a Didactic Poem: also of an Essay on the Picturesque*. London 1795.

Martin, J. R. *The Farnese Gallery*. Princeton 1965.

Mason, W. *Poems*. 3 vols., York 1796–7.

[Matthews, Col. J.]. *A Sketch from the Landscape a Didactic Poem Addressed to R. P. Knight Esq*. London 1794.

Messmann, F. J. *Richard Payne Knight: the twilight of Virtuosity*. The Hague and Paris 1974.

Michaelis, A. *Ancient Marbles in Great Britain*. Cambridge 1882.

Millingen, J. *Some Remarks on the State of Learning and Fine Arts in Great Britain*. London 1831.

Mitter, P. *Much Malign'd Monsters*. Oxford 1978.

Möhle, H. *Die Zeichnungen Adam Elsheimers*. Berlin 1966.

Moor, E. *A Narrative of the Operations of Capt. Little's Detachment* . . . London 1794.

Museum Worsleyanum. 2 vols., n.p. 1794. (Despite the date on the title-page, the first volume of this very limited edition was not published until 1798 and the second later. The text is in Italian and English, but the one is not a close translation from the other. The Italian is in part by E. Q. Visconti.)

Neverov, O. *Antique Intaglios in the Hermitage Collection*. Leningrad 1976.

Nichols, J. *Literary Anecdotes of the Eighteenth Century*. 6 vols., London 1812–15.

Nicolson, B. *John Hamilton Mortimer*, Catalogue of exhibition at Eastbourne and Kenwood House, London 1968.

Niemeijer, J. W. 'P. C. Wonder in England', *Bulletin van het Rijksmuseum*, 1965, pp. 115–23.

Noehden, G. H. *Specimens of Ancient Coins of Magna Graecia and Sicily. Selected from the Cabinet of the Right Hon. the Lord Northwick: drawn by del Frate, a distinguished pupil of Antonio Canova, and engraved by Henry Moses*. London 1826. (200 copies only were printed.)

Oehler, H. *Römische Antiken in englischen Schlössern mit einem Beitrag von Iringard Hiller*. Köln 1980. (The text was translated by Geoffrey B. Waywell for the XI International Congress of Classical Archaeology 3–9 Sept. 1978.)

Oppé, A. P. *Alexander and John Robert Cozens*. London 1952.

Page, W. (ed.). *Shropshire* (Victoria History of Counties of England). 4 vols., London 1908.

Parker, K. T. and Mathey, J. *Antoine Watteau: Catalogue complet de son Oeuvre dessiné*. 2 vols., Paris 1957.

Passavant, J. D. *Tour of a German Artist in England*. 2 vols., London 1836.

Peacock, T. L. *Works*, edited by H. F. B. Brett Smith and C. E. Jones. London 1934.

Pevsner, N. *Herefordshire*. Harmondsworth 1963.

—. *Studies in Art, Architecture and Design*. Vol. I, London 1968. (This volume includes essays on Richard Payne Knight, Uvedale Price, Humphry Repton and — written with S. Lang — the Doric Revival, reprinted from the *Art Bulletin* in the first case and the *Architectural Review* in the others.)

Pinkerton, J. *An Essay on Medals*. 3rd corrected edition, 2 vols., London 1808. (The edition of 1779 is also referred to.)

Popham, A. E. *Italian Drawings . . . in the British Museum: Artists working in Parma in the Sixteenth Century*. 2 vols., London 1967.

Popham, A. E. and Pouncey, P. *Italian Drawings . . . in the British Museum: the Fourteenth and Fifteenth Centuries*. 2 vols., London 1950.

[Porson, R.]. Review of Knight's *Essay on the Greek Alphabet, The Monthly Review*, XIII, 1794, pp. 7–16, 379–85.

Poulsen, F. *Greek and Roman Portraits in English Country Houses*. Oxford 1923.

Pouncey, P. and Gere, J. A. *Italian Drawings . . . in the British Museum: Raphael and his Circle*. 2 vols., London 1962.

Price, U. *Essays on the Picturesque*. 3 vols., London 1810.

Pugliatti, T. 'Pietro Paolo Bonzi paesista', *Quaderni dell'Istituto di Storia d'Arte medioevale e moderna della Facolta di Lettere, Università di Messina*, I, 1975, pp. 15–23.

Raspe, R. E. *Descriptive Catalogue of gems . . . cast by James Tassie*. 2 vols., London 1791.

Reid, T. *An Inquiry into the Human Mind*. Edinburgh 1764.

Reilly, R. and Savage, G. *Wedgwood: the Portrait Medallions*. London 1973.

Report from the Select Committee on the Earl of Elgin's Sculptured Marbles. London 1816.

Richter, G. M. A. *Catalogue of Greek Sculpture in the Metropolitan Museum of Art, New York*. Oxford 1954.

Robinson, C. J. *The Mansions of Herefordshire and their Memories*. London and Hereford 1872.

Roethlisberger, M. *Claude Lorrain, the Drawings*. 2 vols., London 1968.

Rogers, S. *Recollections of the Table Talk*. London 1952.

Roget, J. L. *History of the 'Old Water-Colour' Society*. 2 vols., London 1891.

Romney, J. *Memoirs of the Life and Works of George Romney*. London 1830.

Rosenberg, J. *Jacob Van Ruisdael*. Berlin 1928.

Rotterdam. *Michael Sweerts en Tijdenoten*, Catalogue of exhibition at Boymans Museum, Rotterdam 1958.

Rowan, A. 'Downton Castle, Herefordshire' in *The Country Seat*, edited by H. Colvin and J. Harris. London 1970, pp. 170–3.

Rowlands, J. *Rubens – Drawings and Sketches*, Catalogue of exhibition at the British Museum, London 1977.

Saint-Non, Abbé de. *Voyage pittoresque de Naples et de Sicile*. Paris 1781–6.

Shaw, Rev. S. *A Tour to the West of England in 1788*. London 1789.

Shearer, E. A. 'Wordsworth and Coleridge marginalia in a copy of Richard Payne Knight's *Analytical Inquiry into the Principles of Taste*', *Huntington Library Quarterly*, I, 1937.

Sheppard, F. H. W. (ed.). *The Survey of London*. Vols. XXXIII–XXXIV (The Parish of St Anne, Soho), London 1966.

Sidey, T. *Amelia Long, Lady Farnborough*, Catalogue of exhibition at Dundee Art Gallery 1980.

[Smirke, R.]. *A Catalogue Raisonné of the Pictures now Exhibiting in Pall Mall*. London 1816.

Smith, A. *Essays on Philosophical Subjects*. Edinburgh 1795.

Smith, A. H. *A Catalogue of the Sculptures in the Department of Greek and Roman Antiquities, British Museum*. 3 vols., London 1892–1904.

—. 'Lord Elgin and his collection', *Journal of Hellenic Studies*, XXXVI, 1916, pp. 163–372.

Smith, J. T. *Nollekens and his Times*. 2 vols., London 1828.

Smith, S. *Letters*, edited by N. C. Smith. 2 vols., London 1953.

Story, Maskelyne, J. *The Marlborough Gems*. London 1870.

Stosch, P. von. *Gemmae Antiquae Caelate*. Amsterdam 1724.

Stroud, D. *Humphry Repton*. London 1962.

Summerson, J. *John Nash*. London 1935.

Swaddling, J. 'The British Museum Bronze Hoard from Paramythia', *Actes du Ve Colloque International sur les Bronzes Antiques*, Lausanne 1979, pp. 103–6.

Swinburne, Henry. *Travels in the Two Sicilies*. London 1783.

Tait, H. *Jewellery through 7000 years*. London 1976.

Thompson, J. R. F. 'David Allan and the Hamilton Portraits', *The Connoisseur*, April 1970.

Tipping, H. A. 'Downton Castle Herefordshire', *Country Life*, 14 July 1917.

Toynbee, J. M. C. *Art in Britain under the Romans*. Oxford 1964.

Tuzet, Hélène. *La Sicile au XVIIIe siècle – vue par les voyageurs étrangers*. Strassburg 1955.

Vey, H. *Die Zeichnungen Anton Van Dycks*. 2 Vols., Brussels 1962.

Victoria and Albert Museum. *Dr Thomas Monro (1759–1833) and the Monro Academy*. Catalogue of exhibition at the Victoria and Albert Museum, London 1976.

Vollenweider, M.-L. *Die Steinschneidekunst und Ihre Künstler in spätrepublikanischer und augusteischer Zeit*. Baden-Baden 1966.

Waagen, G. F. *Works of Art and Artists*. 3 vols., London 1838.

Walpole, H. *Correspondence*. 38 vols., New Haven and London 1937–74.

Walters, H. B. *Catalogue of Bronzes: British Museum*. London 1899.

—. *Catalogue of Terracottas in the Department of Greek and Roman Antiquities*. London 1903.

—. *Catalogue of Silver Plate (Greek, Etruscan and Roman) in the British Museum*. London 1921.

—. *Catalogue of Greek, Etruscan and Roman Gems in the British Museum*. London 1926.

Waterhouse, E. K. *Reynolds*. London 1941.

—. 'Some notes on the exhibition of "Works of Art from Midland Houses" at Birmingham', *Burlington Magazine*, 1953, pp. 305–9.

—. *Gainsborough*. London 1958.

Watkin, D. *Thomas Hope and the Neo-Classical Idea*. London 1968.

Webster, M. 'Zoffany's painting of Charles Towneley's library in Park Street', *Burlington Magazine*, 1964, pp. 316–23.

Whitaker, T. D. *An History of the Original Parish of Whalley*. 2nd ed., London 1806.

Wilde, J. *Italian Drawings . . . in the British Museum: Michelangelo and his Studio*. London 1953.

Wilkins, W. *The Civil Architecture of Vitruvius . . . with an Introduction containing an historical view of the rise and progress of architecture amongst the Greeks*. London 1812. (Lipscombe, 1980, p. 64, points out that this in fact appeared in 1813 and 1817. The *Introduction* was by Lord Aberdeen and was published, slightly modified, as *An Inquiry into the Principles of Beauty in Grecian Architecture*, London 1822.)

Williams, D. E. *The Life and Correspondence of Sir Thomas Lawrence*. London 1831.

Wilton, Andrew. *Classical Sites and Monuments*. Catalogue of exhibition at the British Museum (Department of Prints and Drawings), London 1971.

—. *The Life and Work of J. M. W. Turner*. London 1979.

—. *The Art of Alexander and John Robert Cozens*. Catalogue of exhibition at the Yale Center for British Art, New Haven 1980.

Winckelmann, J. J. *Storia delle arti del disegno presso gli antichi*, 3 vols., Rome 1783–4. (Knight seems to have used this, the edition of Carlo Fea, or the French editions of Winckelmann's *Geschichte* of 1763–4.)

Windham, W. *The Diary of the Right Hon. William Windham 1784–1810*, ed. Mrs H. Baring, London 1866.

Wyndham, M. *Catalogue of the Collection of Greek and Roman Antiquities in the possession of Lord Leconfield*. London 1915.

Catalogue

Only essential literature is cited. Dimensions are given in centimetres, height before width. A single measurement indicates height. The weights not the dimensions of coins are given.

[CAMEOS AND INTAGLIOS]

Hellenistic, first century BC

1 *The Entertainment of Silenos*

Sardonyx cameo; unbacked, with missing fragment supplied in gold, mounted as a gold finger ring: 2.6 × 2.8
Lit.: Knight MS (Gems), no. 90; Walters, 1926, no. 3498; Vollenweider, pp. 34, 100, plate 25 (1) & (2)

Knight was, understandably, enthusiastic about the stone, the carving and the conservation of the surface of this piece which he noted as coming from the Strozzi collection – probably the most important in Rome. Gertrud Seidmann points out that the cameo has recently been associated with Sostratos, a Greek artist who signed a celebrated cameo (of Victory in a chariot) which passed from the collection of Pope Paul III to that of Lorenzo il Magnifico, and eventually to the Farnese (now Museo Nazionale, Naples)

Hellenistic, or Roman of the early Imperial period

2 *Infant Dionysos Riding upon a Panther Escorted by a Faun and Followed by a Nymph*

Amethyst intaglio; unbacked, mounted as a gold swivel ring: 1.5 × 1.7
Lit.: Knight MS (Gems), no. 13; Walters, 1926, no. 1536

Knight noted that this gem came from the Borghese collection – one of the most important in Rome. Prince Camillo Borghese's financial difficulties led him to sell a number of smaller items before his brother-in-law, the Emperor Napoleon, purchased the best of his ancient marbles in 1807. The gold of the mount is unusually pale to suit the stone

Hellenistic or Roman of the early Imperial period   Colour Plate III

3 *Profile head of 'Men'*

Sardonyx cameo, with some small fragments supplied in gold; unbacked, mounted as a gold swivel ring: 2.2 × 2.1
Lit.: Knight MS (Gems), no. 62; Walters, 1926, no. 3569

A flourish of escaping rich brown locks carved out of the highest stratum contrasts with the serene immobility of the beautifully modelled face. Walters regarded this as an Amazon, but gave no reason for the Phrygian cap and diadem, both of which, together with the beautiful hair, might suggest Paris. However, Knight, as Gertrude Seidmann and Martin Henig point out, was correct to identify it as the male oriental moon-god (cf. Lane, II, p. 166 and plate lxi.g.9, and see Raspe, I, pp. 150–1). It came, Knight claimed, from the Borghese collection (cf. cat. no. 2)

Hellenistic or Roman of the early Imperial period

4 *Actaeon*

Fragment of a sardonyx cameo; unbacked,
mounted as a gold finger ring. 1.5 × 1.8
Lit.: Knight MS (Gems), no. 3; Walters, 1926,
no. 3555

Knight recognized this as Actaeon because a figure in the
same pose beating down his hounds appears in a relief
discovered by Gavin Hamilton in 1774 which was in
Townley's collection (A. H. Smith, III, no. 1568) — another
appeared on a Greek metope found in 1831 at Selinus. The
stratum out of which the flesh is carved is skilfully graduated
from opaque to translucent white; the higher golden brown
stratum is retained for hair and cloak
TRUSTEES OF THE BRITISH MUSEUM

Hellenistic or Roman of the early Imperial period

5 *Head of Medusa (Gorgoneion)*

Sardonyx cameo of very irregular shape;
unbacked, and mounted as a gold swivel ring.
2.0 × 2.0
Lit.: Knight MS (Gems), no. 65; Walters, 1926,
no. 3545

Clear evidence of deft use of the miniature drill is to be
found in the pupils, below and above the mouth, and also in
the curls and snakes which, fashioned out of the higher
pale stratum where it is in lowest relief and slightly translucent, appear pale blue. Knight considered this cameo as of
the highest quality. He also noted that it came from the
same place as the previous item in his catalogue — this
however has no provenance. This error originates from
the way his catalogue is composed of entries cut from an
earlier draft. It may be that he is referring back to no. 62
which came from the Borghese collection or, possibly, to
no. 52 (cat. no. 18) which is, like this cameo, violently
chipped on the reverse. Gertrud Seidmann points out that
there is a similar work of comparable quality in Berlin
(Furtwängler, 1900, I pl. lii, 4)
TRUSTEES OF THE BRITISH MUSEUM

Hellenistic, or Roman of the early Imperial period

6 *Head of a Bacchante*

Sardonyx cameo; backed, and mounted as a
heavy gold finger ring. 2.4 × 1.9
Lit.: Knight MS (Gems), no. 12; Walters, 1926,
no. 3493

For Walters this was a head of Ariadne, but Knight's idea —
that it represented a Bacchante — seems just as reasonable.
He considered it, fairly, as the work of a skilful rather than
an inspired artist, using a stone — the Indian sardonyx —
with rich, dark strata which was most highly prized. The
upper stratum is retained for the leaves in the hair as with
the *Flora* (cat. no. 19), but the carving is stiff by comparison
TRUSTEES OF THE BRITISH MUSEUM

Hellenistic, or Roman of the early
Imperial period   Colour Plate III

7 *Profile Head of Zeus Crowned with Laurels*

Sardonyx cameo; unbacked, mounted as a gold
swivel ring: 2.5 × 2.3
Lit.: Knight MS (Gems), no. 53; Walters, 1926,
no. 3419

Knight noted that the cutting here has been accomplished
without the use of the drill and the treatment of the hair and
beard is, in consequence, unusually linear. The sublime
character of the god is admirably enhanced by the 'misty'
effect of the upper, brown stratum where in lowest relief
TRUSTEES OF THE BRITISH MUSEUM

Roman, first century AD

8 *Eros Pursuing Locusts and a Butterfly*

Onyx cameo; unbacked, mounted as a gold
finger ring: 1.25 × 1.6
Lit.: Knight MS (Gems), no. 26; Walters, 1926,
no. 3456

Sporting Erotes were popular on cameos. The butterfly
was — or rather could be — a symbols of the soul, and Knight
noted that it appeared commonly on gems but that 'there
is no trace of it upon any coin', because, he suggested, it was
'a subject more applicable and interesting to individuals
than communities' (Knight, 1818, p. 136). In style the
work is clearly close to that of cat. no. 1, although the
surface is less well preserved
TRUSTEES OF THE BRITISH MUSEUM

Roman of the early Imperial
period   Colour Plate III

9 *Profile bust of Athena*

Arabian sardonyx cameo; unbacked, mounted as
a finger ring: 2.0 × 1.5

Lit.: Knight MS (Gems), no. 70; Walters, 1926, no. 3444

As Knight acutely observed, the transparent highest stratum of this stone has been retained to give a sheen to the armour of the goddess, although it appears at first to be merely a polish on the white stratum used for the flesh

TRUSTEES OF THE BRITISH MUSEUM

Roman, second half of the first century AD

10 *Profile head of a Roman Lady*

Arabian onyx cameo; unbacked, mounted as a gold finger ring: 2.8 × 2.0
Lit.: Knight MS (Gems), no. 55; Walters, 1926, no. 3609

Knight admired both the stone and the carving, considering the latter as remarkable since art was, he believed, at this date, in decline. He thought it represented Julia, wife of Titus, daughter-in-law of the Emperor Vespasian. The elder Agrippina and, more recently, Domitia have also been suggested, but the hairstyle is impossible for the former. It is safest to consider it as an unknown Flavian princess

TRUSTEES OF THE BRITISH MUSEUM

Roman of the early Imperial period

11 *Athena Leaning on her Shield, Holding a Spear and Contemplating a Helmet*

Fragment of a carnelian intaglio, restored in gold; unbacked, mounted as a gold swivel ring: 1.7 × 1.6
Lit.: Knight MS (Gems), no. 68; Walters, 1926, no. 1143

The signature on this gem was considered as a modern addition by Walters

TRUSTEES OF THE BRITISH MUSEUM

? Italian, sixteenth century

12 *Nude Youth, Standing in Profile by an Altar with Column and Statue of Cupid Behind*

Sardonyx cameo; unbacked, mounted as a gold finger ring: 1.5 × 1.2
Lit.: Knight MS (Gems), no. 5; Dalton, no. 206

Knight catalogues this as a 'nudus et imberbus Hymen', which seems a sensible identification. He believed it to be ancient, but Dalton considered it as a sixteenth-century forgery

TRUSTEES OF THE BRITISH MUSEUM

? Italian, sixteenth century

13 *Seated Male Pulling at Skirts of Passing Maenad*

Onyx cameo; unbacked, mounted as gold finger ring: 2.5 × 1.85
Litt.: Dalton, no. 133

This lively relief from Charles Townley's collection (it is marked T23), which Knight helped the museum to acquire in 1814, although signed Sostratos (for whom see cat no. 1), is clearly carved in a sixteenth- or possibly seventeenth-century style, influenced by ancient sculpture rather than by ancient cameos

TRUSTEES OF THE BRITISH MUSEUM

? Italian, eighteenth century

14 *Profile Portrait of an Unbearded Man*

Carnelian intaglio; unbacked, mounted as a gold finger ring: 1.2 × 0.9
Lit.: Dalton, no. 1124

Dalton catalogued this as from Knight's collection but an 'RPK' number is not now to be seen on the inside of the ring. The hair brushed forward in this manner is found in Roman portraiture of the Republican period, and the exaggerated tendon in the neck is a common feature in portraits, especially coin portraits, of Roman rulers. Dalton considered it as a sixteenth-century imitation of the antique, but Hugh Tait and Charlotte Gere point out that it is more likely to date from the eighteenth century

TRUSTEES OF THE BRITISH MUSEUM

? Italian, eighteenth century

15 *Profile Bust of a Hero with Weapons Behind*

Carnelian intaglio; unbacked, mounted as a gold swivel ring: 2.6 × 1.8
Lit.: Knight MS (Gems), no. 1; Dalton, no. 819

Dalton catalogued this as an eighteenth-century imitation or forgery, Knight as an ancient gem representing Achilles. He acquired it from the posthumous sale at Gerard's on 13–17 June 1785 of the antiquities of the lawyer Matthew Duane (for whom see pp. 67, 99). It was in fact lot 95 on the third day — the 'bust of a young warrior, beautiful sard; and of the best Greek work'. This gem, the catalogue continues, 'formerly belonged to Mons. Marriet [Mariette] and is published by Count Caylus', in whose *Recueil d'Antiquités*, however, it is not to be found

TRUSTEES OF THE BRITISH MUSEUM

? Italian, eighteenth century

16 *Faun Prancing Intoxicated, with Panther Skin Flying*

Sard intaglio, unbacked, mounted as a gold finger ring: 2.2 × 1.2
Lit.: Knight MS (Gems), no. 41; Dalton, no. 728

If this gem is, as Dalton proposed, modern then it is certainly modelled on the antique, for the figure appears frequently in ancient gems and cameos (see, for instance, Neverov, Plate 80; Vollenweider, plate 9). Knight cannot have been unaware of this since it was commented upon by Mariette, who published one in the French royal collection (II, no. xl) — another, published by Stosch (no. xlix), was in the collection of the Grand Duke of Tuscany, and this gem according to Knight came 'e museo Riccardiano Florentiae'

TRUSTEES OF THE BRITISH MUSEUM

? Italian, eighteenth century

17 *Winter as a Female Hunter Carrying Game*

Onyx cameo, unbacked, mounted as a gold finger ring: 3.3 × 2.3
Lit.: Dalton, no. 208

This beautiful cameo, from Charles Townley's collection, was acquired by the Museum in 1814 from Peregrine Towneley — a transaction which Knight, made a trustee in the same year, helped to organize. The same figure appears on one of Townley's ancient terracotta plaques purchased from Nollekens (Walters, 1903, pp. 395–6, no. D584) and in a notable sarcophagus relief of the wedding of Peleus with Thetis in the Villa Albani which Townley would have known since Winckelmann published it in his *Monumenti Antichi Inediti* (tav. cxi) and which was copied in England (for instance as the overmantle designed by Sir William Chambers for the Hall at The Hoo, Herts.). It would be interesting to know whether Townley concluded from this that the cameo was a modern copy, as Dalton did, whether indeed he had commissioned it as such, or whether he considered it as an ancient copy. It is not among the gems in his collection catalogued by Raspe

TRUSTEES OF THE BRITISH MUSEUM

? Italian, early nineteenth century   Plate 36

18 *Head of Jupiter*

Onyx cameo of irregular shape; unbacked, framed in gilt metal: 5.0 × 4.0
Lit.: Knight MS (Gems), no. 52; Dalton, no. 53

Dalton catalogued this as sixteenth-century work and modern authorities have agreed (although others are uncertain that it is not ancient). Knight in his catalogue notes that it was discovered when a marsh was drained under Pius VII — so if not ancient it seems likely to be an imitation of the early nineteenth century. The relief, which is (as Knight noted) perfectly preserved, has been flattened to keep within the stratum (the nose thus projects no further than the curls of the beard or forehead). It seems adapted in design to the fragmentary shape of the stone which, however, is violently chipped under the beard and on the back. Similar chipping is found on the back of at least one other cameo in Knight's collection (cat. no. 5) and was not uncommon on ancient gems found in the Campagna — a phenomenon oddly explained by Francesco Ficoroni as due to grave-thieves in the Dark Ages hacking them from the diadems of precious metal in which they were mounted and then discarding them

TRUSTEES OF THE BRITISH MUSEUM

                                          Plate 39
Probably Benedetto Pistrucci (1784–1855)

19 *Head of Flora*

Irregular fragment of a carnelian breccia cameo mounted as a gold finger ring: 2.3 (length)
Lit.: Knight MS (Gems), no. 46; Dalton, no. 176; Tait, no. 397

Acquired by Knight from the dealer Angelo Bonelli and believed by him to be an ancient work, this was later said by Pistrucci to be a forgery he had created in Rome. The claim, which Knight never accepted, was used to discredit him as a connoisseur (see pp. 74–5). Hugh Tait remarks that the style of the piece suggests that the work was modern and he identifies the flowers as roses (which are left in the red stratum), poppies, and perhaps marguerites

TRUSTEES OF THE BRITISH MUSEUM

[ANCIENT COINS]

20 *Silver Tetradrachm of Athens*

c. 510 BC; 16.95 gm; reverse
Lit.: Knight, 1818, p. 141; Knight, 1830, p. 31, D.6; *Coins of the Greeks: Athens*, no. 26

This coin of Athens (where not only the imagery but also the style remained remarkably constant and, Knight believed, relatively unenterprising) comes from Knight's collection. The hole in the coin which appears in others of this type in Knight's collection was probably made by peasants who used it as an ornament. Noting that the owl was the proper symbol of Athena (shown on the obverse) Knight pointed out that it is a bird 'which seems to surpass all other creatures in acuteness and refinement of organic perception' and added a curious footnote concerning the 'nocturnal clamors of the screech-owl'

21 *Silver coin of Acanthus*

> *c.* 480 BC; 17.36 gm; obverse
> Lit.: Knight, 1818, p. 98; Knight, 1830, p. 67, B.1; Head, I.B.7

The member of the cat family portrayed in this vigorous design sinking its claws and fangs into the rump of a bull is clearly spotted but is now identified as a lioness. Knight, who was aware that contests of this kind generally involve lions and bulls, considered this as a leopard, which animal as a companion of Bacchus signified, he thought, the 'destroyer accompanying the generator'

22 *Small electrum coin of Cyzicus (in Mysia)*

> *c.* 450–400 BC: 1.33 gm
> Lit.: Knight, 1818, p. 100, note 3; Knight, 1830, p. 3, A.1; *Coins of the Greeks: Cyzicus*, no. 92

This was catalogued by Knight as a gold coin. He was of course aware of the impurity of early gold coinage, dwelt on by Pliny (see Knight, 1822, p. 7) but the distinction between gold and electrum (an alloy of gold and silver) was not then observed in numismatic catalogues. Coins of Cyzicus were believed in Knight's day to have 'almost wholly vanished' (Pinkerton, I, p. 93). The name of the city did not appear on its coinage, which also employed a bewildering succession of animals as emblems – a constant emblem was, however, the sturgeon, which clue enabled Greenwell to identify the coins of this city in 1887. Comparison with other larger coins reveal that the animal here is a dog – with the sturgeon below. Knight supposed that the dog was a mouse which was reputedly once employed as an emblem of Argos. This interpretation is understandable, but it is odd that Knight felt sure enough about the matter to allow this example to play a part in his discussion of the priapic animals of ancient religion

23 *Silver Tetradrachm of Leontinoi*

> *c.* 460 BC; 17.20 gm; obverse
> Lit.: Knight, 1830, p. 237, A6; *Coins of the Greeks: Leontinoi*, no. 28

See no. 24

24 *Silver Tetradrachm of Leontinoi*

> *c.* 430 BC; 17.40 gm; obverse
> Lit.: Knight, 1830, p. 237, A14; *Coins of the Greeks: Leontinoi*, no. 54

In the catalogue of his collection Knight drew attention to the change of style evident in these two heads of Apollo, the former with parallel lines in the hair and distinct ringlets, the latter with hair far more pictorial in treatment and with less stylization in treatment of eyelids and brows and nasal ridge

Colour Plate II

25 *Silver Tetradrachm of Syracuse*

> *c.* 500 BC; 17.10 gm; reverse
> Lit.: Knight, 1821; Knight, 1830, p. 252, K.24; Head, I.c.30

See no. 26

Colour Plate II

26 *Silver Tetradrachm of Syracuse*

> *c.* 415 BC; 17.32 gm; reverse
> Lit.: Knight, 1821; Knight, 1830, p. 254, K.60; Head, II.c.604

Knight's collection was especially strong in the series of the Greek colonies of Sicily of which those of Syracuse are the most beautiful. Their reverses are adorned with a female head surrounded by dolphins – emblems of generation according to Knight (1818, p. 188) but also 'remarkable for intelligence and sagacity'. It is now generally supposed (but it has certainly never been proven) that this female head invariably represents Arethusa, nymph of the city's freshwater spring. Winckelmann and d'Hancarville supposed her to be Proserpine, doubtless because corn is sometimes to be seen in her hair. Knight suggested 'Proserpine or Ceres'. The Prince of Torremuzza considered them all to be Arethusa: for Noehden some, but not all, represented her (Castellus, p. 75; Noehden, p. 41). Also debated was the status of the coins: Knight insisted, correctly but controversially, that they were not medals. The later of the two coins shown here is signed by Euainetos on the obverse and in miniature letters on the side of the dolphin in front of the chin. This is typical of the extraordinary detail of this work, which, together with the greater freedom and lightness, of the hair especially, distinguish it from the earlier coin, the lucid design of which could not, however, be surpassed

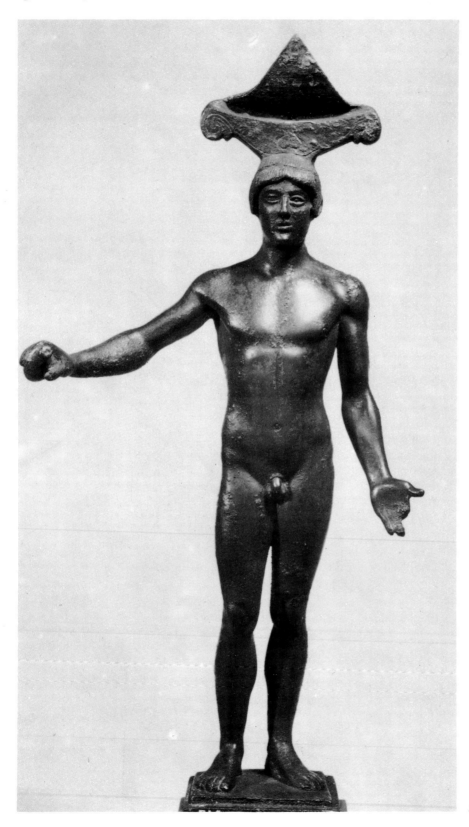

29

27 *Silver Coin of Cnossos*

c. 300 BC; 11.16 gm; reverse
Lit.: Knight, 1818, pp. 73–4; Knight, 1830,
p. 18, C.5; *Coins of the Greeks: Cnossos*, no. 24

The labyrinth was the conventional emblem on reverses of coins of Cnossos. Knight was interested in the evolution of the emblem from far simpler geometric designs commonly found on the punchmarks on the reverses of earlier coins. When, as sometimes occurred, an asterisk, bull or minotaur was placed at the centre of such a geometric design it signified, he believed, 'the male personification of the productive attribute placed in the female, or heat acting upon humidity'

TRUSTEES OF THE BRITISH MUSEUM

28 *Gold Octadrachm of Arsinoe II*

Alexandria 261 BC; 27.82 gm; obverse
Lit.: Knight, 1830, I, p. 208; *Coins of the Greeks: Arsinoe II*, no. 10

Knight's collection included a good set of the superb portraits of the successors of Alexander the Great. This – of Arsinoe II, wife and sister of Ptolemy II – may be the one engraved (by Finden after Courbould) in the second volume of *Specimens* (opposite plate lviii). It is likely to be the 'Arsinoe' which Knight bought in 1787 for 14 guineas (see cat. no. 84) – surely from his cousin Edward Knight who recorded the sale of an 'Arsinoe' for exactly that sum on 19 June 1787 (Kidderminster MS 290)

TRUSTEES OF THE BRITISH MUSEUM

[BRONZES]

Greek, perhaps made in Lokri, *c.* 460 BC

29 *Mirror Stand in the form of a Youth Anointing Himself*

Bronze: 24.8
Lit.: Knight MS (Bronzes), ii.1; Knight, 1809,
plate xv; Walters, 1899, no. 514

This bronze mirror stand – like others of less merit in his collection – was found in the south of Italy and sent by Sir William Hamilton to Knight who described it as 'very ancient Greek, of that period when the art had just begun to emancipate itself from the hard angular lines of the aegyptian style, & to attempt a free imitation of nature, without however aiming at any of the fascinating Embellishments of ideal Grace and Beauty'. He compared it with the heads of Mercury on ancient tetradrachms of Aenos in Thrace

TRUSTEES OF THE BRITISH MUSEUM

Etruscan, *c.* 350 BC

30 *Head of a Youth*

Bronze: 25.0
Lit.: Knight MS (Bronzes), lxx.6; Knight, 1809,
plate xvii; Walters, 1899, no. 1692; Haynes,
p. 23

This head, when owned by Knight, was 'placed upon a modern bust' but Knight had it engraved without it and considered it as ill-suited to the 'antient simplicity' of the head and would have rejoiced at its removal. He recorded that it had been sent from Rome by the Scottish architect and dealer James Byres (who left Rome in 1790) and that it had been discovered in 1771 on the island in Lake Bolsena. His catalogue entry coincides exactly with the views of modern scholars: he noted the significance of the fact that the Romans were reputed to have carried off two thousand bronze statues from Volsinii (this was an Etruscan city now thought to have been at Orvieto, the inhabitants of which were removed to Bolsena, after the sack of 265 BC); he pointed out that one would expect such an Etruscan sculpture to be of more recent date than a work of similar style in Greece which inspired it; and he remarked on the stubble which would not have been found in a Greek work

TRUSTEES OF THE BRITISH MUSEUM

Etruscan, 300–200 BC   Plate 35

31 *Head of a Wrestler*

Bronze: 21.5
Lit.: Knight MS (Bronzes), xxvii.i; Knight, 1809,
pp. xxxiii–xxiv, plates xx and xxi; Walters, 1899,
no. 1614

This fine head, described by Knight as the first item to enter his collection, was found near Rome and sent to London by Jenkins (not purchased there by Knight as is sometimes stated) in 1785. Knight considered that there was too much of 'common nature' in the countenance for this to be the image of a god, but he reckoned it represented a hero and considered the cap as a leather helmet, to which he found a reference in the tenth book of the *Iliad*, which led him to conclude that the subject must have been Diomedes in pursuit of Dolon. A similar head, he believed, was to be seen on an ancient intaglio in the Earl of Carlisle's collection and in an ancient paste given to him by Townley. He noted that the lips had probably originally been enamelled or plated with gold. Although opposed to restoration in general, he filled the eye sockets with glass eyes (and recommended the insertion of such in one of Townley's bronze busts – Knight, 1809, plate xlix). A Greek letter on the interior surface of the bronze was taken by him to be a signature of Rhoecus, briefly mentioned by Pliny, but it certainly is not

? Roman of the early Imperial period

32 *Fragment of a Head of a Youth*

Bronze 16.1
Lit.: Knight MS (Bronzes), lx.21; Knight, 1809,
plates xvii, xix; Walters, 1899, no. 283

Knight acquired this fragment, apparently discarded by ancient vandals who had torn out the precious stones which served as eyes, from the collection of the Duc de Chaulnes in Paris in 1791. He could not determine where it had been found. He believed it to represent Mercury and found in it the appeal of a work created slightly before the 'perfection of art' – something analogous in ancient sculpture to the paintings of 'Lionardo da Vinci'. For Walters it was a Hermes of the 'best period of Greek art'. Today it is regarded as a Roman copy or imitation of a Greek original – suspicions that it is a forgery have been dispelled by tests on the composition of the bronze, the depth of the corrosion and the character of the breaks

? Roman, second century AD   Plate 38

33 *Zeus or Poseidon*

Bronze: 21.9
Lit.: Knight MS (Bronzes), xc.4; liii.4; Knight,
1809, plate xxxii; Walters, 1899, no. 274;
Swaddling

Knight believed that this represented Zeus and by means of dotted lines reconstructed it in *Specimens* as originally holding a sceptre. It was, he wrote, 'of the grandest and finest Greek sculpture of the time of Phidias and his immediate successors'. Today some scholars consider it as a copy or reflection of an original by Lysippos. It was one of the bronzes which was discovered at Paramythia in the early 1790s – for which see pp. 71, 115 – and was valued at £80 by Townley. As Knight realized, the figures probably came from a household shrine, but whereas he, like most subsequent scholars, believed them to have been buried when the Romans invaded Epirus in the second century BC, the site has recently been proposed by Judith Swaddling as the

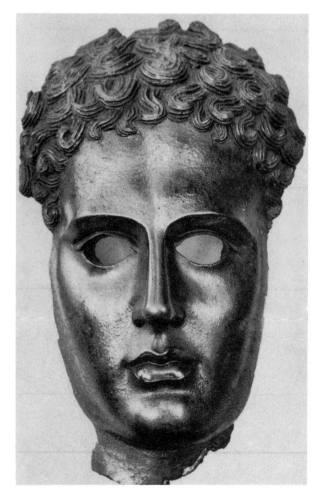

32

Roman town of Photice and she points out that chemical analysis suggests that those which are distinctly Hellenistic in style were in fact cast together with some which look later in style

? Roman, second century AD

34 *Zeus*

Bronze, with silver eyes: 19.6
Lit.: Knight MS (Bronzes), xc.4; liii.4; Knight, 1809, p. xxxii, plates lii and liii; Walters, 1899, no. 275; Swaddling

For the group of bronzes to which this belongs see cat. no. 33. This was the earliest to be acquired by Knight, from a certain Amascari, a dragoman at the Turkish embassy. He contrasted it with the squarer and harder forms of cat. no. 33, considered it as possessing more grace but no less majesty, and proposed that it was a copy of a repetition of the celebrated statue of Jupiter by Lysippos at Olympia, and perhaps an original by that master who was recorded as sometimes working on a small scale. In the plate in *Specimens* he indicated the probable attributes (thunderbolt and sceptre as in cat. no. 45) with dotted lines

? Roman, second century AD   Plate 37

35 *Apollo Stringing his Bow*

Bronze, with silver eyes: 24.8
Lit.: Knight MS (Bronzes), v.2, xc.4; Knight, 1809, plates xliii and xliv; Walters, 1899, no. 272; Swaddling

For the group of bronzes to which this belongs see cat. no. 33. This highly elegant but somewhat boneless figure was, together with a Venus, given the highest valuation (£100) by Townley, and Knight considered that it might have been by Praxiteles – 'for taste and elegance of design, grace and

34

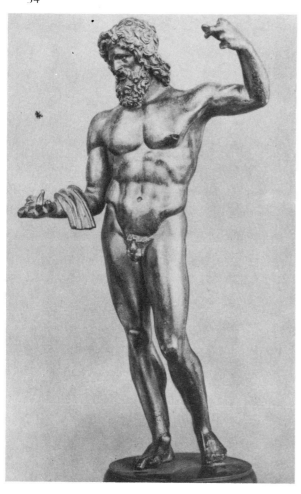

35

ease of action, and delicacy and skill of execution, it is perhaps the most perfect work of art now extant'. He called it an Androgynous Apollo because the hair is 'bound up and plaited according to the female fashion of the most polished periods of Graecian Elegance'

Roman, probably of the second or third century AD

36 *Terminal Figure, Bearded and Priapic*

Bronze: 19.0
Lit.: Knight MS (Bronzes), lx.9
Catalogued by Knight as a priapic Mercury, and as one of the works he acquired from the notorious cabinet of Senator Quirini

? Roman of the second or third century AD

37 *An Hermaphrodite Lifting its Drapery to Inspect its Erect Penis*

Bronze: 8.0 (without added brass pedestal)
Lit.: Knight MS (Bronzes), xlvii.1
One of the more charming items acquired by Knight from the notorious cabinet of Senator Quirini, this is also one which looks as if it may not be ancient. The end of the left foot is broken, perhaps by a screw-hole made to fix the figure to its pedestal

Egyptian, of the Graeco-Roman period   Plate 41

38 *Seated Ram-headed Deity*

Bronze: 66.0
Lit.: Knight MS (Bronzes), iii.i; Knight, 1809, p. iv; Knight, 1818, pp. 149–50
Knight noted that although Jupiter was not uncommonly identified with Ammon by appropriating his horns, Herodotus recorded that the Egyptians worshipped Ammon in the form of a human with the head of a ram 'in the celebrated oracular temple in Libya, as well as that of Thebes'. In the plate of the figure engraved by Agar for *Specimens* Knight included a base adorned with a relief after a medal of Myndus showing what he imagined to have been the 'head ornament' of the original. Despite the distaste he expressed, in the *Progress of Civil Society* (p. 92), for the monstrous gods of Egypt – 'the mystic symbols of a gloomy creed' – by 1805 he admired the severe dignity possessed by this figure, its 'breadth and sharpness' and 'easy flow'. He pointed out correctly that it was highly curious because the three pieces of bronze of which it is composed are solid. They were, he believed, not cast but hammered together, and chiselled. Thus this was 'one of the most antient monuments of imitative art extant'. It was

purchased by the Duc de Chaulnes in Cahira in Upper Egypt from a person who had bought it from the Thebaid. Peter Funnell has found a letter in the Towneley Hall Papers (DDTo, uncatalogued) written by the Abbé Tersan to Charles Townley from Paris on 13 April 1791 when he was assisting Knight in a game of elaborate double-bluff with the dealer Juliot who had acquired the Duc de Chaulnes' collection and wished to sell it entire. Knight wanted the 'plums' and this piece above all. Juliot was persuaded to part with it for a mere 15 louis on the grounds that its great antiquity was doubtful, but the dealer sensed he had been tricked and raised his prices to Knight's disadvantage

Punjab Hills, ? eighteenth century

39 *Vishnu seated on Garuda*

Bronze: 28.0
This is one of a set of four figures from the collection of Charles Townley acquired by the Museum, with Knight's help, from Peregrine Towneley in 1814. It is marked T25. Knight owned some oriental bronzes and shared Townley's interest in the ancient religion of the East, sending him for instance on 24 October 1782, some 'uncensored' translations of 'Shanscrit' hymns made by his neighbour Mr C. W. Boughton Rouse (whose son shortly before Knight's death was to marry one of Knight's nieces). See Towneley Hall Papers, DDTo, box 46, folder H ('Memoranda and Quotations relative to antiquities in my collection and elsewhere')

? eighteenth century, Italian

40 *Vessel*

Bronze: 34.6
Lit.: Knight MS (Bronzes), lxiv.1; lxxxix.5
According to Knight's catalogue this was found at Praeneste (Palestrina) in 1786 near the Temple of Fortune – an etching by Skelton illustrates the vessel together with a group of other bronzes, including an Etruscan cista, all allegedly discovered in this same *Scavo* (this is bound in a volume of plates discussed in cat. no. 78). Since these other items seem all to have been in Townley's collection, Knight perhaps acquired this piece from his friend. In any case it appears in Lawrence's portrait of Knight exhibited in 1794 (cat. no. 184). As Knight noted, the handles were different in style and of 'a different kind of Brass', of the wrong size and could not originally have belonged in their present position even if they were discovered together with the vessel. They were, he thought, worthy 'of the time of the Macedonian Kings'. He noted that they were not identical; but it is not necessary to conclude as he did that they do not come from 'the same mould or model' since the differences are of the sort rough casting results in. The

antiquity of both vessel and handles is now doubted

? Italian, early nineteenth   Colour Plate V
century

41 *Striding Etruscan Warrior*

Bronze: 38.6
Lit.: Knight MS (Bronzes), lviii.3; *Specimens*, II,
plate iv; Walters, 1899, no. 455

This simply posed but exquisitely detailed figure was
recorded in Knight's catalogue as having been brought to
England by Major Balgrove from Italy. (The date is trimmed
but is given as 1813 in the Museum's register.) Knight
claimed that it came from the Gallery of the Grand Duke of
Tuscany, but, as was recognized by J. B. S. Morritt soon
after Knight died, a very similar figure remained in that
collection (then in the Uffizi, now in the Museo Archeo-
logico). The inaccurate reproductions of the Florentine
figure (e.g. in Hope's *Costume of the Ancients*, Plate 34)
prevented recognition that they were identical but photographs recently revealed this — indeed Knight's figure even
reproduces the accidentally distorted foot of the Florentine
piece. Such reproductions were never made in early
antiquity and so this must be modern work, indeed a
forgery; but it is of quite extraordinary quality. The
Florentine bronze is now admired as an important Etruscan
work of about 450 BC. It was considered as Etruscan in
Knight's day and was known to have been found at Todi
(anciently an Etruscan city). Nevertheless, Knight believed
his figure to be Greek and related it to descriptions of
warriors in Homer. He also compared the helmet with its
horse-hair crest to those on the most ancient coins of
Athens and noted that the shirt appeared to consist of

'narrow strips sown together according to the primitive
mode of weaving by hand without a loom as it is still
practised in the interior of Africa'

[SILVER]

Roman, ? second century AD

42 *Part of a Cylindrical Bowl*

Silver: 4.3 (diameter: 7.8)
Lit.: Knight MS (Bronzes), lxxxix.70; Walters,
1921, no. 138

This is one of seven pieces of silver plate 'found together in
the month of May 1785, carefully placed one in the other
under a great stone, which obstructed the plough of a
peasant in a field near the village of Caubiac, six leagues
from Toulouse'. They were purchased of Monsieur Carnac,
'Lord of the Soil of Caubiac', by the Abbé Tersan, who sold
them to Knight in 1790. After the discovery, a thorough
search was made of the neighbourhood and the ruins of the
foundations of a small temple were discovered. This Knight
supposed to have been perhaps dedicated to Bacchus
(Caubiac being anciently written Colbiac and Calbac
'which is an easy corruption of Collis Bacchi') and the
plate to have served therein and to have been concealed by
'pious heathens' from the Christians. The dionysiac figures,
masks and emblems on this and all the other pieces in the
hoard clearly suggested this idea. But such decoration
would not be improbable in domestic plate. Knight noted
that the reliefs were 'slightly' and in some cases 'hastily and
negligently finish'd' but were 'designed and wrought with
admirable Truth, Intelligence and Effect'

42

Roman, ? second or early third century AD

43 Part of a Skillet

Silver: 14.3 (length of handle)
Lit.: Knight MS (Bronzes), lxxxix.61; Walters,
1921, no. 189; Toynbee, pp. 305–6

The portion of the rim is adorned with water deities and, where it connects with the handle, with Ariadne and Bacchus. On the handle we see Mercury seated below a canopy with a pair of rustic labourers resting, and, at the end, a female bust (unidentified by Knight, but Juno and most recently Diana have been suggested) rising from a flower. This is one of 'seven articles . . . the Remains of a Roman Table service of plate found in the Estate [Capheaton] of Sir John Swinburne Bart in Northumberland; which was immediately broken to pieces, and secretly sold to a silversmith in Kirkharle by the labourers, who discovered it; so that these fragments only were preserved by the landed proprietor' who deposited them in Knight's collection. (It may be that Knight knew Swinburne's neighbour Sir Charles Monck of Belsay, a keen hellenist and patron of Knight's friend William Gell.) The disparate quality of the enrichments on the various articles led Knight to assign them to different periods between 'the time of Augustas' and that of 'Septimius Severus, or even later'. This he thought came mid-way between the two extremes

Roman, second or early third   Colour Plate IV
century AD

44 Tyche

Silver with some gold plating: 14.0
Lit.: Knight MS (Bronzes) xxiv.1; Knight, 1818,
p. 153; Walters, 1921, no. 33

In March 1764 a labourer digging in a vineyard at Mâcon hit a hard lump with his spade: this consisted of a group of silver figures and many thousand gold and silver coins compacted together. The Tyche had been published posthumously by Caylus (VII, pp. 239, 250, plate lxxi) but Knight was scornful of his imprecision over the curious combinations of silver and gold. Walters catalogued it as the tutelary deity of a city, perhaps Massilia, the ancient Marseilles, but Knight considered it to represent Cybelè or the universal mother, who is 'mixing the productive elements of heat and moisture, by making a libation upon the flames of an altar from a golden patera, with the usual knob in the centre of it, representing, probably, the lingam'. This is not now thought likely, but the wings do certainly support the 'presiding deities of the planets, placed in order of the days of the week' with the busts of Dioscuri below and, in the cornucopia, held in the left hand, the busts of Apollo and Diana. Knight felt that this figure and its companions, all of which he acquired, were exquisite but lacked grandeur of character, and the style he considered as belonging to the 'latest period of fine art, that of Trajan

or his immediate successors', and since the coins found with it were none later than Gallienus (AD 253–68) he thought it likely that the treasure was hidden 'during the troubles and confusions of that reign'. Walters considered the figures likely to be a little later in date than Knight supposed

Roman, second or early third century AD

45 Jupiter Holding a Thunderbolt

Silver, with some gold plating: 6.5 (excluding base)
Lit.: Knight MS (Bronzes), liii.9; Walters, 1921,
no. 27

Part of the 'Mâcon horde', for the discovery of which, and for Knight's view of the style and date of this figure, see cat. no. 44

Roman, second or early third century AD

46 Mercury with a Purse

Silver, with some gold plating: 14.0 (including ancient base)
Lit.: Knight MS (Bronzes), lx.12; Walters, 1921,
no. 29

Part of the 'Mâcon horde', for the discovery of which, and for Knight's view of the style and date of this figure, see cat. no. 44

Nuremberg, Germany, c. 1630–40

47 Cup in form of a Columbine Flower

Silver: 20.1
Lit.: Knight MS (Bronzes), lxxxix.84; Catalogue of
Plate, no. 103

Cups of this traditional late Gothic form (but with novel Renaissance ornament) were required of Nuremberg apprentices on admission as Masters of the guild. Knight, understandably, supposed this example to be Italian work of the sixteenth century, and proceeded with a characteristic mixture of caution and hyperbole to observe 'As Benevento [sic] Cellini is the most celebrated artist in this way, all works of great Excellence are attributed to him, & this is unquestionably the most excellent now known'. He noted that the six compartments of the upper part of the bowl are filled with compositions from Ovid's Metamorphoses 'relative to art' and that there was a 'symbolical genius with an appropriate Emblem and Inscription below'. He continues: 'It was purchased at Delhi in Hindostan, whither it had probably been carried by some Venetian merchant as a present to the Mogul'

47

48

[MARBLE]

Roman, first century AD

48 *Bust of a Boy*

Greek marble (tip of nose and lobe of ear and
patches of drapery restored): 32.0
Lit.: Knight MS (Bronzes), lxx.8; *Museum
Marbles*, XI, plate xxvii; A. H. Smith, III, no. 1936
This attractive piece from Knight's collection — originally
wearing ear rings — is obviously a portrait of the early
Imperial period and by the mid nineteenth century it was
thought that it possibly represented Nero. Knight, however,
with caution uncharacteristic of his period, was content to
describe it as of an 'unknown boy' — adding justly that it
was 'well preserved' and 'of moderate sculpture, though of
a natural, simple unaffected character'

Roman, of the first or second century AD

49 *Head from a Copy of a Greek Sculpture of an Athletic Victor*

Fine grained Greek marble (of excellent
preservation, retaining original polish but with a
few chips, the tip of the nose and lobe of the
right ear restored): 18.0 (excluding modern bust)
Lit.: Knight, 1809, plate xxx; Michaelis, p. 609;
Furtwängler, pp. 161–5; Wyndham, pp. 44–5;
Richter, p. 34
It is possible that this superlative copy of a beautiful Greek
original was the head published by Caylus (II, p. 142 and
plate xlviii, no. 2) as formerly in the collection of the Comte
de Pontchartrain, Chancellor of France at the close of the
reign of Louis XIV, which was, however, mounted on a
draped bust (which Caylus deplored). It may have been
among the ten busts acquired for Lord Egremont's collec-

49

tion at Petworth (before 1768) from the Lyde Browne collection, but it is more likely to have been taken to England by Matthew Brettingham the Younger whose enterprise in forming the collections at Petworth and Holkham Hall Knight commended. A cast of this head (defective in the lips) may be seen above a door of the drawing room at Holkham where the plaster casts were supplied by Brettingham. This cast is stamped 'Ptolemy', an identification which must have been suggested by the similarly curled hair and diadem (or royal fillet) on the coin portraits of Ptolemy I. Knight considered the head to belong to 'some canonical hero of poetical mythology or fabulous history but of whom it is vain to conjecture'. The fillet, however (which is unusual in that the ends are tucked in on each side rather than tied at the back) belongs to an athletic victor. Inspection of the top of the head suggests that one of his arms originally rested there, but our reconstruction of the action of the figure is impeded by the bland modern bust from which Knight rightly wished the head to be 'delivered'. Furtwängler argued that the head was copied from an original statue by Kresilas of the fifth century BC (Richter, considers a work of the fourth century more likely). Knight, like Furtwängler, was fascinated by the way that the sculptor, although still giving each lock of hair separate attention, relished their tangled freedom. Richter lists other replicas of inferior quality and preservation

NATIONAL TRUST (PETWORTH HOUSE)

Roman, mid second century AD

50 *Head from a Copy of a Colossal Bronze Statue of Apollo*

Parian marble (front curls, nose and ear lobes restored): 46.0
Lit.: Knight, 1809, p. XXV, plates iv and v;
A. H. Smith, I, no. 208

This head is from the collection of Knight's friend Charles Townley which Knight helped the Museum to acquire in 1805. It was recognized by Knight as a copy of an early Greek bronze whose severe style had been somewhat softened to gratify the taste of the court of the Emperor Hadrian (at whose villa it is likely to have been found). He was particularly interested in the stylization of the hair, which he related both to a remarkable bronze head found at Herculaneum and illustrated in the *Bronzi d'Ercolano* (cat. no. 75) and to the heads of Apollo on the silver tetradrachms of Leontium (see cat. no. 23). We do not know what Townley thought of the head because he acquired it late in life, after the compilation of his catalogues, at the sale of Lord Cawdor's collection (Skinner and Dyke, 5–6 June 1800) where it was lot no. 69. According to a marked copy of the catalogue (Dept. of Prints and Drawings, British Museum), it was bought for 29 guineas

TRUSTEES OF THE BRITISH MUSEUM

50

51

Roman, of the mid second century AD

51 Head of a Copy of a Greek Statue of Hermes

Pentelic marble (parts of the nose and ears and most of the brim of the hat restored): 60.5 (including modern bust)
Lit.: Knight, 1809, plate li; Michaelis, p. 467, no. 88

This pensive male head of a type first created by Polyclitus in the fifth century BC was excavated at Hadrian's villa by Gavin Hamilton in 1769 and was acquired in 1771 by the second Earl of Shelburne (later first Marquis of Lansdowne) for £55. Knight considered 'the execution as perfect as the design is beautiful'. In a sale catalogue drawn up (probably by Henry Tresham) in 1810, it was observed that 'copying from plaister casts of this bust has been a source of perennial income to Sculptors at Rome; there is scarcely a collector of modern works in Europe; that has not in his possession an imitation of this marble', which explains how Thorvaldsen was able to employ it as a model for the head of his famous *Mercury about to slay Argus*. Throughout the nineteenth century it was 'probably the most popular specimen' among the antique sculpture at Lansdowne House and when this collection was auctioned on 5 March 1930 (by Christie's) it was retained by the family (or re-purchased, perhaps, for in one sale catalogue it is clearly marked as 'bought Reid £241 10s 0d')

THE EARL OF SHELBURNE, BOWOOD, WILTSHIRE

Roman, late second century AD

52 Fragment of a Portrait Head

Italian marble (badly weathered): 20.0 × 23.0
Prov.: Purchased by Henry Blundell; by descent

52

53

to Colonel J. Weld by whom presented 1959
Lit.: Blundell, 1803, no. ccccxxxviii

This fragment, which was until recently clad in lichen, may be discerned in old photographs inside a marble basin in the interior of the garden temple at Ince Blundell Hall (Poulsen, fig. 19). It was displayed as a fragment and would indeed have been impossible to restore effectively. Henry Blundell, who acquired it, observed that it was 'known by the eye as for Commodus' and he compared it with a bust of that emperor at Castle Howard, which does indeed have elaborately drilled hair of similar style and a similar cutting of the eye — so too do busts of the young Marcus Aurelius

MERSEYSIDE COUNTY MUSEUMS

Roman, probably of the second century AD

53 Head of 'Jupiter Serapis'

Pentelic marble (modius, back of hair and part of beard, and copper rays restored): 48.0 (including base)
Prov.: Purchased by Henry Blundell; by descent to Colonel J. Weld by whom presented 1959
Lit.: Blundell, 1803, no. cxiii; Michaelis, p. 367, no. 151; Ashmole, no. 151, plate 18

Ashmole considered this 'head of Sarapis' (the rays he notes identify the god with Osiris who shines alike on the quick and the dead) as perhaps from a reduced copy of an earlier, hellenistic, seated statue. Blundell, who acquired it, directly or indirectly from Rome, noted that it had been discovered in ruins on the Via Appia and considered that it possessed 'great majesty and dignity of character'. He seems, however, to have esteemed still more highly a copy of a head of the same subject in the Vatican carved out of a Greek marble cornice by Angelini, and purchased from Giovanni Volpato (Blundell, 1803, no. xcix)

MERSEYSIDE COUNTY MUSEUMS

54

Roman, probably of the second century AD

54 *Hope*

Italian marble (head, arm holding drapery, extended hand and other parts restored): 80.0 (including base)
Prov.: Purchased by Henry Blundell; by descent to Colonel J. Weld by whom presented 1959
Lit.: Blundell, 1803, no. xxviii; Blundell, 1809, plate 22; Michaelis, p. 350, no. 40; Ashmole, no. 40, plate 17

There are numerous neo-Attic interpretations of this popular archaic Greek prototype and it was adopted as a personification of Hope on Roman coins. Recognizing that the style was archaic, Blundell called it Etruscan — the sort of solecism which made his learned friend Townley despair. Blundell was sceptical of the theories propounded by 'D'Ankerville', Townley and Knight and he considered the lotus flower to be simply a 'symbol of delight' but noted that the figure was called an Isis 'by some ingenious mythologists . . . This they pretend to prove from the lotus in the hand being an emblem of generation'. The statue was kept in the Pantheon at Ince Blundell Hall (see Poulsen, fig. 16)

MERSEYSIDE COUNTY MUSEUMS

Roman copy, probably of the second century AD   Plate 40

55 *Head from a Copy of a Hellenistic Statue of Niobe*

Pentelic marble (tip and most of the left side of the nose restored): 87.5 (including modern bust)
Lit.: Knight, 1809, plates xxxv–vii; Michaelis, p. 227, no. 5; Oehler, Kat. I, Taf. 16; Haskell and Penny, no. 66

This head seems to have been known to Winckelmann and his editor Carlo Fea from a cast which remained in Rome where it had been acquired by the sculptor, restorer and dealer Joseph Nollekens, who sold it to the Earl of Exeter who in turn gave it to Nollekens's patron the Earl of Yarborough, a keen collector who inherited the great collection of antiquities formed by Sir Richard Worsley. The head was always recognized as copied from the same original as was the very celebrated statue of Niobe in the Medici collection, but it has often been considered as superior. Knight even thought that it was 'probably' a fragment of the original statue of which the Medici was a copy. He admired — as did all commentators at that date — the blend of 'maternal tenderness', 'regal pride' and 'earnest supplication' in the expression

THE EARL OF YARBOROUGH

? Roman, of the early Imperial period

56 *Head of a Hero*

Italian marble (badly stained and extensively reworked, with neck and breast, chin, nose and part of the lower lip restored): 45.0 (including helmet)

Lit.: Knight, 1809, plate liv; Michaelis, p. 608, no. 23; Wyndham, pp. 42–3

Knight, who was fully aware of the dismal condition of this head, probably acquired for Lord Egremont's collection at Petworth by Matthew Brettingham the younger, was, nevertheless, deeply impressed by its 'grandeur or character and expression' which would, he felt, be discerned if only 'a single brow remained', and he suggested it was a fragment of a copy of a bronze by Lysippos perhaps of Ajax about to kill himself or carrying off Achilles. Michaelis, on the other hand, found the expression mannered and suspected it was a modern pastiche. Whatever its status, it is clearly related in style to the famous head from the Pergamene group of Menelaus and Patroclus of which one copy exists in the Vatican

NATIONAL TRUST (PETWORTH HOUSE)

? Bartolommeo Cavaceppi (1716–99)

57 *Female Hand on Elaborate Plinth*

Italian marble (hand); 'Granito rosso di Assuan' (base); imperial porphyry (column); 'Breccia di Settebasi' (sphere): 58.0

Prov.: Purchased by Henry Blundell; by descent to Colonel J. Weld by whom presented 1959

Lit.: Blundell, 1803, no. ccccxxii

This is one of three hands, antique, but mounted on plinths of modern workmanship (made, however, from Roman fragments) in Blundell's collection. The others were nos. ccccxx and ccccxxix in his 1803 catalogue. Of these the former was noted as being acquired from Cavaceppi who would seem likely to have supplied all three. No scholar surveying the collection during the last century seems to have cast even a disdainful eye upon this bizarre relic

MERSEYSIDE COUNTY MUSEUMS

Italian, late eighteenth century

58 *Bust of Homer*

Italian marble: 61.0

Lit.: Blundell, 1803, no. clxvi; Poulsen, p. 115; Ashmole, no. 168

This bust was not, as Poulsen supposed, a forgery. It was correctly described by Blundell himself (who was admittedly often muddled, as well as deceived, about the status of his possessions) as a 'copy of that most celebrated bust of Homer, formerly in the Farnese Palace at Rome, but now at Naples' (e.g. in the Museo degli Studi, now Museo Nazionale). Another version of the prototype was in Townley's collection. For the benefit of the uneducated visitors to Ince, the far from learned Blundell added: 'Homer lived about 1000 years before Christ; yet his works remain, and render him Immortal as the Prince of Poets'. He was clearly ignorant of the great debates about Homer to which Knight contributed (see pp. 8–9).

MERSEYSIDE COUNTY MUSEUMS

? Joseph Nollekens (1737–1823)

59 *Copy of the so-called Bust of Clytie*

Italian marble: 64.0

Lit.: Dallaway, p. 322; J. T. Smith, I, pp. 263–4; A. H. Smith, III, pp. 147–8

The original marble of which this is a copy was acquired in 1772 by Charles Townley from the Caetani d'Aragona family (Principi di Piedmonti, Duchi di Laurenzano) at Naples near where it was said to have been found (Plate 32). In early lists of his antiquities Townley called it a *Bust of a woman ending in a sunflower* — and his friend the sculptor Nollekens, who perhaps restored it, simply regarded it as a portrait of the sculptor's model — but Townley also called it *Clytie* (who was transformed into a flower when deserted by Helios). He noted that he purchased it for the high price of £95, but he valued it at the extraordinary sum of £500 (Towneley Hall Papers, DDTo, box 46, uncatalogued) and it was the most celebrated item in his collection — indeed no antique sculpture in late eighteenth-century England was more admired. Although still popularly known as *Clytie*, scholars have long dismissed the combination of bust with a flower as 'probably' of 'no special significance' and considered it as a portrait, probably of the Augustan period, and perhaps of Antonia, daughter of Mark Antony and mother of Germanicus. By the 1780s, however, Townley and his circle had detected a mystic significance in the bust — as Aphrodite/Isis with the Lotus — a mystic emblem of passive generation. Nollekens 'always had a copy of it in marble purposely for sale' and after the Townley marbles had been acquired for the British Museum in 1805 he sold the last of these to John Towneley for 100 guineas — this example, was presented to Towneley Hall by Mrs Sharrocks of Cleveland Mount, Burnley, in 1946, and given its local provenance may, as Susan Bourne points out, have been acquired when the contents of Towneley Hall were sold in about 1901. John Kenworthy-Browne points out that Nollekens made his bust of Caroline Princess of Wales in the form of Clytie. He also seems to have imitated the hair for his beautiful figure of Mrs Howard of Corby at Wetherall, and modified it for Emma Hamilton (cat. no. 61)

TOWNELEY HALL ART GALLERY AND MUSEUM, BURNLEY BOROUGH COUNCIL

? Joseph Nollekens (1737–1823)

60 *Herm Bust of Charles Townley*

Italian marble: 44.5
Inscribed: *Nollekens Ft. 1807* (on reverse and on
one side); *CHARLES TOWNLEY* on obverse
Lit.: J. T. Smith, I, p. 266n

Smith records a posthumous bust made by Nollekens of his
friend using a 'face-mask', and the herm form (which
Nollekens had used before) may have seemed appropriate
for a connoisseur of 'Greecian' art and, perhaps, for a posthumous portrait. Smith mentions that Knight donated a
head of Townley by Nollekens to the British Museum, but
this it has not been possible to trace. The Greek inscription
below the sitter's name may be translated 'knowledge of
the old fosters clear understanding of the new'

LORD O'HAGAN, ON LOAN TO TOWNELEY HALL ART
GALLERY AND MUSEUM, BURNLEY BOROUGH COUNCIL

Joseph Nollekens (1737–1823)

61 *Bust Portrait, perhaps of Emma Hamilton*

Italian marble: 58.3 (including base)
Signed: *Nollekens F*^{t.}
Prov.: Christie's, 21 Jan. 1965, lot 11
Lit.: Jaffé, p. 47

61

For the Hamiltons and their friendship with Knight see
pp 70–1. The theatrical character of this portrait suggests
Lady Hamilton's accomplishments but for this reason also
it can only be an approximate likeness, and it is not entirely
certain that this bust represents her. As Mrs Jaffé has
pointed out, Emma sat to a number of artists in 1791.
Knight owned an oval pencil drawing of her made by
Lawrence in that year (Oo.5–22), and it is likely that
Knight was the gentleman whom Lawrence refers to in a
letter as having arranged the sitting. This bust may be
related to heads of Niobe such as cat. no. 55

VISITORS OF THE ASHMOLEAN MUSEUM, OXFORD

Imitator of Joseph Nollekens

62 *Bust portrait of Charles James Fox*

Italian marble: 60.0 (including base)

This is an unsigned copy of Nollekens's admired portrait
of the great Whig politician with cropped hair (modelled in
about 1802) which is, in many versions, supplied with
antique drapery. It is, conceivably, by Nollekens's chief
carver Goblet who, as John Kenworthy-Browne points out,
seems to have continued working in his master's studio
producing unsigned copies after Nollekens ceased to be
active himself in 1816, but more probably it is of later date
and, perhaps, by Nollekens's assistant Sebastian Gahagan.
Fox was not only Knight's mentor in politics. They shared a
passionate interest in literature – we find them in the
1790s consulting with Parr over Lycophron (Johnstone,
VII, p. 304) and discussing the relative merits of *Lear* and
Macbeth with Price, Beaumont, Marchant and Westall
(Farington, 4 May 1796)

LT-COLONEL SIR WALTER BROMLEY DAVENPORT,
CAPESTHORNE HALL

Peter Turnerelli (1774–1839)

63 *Sir Joseph Banks*

Italian marble: 52.0 (excluding plinth)

Banks, one of the most eminent scientists of his time, was a
friend and a near neighbour of Knight in Soho Square.
From about 1791 he was also a close friend of Knight's
brother Thomas Andrew, whose public career he actively
promoted. This bust was ordered by Council of the Royal
College of Surgeons on 8 July 1813, exhibited (perhaps as a
plaster) at the Royal Academy in 1814 (786), and paid for
on 20 December of that year (for 100 guineas). The Board
of Curators were dissatsified with the bust and wished him
to carry out further work on it. There is a replica at the
National Maritime Museum

PRIVATE COLLECTION

John Bacon the Younger (1777–1859)
64 *Portrait of Richard Payne Knight*

Italian marble: 46.0
Signed and dated *J. Bacon, Junr. 1812*

Bacon's success in obtaining commissions for patriotic memorials in St Paul's from the Committee of Taste seems to have been due to Knight's high opinion of his merits (Farington, 14 June, 1810). The exact provenance of this head is unknown, but it is likely to have been connected with Knight's bequest to the Museum. Bacon exhibited portraits of Knight at the Royal Academy in 1811 (954) and 1812 (931) – the former no doubt the plaster after the clay model and the latter this marble bust

TRUSTEES OF THE BRITISH MUSEUM

64

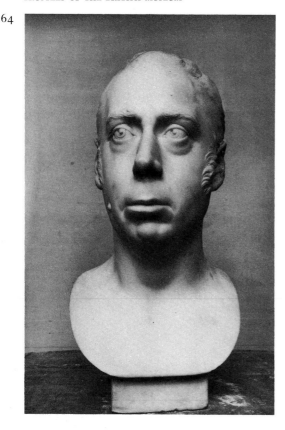

John Bacon the Younger (1777–1859)
65 *Portrait of Richard Payne Knight*

Italian marble: 57.2
Signed and dated *J. Bacon, Ft May 1814*

This is made from the same model as no. 64 but with metal drapery crudely cemented to make it a 'bust' rather than a 'head'. It was acquired by the National Portrait Gallery in May 1972 from Cyril Humphris but no provenance is available

NATIONAL PORTRAIT GALLERY, LONDON

Sir Francis Chantrey (1781–1841)
66 *Charles Long, Lord Farnborough*

Italian marble: 74.9
Prov.: Purchased from Mawers Ltd., 1925

Knight's cousin, Thomas Johnes, was an important patron of Chantrey, who also stayed at Downton with Knight's brother (they were both friends of Sir Humphrey Davy). According to Chantrey's MS ledger (p. 101), he received a commission to make a bust of Charles Long from Long's father-in-law Sir Abraham Hume in 1819, and was paid £126 for it on 6 January – this must be the bust of Long shown at the Royal Academy in 1820 (1046) and, it seems, the one exhibited here. A duplicate was ordered in 1833, was ready a year later and paid for in 1842 (*ibid.*, p. 258) – this is probably the example in the National Gallery. Charles Long (1761–1838) was a protégé of Pitt, by whom he was made firstly Joint Secretary of the Treasury in 1791 (resigned 1801) and then Lord Commissioner of the Treasury in 1804. In 1806 he was made Secretary of State for Ireland and in 1810 Joint Paymaster General. He was created Baron Farnborough in 1826. An important collector, he was still more important as the 'Spectacles' of George IV. He was, with Knight, the most powerful figure on the Committee of Taste – and equally influential as a Trustee of the British Museum, and of the National Gallery, and as Deputy President of the British Institution. He was, despite political differences, a close friend of Knight, at least before he was an intimate of the Regent

NATIONAL PORTRAIT GALLERY, LONDON

[MISCELLANEOUS]

67 *Cast of the Head of the Horse of Selene from the East Pediment of the Parthenon*

Resin: 53.3
Lit.: Haydon, 1818

The marble head of which this is a replica was the subject of special claims made by the English painter Benjamin Robert Haydon in a pamphlet which he designed for European dissemination. He considered it incomparably superior to the heads of the horses of Saint Mark, just as he considered the *Theseus* to be finer than the *Apollo Belvedere* (see also cat. no. 145)

BRITISH MUSEUM PUBLICATIONS LTD

68 *Cast of the Front Portion of the 'Leconfield Aphrodite'*

Plaster: 33.0
Lit.: Knight, 1809, plates xlv and xlvi;
Furtwängler, pp. 343ff; Wyndham, pp. 118–23;
Oehler, Kat. 82, Tafs. 12–15

Knight was the first person to declare that the head at Petworth from which this cast was made was an original Greek work of exceptional quality and to propose that it was a fragment of the original statue, perhaps by Praxiteles, of which the Medici Venus, then the most generally admired of all statues, was an imitation. Furtwängler, who saw the head in 1888, came to the same conclusion, and scholars still share this opinion, with the result that the marble is now too valuable to be loaned

VISITORS OF THE ASHMOLEAN MUSEUM

Giovanni-Battista Serabaglio (*fl.* 1560s)

69 *Head of a Boarspear*

Steel, with parts gilded: 46.4
Lit.: Knight MS (Bronzes), vii.11

Knight had one or two pieces of Renaissance metalwork in his collection. This was given him by the first Marquis of Lansdowne. Knight catalogued it as Florentine work of the sixteenth century. It is adorned with heads of Adonis and Diana which he considered as portraits of the 'two personages, under whose patronage it was executed, that is of Duke Alexander dei Medici and his Duchess'. The attribution to the Milanese craftsman Serabaglio has been made on account of the similarity of this piece to a boarspear purchased from him by the Archduke Ferdinand II in about 1560 (*Waffensammlung*, Vienna — see Thomas, Gamber and Schedelmann, *Arms and Armour*, 1965, no. 45)

TRUSTEES OF THE BRITISH MUSEUM

70 *Cast from a Plaster Cast of an Ivory Relief of the Discovery of Callisto*

Resin: 11.2 × 16.2
Lit.: Knight MS (Bronzes), xvi.1; Rowlands, p. 42

The ivory relief of which this is a reproduction was an exceptional item in Knight's collection — although he did also own a hone stone relief after Dürer — and he perhaps acquired it because of the relationship which he recognized between it and a drawing of the three nymphs in the left foreground — a drawing (Oo.9–54) now considered as by Rubens but then believed to be by Van Dyck, which Knight noted as 'given to me by the Hon Mrs Damer, who inherited it, thro' Lord J. Campbell from her uncle Archibald Duke of Argyll' — mistakenly, it seems, for the drawing was actually purchased at W. Y. Ottley's sale. The ivory was not in Knight's house when he died, so was not part of the bequest, but his niece, Mrs Stackhouse Acton, presented a cast in 1875. The present whereabouts of the ivory is unknown (it is not at Acton Scott Hall), but there are other examples of work in this medium derived, as this one was, from one of a series of sixteen reliefs of episodes in Ovid's *Metamorphoses* modelled in clay by Jacob Cobaert after designs by Guglielmo della Porta, probably in the 1550s

PRIVATE COLLECTION

71

Venetian, *c.* 1500

71 *Ball of Millefiori Glass*

Diameter (from hole to hole): 4.0
Lit.: Knight MS (Bronzes), xii.1

This curious object was 'plough'd up in a part of the forest of Ormesby in Lincolnshire, that had not been before till'd, in the year 1805, and', Knight continued, 'was given to me by Joseph Banks. From the circumstances of its being so found; and of nothing in any degree similar having been discovered in Herculaneum, Pompeii, or any other ruin'd City of the Greeks or Romans, there can be no doubt of its being a specimen of those works in this material, for which the ancient Phoenicians of Sidon were once so famous, and which they brought here to exchange with the barbarian natives for the gold of Ireland and the tin of Cornwall.' He thought that it might have served as a knob on the top of a helmet such as are mentioned in Homer. He had it polished, but left one side as it had been found, considering its corrosion as proof of its antiquity. A devastating note on the glass ball is added to Knight's catalogue (p. 309) by J. B. S. Morritt: 'I have since . . . bought beads exactly similar, also perforated like this at Florence. They were of old Venetian manufacture, & adorned old Italian cabinets as knobs. They are no longer made now & I was told that the secret by which the enamel was embedded in the glass without being fused was now lost'. Such balls, recorded as being made in Venice in about 1500, are noted in Apsley Pellatt's *Curiosities of Glass Making*, London 1849, pp. 22, 141

TRUSTEES OF THE BRITISH MUSEUM

Thomas Adye (died before 1762)

72 *Mahogany chest*

Height (including legs and Ivory figure): 37.0; width (including base projection): 36.0; depth: 28.0
Lit.: Harcourt Smith, pp. 34–40; Society of Dilettanti Papers, I, ff. 13, 14v, 15, 27, 258; Haskell and Penny, pp. 48–9

The front of this chest is an imitation, doubtless made from a print, of the colossal porphyry sarcophagus which was long admired in the church of S. Costanza, Rome (but which was later removed to the Museo Pio-Clementino) and which, because of the vine ornament (emblematic of the Eucharist) was known from the Renaissance onwards as the Tomb of Bacchus, although it is in fact an early Christian Imperial sarcophagus. The members of the Society of Dilettanti, whose 'Books, Papers and Money' the chest was made to hold, are likely to have been attracted by the confusion of Christian and pagan imagery. The idea was, it seems, Sir James Gray's – at least he supplied the Society's 'scultore', Adye, with designs. The latter was paid 15 guineas out of forfeit money for his work on 1 May 1837. The lid, decorated with affronted goats and panthers, departs from the ancient prototype and seems to be derived from a seventeenth-century pattern book. It was an addition designed by Knapton (see no. 182) for which Adye was paid 11 guineas on 7 January 1739–40. Two months later an additional ornament – an ivory figure of a reclining and inebriate Bacchus – was deemed necessary. Knapton and Sir John Hawden were involved in the design and in April 1744–5 Adye was paid 10 guineas for the figure. In 1767 a design for the back was solicited from Nicholas Revett but nothing was, it seems, done until 1780 when Christopher Fuhrlong undertook repairs and carved the mahogany panel which was stuck on the back together with an ivory copy of the antique relief of Perseus and Andromeda in the Capitoline Museum which was presented by Sir John Taylor

THE SOCIETY OF DILETTANTI

Thomas Adye (died before 1762)

73 *Mahogany Balloting Box*

Height: 42.0; width: 40.0; depth (excluding projecting figure): 22.0
Lit.: Harcourt-Smith, pp. 26–9, 47

The figure of Justice (with swords, scales and book) surmounts the aperture into which balloting balls are dropped. Over the drawer marked 'Aye' are a radiant mask and a lyre, emblems of comedy and music, together with a merry bacchic head, but over that marked 'No' are a glum head and the owl and gorgon-shield which forbode and repel evil. There is a frieze carved with further emblems of Bacchus and, on either side, reliefs copied from immensely popular and commonly reproduced reliefs by François

Duquesnoy of putti at play. The box was commissioned 1 May 1737 and completed by 7 May 1738 for the Society of Dilettanti by their 'scultore', Adye, who was paid 6 guineas for materials and a further £25 upon completion. The Society's 'limner' Knapton (see cat. no. 182) was thanked for the design but Justice at least must be Adye's creation, since he devised very similar but larger and marble allegorical females to perch upon the sarcophagi of Charles Sergison (d. 1732) at Cuckfield, Sussex, and of William Mitchell (d. 1745) at Fowlmere, Cambs.

THE SOCIETY OF DILETTANTI

Etruria, Factory of Josiah Wedgwood (opened 1769)

74 *Charles Townley*

Blue Jasper, white relief: 9.3
Sitter's name impressed below truncation of bust
Prov.: Charles Townley; by descent
Lit.: Reilly and Savage, p. 323

This profile portrait is close enough to that in Zoffany's painting (cat. no. 210) to suggest that this was Wedgwood's source, although this is by no means certain. There was also a medallion portrait by Tassie made in 1780

SIMON TOWNELEY, ESQ.

[BOOKS]

75 *Bronzi d'Ercolano*

Volume I (Naples 1767)

This is the fifth of eight volumes of the *Antichità di Ercolano* which appeared between 1757 and 1796 edited by the Accademia Ercolanense, at first for presentation only. It was through these volumes that the learned world chiefly studied the treasures disinterred at Herculaneum and Pompeii, for although travellers visited the Museum at Portici – Knight must have done so – they were forbidden even to make notes there. The volume is open at Tav. LXXI showing a bronze head (now in the Museo Nazionale at Naples and no. 850) thought perhaps to represent Apollo and to be an ancient Greek work but produced in the Sicilian or Italian colonies. This plate is engraved by Nolli after a drawing by Giovanni-Battista Casanova (1730–95) a Venetian who worked in Rome in the 1750s and 1760s encouraged by Mengs and Winckelmann. Knight obtained from Hamilton a single lock of hair $2\frac{1}{2}$ inches long presumably from a similar head and this he considered 'of finer sculpture than anything now extant' (MS (Bronzes), no. XLVII–10). This head, he realized, provided important evidence for the way in which such locks were cast and chased separately in elaborate Greek bronzes of the 'best period' – d'Hancarville (II, pp. 16–17) and Winckelmann (II, p. 35) had made a similar point

PRIVATE COLLECTION

James Sherriff   Plate 9
76 *The Downton Terrier*

Prov.: R. P. Knight; by descent
This manuscript terrier (that is 'register of landed property')
consists of maps drawn – clearly by the same hand – with
picturesque vignettes and rococo cartouches on vellum.
Some of the cartouches are signed by Sherriff and one or
two are dated (in every case, 1780). The volume is open
to show a view – the only one in the volume, and not,
apparently, originally a part of it – signed by Sherriff and
portraying the new bridge and house. It is in pen and ink
with wash in a style imitative of, and perhaps preparatory
for, a print. The exterior of the house was complete by
1780 and this is the earliest surviving record of it
D. P. H. LENNOX, ESQ.

d'Hancarville, Pierre François Hugues, 'Baron'
77 *Antiquités etrusques, grecques et romaines*
tirées du Cabinet de M. Hamilton envoyé
extraordinaire et plenipotentiare de S. M.
Britannique en Cour de Naples

Volume IV (Naples 1776)
The title-page of the first volume of this book is dated 1766,
those of the second, third and fourth, 1767, but as Professor
Haskell has pointed out, the second appeared in 1770 and
the third and fourth in 1776. The parallel English translation is not sustained in all volumes and by the second
volume it had been decided to publish ancient vases – for
the book was chiefly devoted to illustrating these – in the
collections of the Pope, the Grand Duke of Tuscany, the
King of France, the Prince of Biscari as well as Sir William
Hamilton. Surely the most beautiful and luxurious of all
archaeological anthologies ever published, it also set new
standards with the precision of its reproductions – standards
which were as important for the Society of Dilettanti in
England as were the ingenious speculations of d'Hancarville
in the letterpress. This volume is open to show the first
page of Chapter III with an initial letter worthy of Piranesi,
printed in black and brown inks, unsigned but identical in
style to those elsewhere in these volumes signed by C.
Pignatori (etcher) and G. Bracci (designer), together with
an etching of a group of terracotta plaques and a pair of
bronzes, the former printed in red ink, the latter hand-
tinted with a green wash, probably the work of the same
artists
VISITORS OF THE ASHMOLEAN MUSEUM, OXFORD

78 *Album of Etchings of Bronzes in the*
Collection of Charles Townley

It seems that Townley commissioned a series of etchings
of his bronzes from William Skelton (see cat. no. 91)
during the 1780s and then had these bound up for

presentation. The copies known to us all differ slightly.
Thus for instance, the one in the British Library includes a
large folding plate of items discovered at Praeneste (see no.
40) which is not present here, whereas additional material
on antiquities is included in this copy. The volume is open
at the only plate in it which is dedicated to an item in
another collection – an engraved Etruscan mirror which
Knight acquired from the Gaddi family in Florence, catalogued by Walters as showing the 'Reconciliation of
Teuthras and Augè by Aphrodite' (Knight MS (Bronzes),
lxxxix. 46 and Walters, 1899, no. 628)
TRUSTEES OF THE BRITISH MUSEUM

Plate 29
79 *An Account of the Remains of*
the Worship of Priapus lately existing at
Isernia . . .

London 1786 (privately published)
This extraordinary book is discussed in detail on pp. 50–64.
Despite the date on the title-page of 1786, it may not have
appeared until early in the following year – see British
Library Add. MS 34048, ff. 36–7 (Hamilton to Banks,
29 May 1787). The Dilettanti Society Papers contain
(vol. I, between f. 315 and f. 340) numerous references to
the making of the prints supervised by Knight between 1783
and 1786. It is opened to display the group of wax votives
presented by Hamilton to the British Museum. Fragments
of one of these fragile objects survive. The Society of
Dilettanti were discovered by the present Secretary to
possess no copy of this book, but he was able to purchase
this copy which originally belonged to Nathaniel Marchant,
the gem engraver
THE SOCIETY OF DILETTANTI

R. P. Knight   Plates 22 and 23
80 *The Landscape, a Didactic Poem*

London 1794
This poem, which is discussed on pp. 10, 47 is here open
to reveal the etching of a park 'dressed in the modern style'
which was contrasted with the same scene 'undressed'.
The idea of such a contrast was perhaps suggested by
Repton's practice in his Red Books (see cat. nos. 82 and 83).
The etchings are by Benjamin Pouncy (d. 1799), the
brother-in-law and pupil of Woollett, made after drawings
by Hearne, another pupil of Woollett, obviously under
Knight's supervision. The collaboration continued, as
Farington reported on 6 July 1794: 'called on Hearne. –
Pouncy is making one set of *finished* etchings from his
designs. The specimen is worked up to the effect of Vivares
prints [the landscape engravings of François Vivarès],
retaining a great portion of the freedom of a loose etching.
Baker, suggested this scheme to them from the specimen
of etching in Knight's poem . . .'
THE BRITISH LIBRARY

Anonymous, but supposed to be Colonel John Matthews

81 *A Sketch from the Landscape, a Didactic Poem Addressed to R. P. Knight Esq. with Notes, Illustrations and a Postscript*

London 1794

This squib was published briskly after *The Landscape* and reflects the popular controversy surrounding Knight's poem. The book is open at the title-page, which features an engraving (unsigned) of Knight emptying a chamber-pot (or 'jordan' as this vessel was then known) upon a classical cenotaph honouring 'Capability' Brown to the distress of the gardeners who, equipped with scythes, mattocks, spades and a plan are seated in its shade. The chamber-pot is a joke at the claims made by Knight for the superiority of common vessels in antiquity (cf. cat. no. 90). The end of the poem outrageously proposes that Knight should be honoured with a colossal topiary statue as the priapic god of gardens and there is a wood-engraving showing this – from behind – with two approaching ladies astonished by it, serving as a vignette

THE BRITISH LIBRARY

Humphry Repton (1752–1818)

82 *'Red Book' for Tatton Park, Cheshire*

Lit.: Stroud, pp. 78–9

Repton first visited Tatton, perhaps at the suggestion of Samuel Wyatt who was employed there as architect by

William Tatton Egerton, in early November 1791 and completed this Red Book, which has remained in the house ever since, in February 1792. The proposals which it attractively illustrates were not carried out by Repton but seem to have provided hints for a rival landscapist at a later date. The work is open to exhibit a view of the house as Wyatt hoped to complete it, seen across water and parkland disposed very much in the manner of Brown – something Knight and Price would have disliked. Knight chanced to see at a bookseller's an extract from this Red Book which Repton was proposing to use in his anthology *Sketches and Hints on Landscape Gardening*. In it Repton suggested promoting the Egerton's self-importance by putting their arms on mileposts, and Knight ridiculed this in a note to *The Landscape*

NATIONAL TRUST

Humphry Repton (1732–1818)

83 *Red Book for Attingham Park, Shropshire*

Lit.: Stroud, p. 107

The attacks on Repton by Knight and Price in the mid 1790s did not halt his success. This Red Book for Attingham Park was commissioned by the 2nd Lord Berwick in 1797 and has remained in the house ever since. In this case Repton carried out his proposals, and they survive in part. It is open to display a view of the park which would have been deemed vapid by Knight and Price; in such country, however, greater wildness would have produced untidyness rather than grandeur or richness

NATIONAL TRUST

82

Richard Payne Knight

84 *Notebook*

Prov.: R. P. Knight; by descent to Major
Kincaid-Lennox, by whom presented 1963
In two pages of this notebook (we show the first) Knight
entered an abbreviated record of the coins he acquired at
fairly regular intervals between 1785 and 1806 in which
period, if this record is complete, he expended over £3000.
He bought at auction (at Christie's for instance) and from
dealers (Miles, apparently acting for Millingen) and from
collectors who also acted as dealers (the Abbé Tersan, Sir
William Hamilton). For the two biggest purchases, see
pp. 70, 73

85 *Specimens of Antient Sculpture*   Plate 5

Volume I (London 1809)
The publication date on the cover of this volume is 1810,
but it was described as 'about to be published' in March
1808 (Cust, p. 128). It is the first of the two superb folios
sponsored by the Society of Dilettanti prepared by Knight
and Townley. It is discussed on pp. 7, 76. It is here shown
open at plate v, an engraving of Townley's head of Apollo
(cat. no. 50) by John Samuel Agar made under Knight's
direction and praised by him in the text. Few photographic
illustrations are more reliable or informative than Agar's
prints, which are the finest ever made of sculpture. The
small dotted lines unobtrusively indicate restorations, for
instance on the bridge of the nose

86 *Specimens of Antient Sculpture*

Volume II (London 1835)
1835 appears on the title-page but the plates are dated
'Feby. 1834'. This is the long-delayed sequel to no. 85.
The introductory text was by J. B. S. Morritt, who also
compiled the notes to the plates with assistance from
Christie, Hope and Westmacott and reference to Knight's
notes. All the best plates employed had been made long
before under the supervision of Knight and Townley. The
volume is open at a later one, Plate XIII, engraved by T. A.
Denn after H. Corbould with exactly the sort of meretricious
appeal which most irritated Knight. Moreover the object
illustrated, the Weddell Venus at Newby Hall, Yorkshire,
was just the class of sculpture ('heterogeneous compositions
of parts not originally belonging to each other') which was
carefully excluded from Volume I. In this case a head of
the 'Pudicitia' type had been reworked by Pacili and
matched with a restored and reworked torso of a Venus of
the Medici type acquired from the Barberini by Gavin
Hamilton (it was sold by Jenkins to William Weddell in
1765 for a fabulous sum). Morritt's scholarship was also
woefully inadequate. He corrects Knight for describing the

Lansdowne 'Antinous' as a Hermes instead of a Meleager
and believed the Medici Venus to be the type of the Cnidian!
Knight's introductory text for this volume, already published separately, was printed as an appendix, in response
to pressure probably applied by Lord Aberdeen. Morritt,
doubtless encouraged by the Society's secretary W. R.
Hamilton, clearly detested Knight. The former had been a
champion of Lord Elgin, the latter had been Elgin's private
secretary and had taken Pistrucci's side in his quarrel
with Knight (Banks Letters, XIX, ff. 269–81), indeed he
probably first circulated the story of the *Flora* to discredit
Knight (see cat. no. 19)

[PRINTS]

Charles Turner (1774–1857) after Sir Joshua
Reynolds

87 *Members of the Society of Dilettanti*

Mezzotint: 50.2 × 37.5
Lit.: Cust, pp. 221–3; Harcourt-Smith, pp. 69–75
See cat. no. 88

William Say (1768–1834) after Sir Joshua
Reynolds

88 *Members of the Society of Dilettanti*

Mezzotint: 46.4 × 37.5
Lit.: Cust, pp. 221–3; Harcourt-Smith, pp. 69–75
These prints reproduce the group portraits painted by
Reynolds between 1777 and 1779 for the Society to record
a meeting on 2 March 1777 at which Sir William Hamilton
was introduced as a new member (Plates 3 and 4). The
artist was evidently at work on the pictures in February
1778 when the Society noted with disapproval that he had
not sent back the 'toga' (Papers of the Society of Dilettanti,
I, f. 251). In cat. no. 87 Hamilton points to one of the four
volumes publishing his collection, the last of which had
appeared in the previous year (see cat. no. 77). Surrounding
him are Sir John Taylor (standing, left – see cat. no. 72),
Sir William Watkins Wynn (on the left in robes of President
of the evening), Richard Thompson of Escrick (behind
Hamilton's chair, in the robes of Arch-master), Walter
Spencer-Stanhope (conversing with the former), Stephen
Payne-Gallway of Tofts Hall, Norfolk (seated drinking),
and John Smyth of Heath Hall, Yorkshire (seated, far right).
In this print we see Lords Mulgrave, Seaforth and Car-
marthen seated at the table and, standing, Lord Dundas
(on the left), Hamilton's nephew, Charles Greville, John
Charles Crowle (Secretary, in robes of office) and on the
extreme right Joseph Banks (the next secretary). Each man
painted paid the artist £35. Brinsley Ford has corrected the
peculiar notion that the standing men in cat. no. 88 are
making lewd gestures in reference to priapic symbolism.

They are clearly inspecting gems. Exactly what is displayed so meaningfully by Sir John Taylor is, however, a mystery. The pictures exhibit some of the most active spirits (as well as some of the merely affluent members) in the Society in the period immediately previous to Knight's involvement with it

TRUSTEES OF THE BRITISH MUSEUM

T. Medland after Humphry Repton (1752–1818)

89 *Trade card*

Engraving: 9.5× 11.0

This elegant card, copies of which are often found in Repton's Red Books, is an eloquent testimony to Repton's extensive practice for which see cat. no. 83

DOROTHY STROUD

James Gillray (1756–1815)

90 *A Cognocenti contemplating ye Beauties of ye Antique*

Etching, hand coloured: 35.0× 25.7
Inscribed: *Feby. 11th 1801 by H. Humphrey 27 St. James's Street*
Lit.: George, VIII, no. 9753

Sir William Hamilton's interests in ancient art are here ridiculed together with his ignorance of or compliance in his wife's liaison with Lord Nelson. The portraits of the couple, entitled Cleopatra and Mark Antony, are rudely linked by the horns of Apis. In other pictures Vesuvius erupts and the derelict, cuckolded Emperor Claudius looks the other way – antlers crowning the frame. The old connoisseur is shown contemplating a defaced bust of Lais, the most celebrated courtesan of the ancient world. Around him are the sorts of erotic, exotic, archaic and grotesque curiosities with which Hamilton in the previous decade had supplied Knight. Nelson and the Hamiltons were entertained by Knight at Downton in the summer of the year following

TRUSTEES OF THE BRITISH MUSEUM

William Skelton (1763–1848)

91 *Charles Townley's Visiting Card*

Engraving, 6.8× 9.9
Lit.: J. T. Smith, I, p. 165n

Smith wrote that Townley was 'so enamoured with his favourite busts of Isis [*Clytie*, cat. no. 59], Pericles, and Homer, the most perfect specimens of ancient art, that he employed the hand of Skelton, Sharpe's favourite pupil, to engrave them upon a small plate, which he used as his visiting card. This elegant performance, always considered a great rarity, was left only at the houses of particular persons, so that an impression of it is now greatly coveted by the collectors of such *bijoux*'

SIMON TOWNELEY, ESQ.

William Skelton (1763–1848) after Henry Howard (1769–1847)

92 *Plate from 'Specimens'*

'Proof from acqua fortis' (i.e. etched first state) of engraving: 33.0× 23.5
See cat. no. 93

TRUSTEES OF THE BRITISH MUSEUM

William Skelton (1763–1848) after Henry Howard (1767–1847)

93 *Plate from 'Specimens'*

'Proof before the last finishing touches' of engraving: 33.0× 23.5

This and 92 are proofs of Plate XXX of *Specimens*, Volume I (86) illustrating the Petworth Athlete (no. 49) which have been preserved among Townley's papers in the British Museum. The first is dated 1801 and the second 'Feb. 1802'. In the preparation of plates for *Specimens* Skelton worked under Townley's direction and Agar under Knight's. Of this plate Knight observed, justly, that it 'adequately represented . . . the beauty, delicacy and simplicity in the character and expression of the features; and the luxuriance and elegance in the composition and distribution of the hair', but he added that 'the mixture of sharpness and softness in the one, and of elasticity, crispness and flexibility in the other, cannot be conveyed in any such imitation'

TRUSTEES OF THE BRITISH MUSEUM

William Skelton (1763–1848) after Henry Howard (1769–1847)

94 *Plate from 'Specimens'*

Engraving with etching: 14.7× 21.2

This neo-Attic relief of a youth with a horse and his dog in Townley's collection (A. H. Smith, III, no. 2206) was discovered in Hadrian's villa by Gavin Hamilton in 1769 and was believed by Knight and Townley to represent one of the *Dioscuri*. It cost Townley £40 (Towneley Hall Papers, DDTo, Box 46, uncatalogued). Knight supposed it a Greek original rather than an archaizing piece and related the style of relief to the coins of Selinus and Tarentum for its 'rigid severity' and 'long, bony and meagre' forms. He was also interested in the flattened quality of the relief, which he compared with that of the Parthenon frieze and considered a style devised for the decoration of architecture. He is here developing the reflections of d'Hancarville on the 'sorte de relief applati' of the Portland Vase (II, p. 85 and pp. 143–4n). The existence of this impression in Townley's papers shows that the plate was ready before he died in 1805, although only published in 1809 as Plate XIV of *Specimens*, vol. I

TRUSTEES OF THE BRITISH MUSEUM

William Skelton (1763–1848) after Henry Howard (1769–1847)

95 *Plate from 'Specimens'*

Engraving with some etching: 27.5 × 19.8

The existence of this impression in Townley's papers in the British Museum shows that the plate was made before his death in 1805 and over thirty years before it appeared in the second volume of *Specimens* (as plate lviii) when the text opposite it disowned responsibility for its selection, attributing this to Knight. It shows the Bronze Ceres with a Calf at Strawberry Hill which Knight had already illustrated in his 1786 *Discourse* (VIII, fig. 1) and which he believed exhibited Ceres 'as the personified principle of the productive power of the Earth' (1818, pp. 26–7). The bronze was sold at auction in 1842 to a Mr Cope for £73 10s and has not since been traced (Michaelis, p. 69, note 172). Horace Walpole, who owned it, was no admirer of the Dilettanti or of Knight's theories but agreed with their polite request to illustrate it. He regretted that he could not see Knight's bronzes 'which I excessively admire' (Farington, 22 April 1794; 24 July 1796)

George Cruikshank (1792–1878)

96 *The Antiquarian Society*

Etching, hand-coloured: 17.5 × 36.55. Published 1 June 1812 by M. Jones
Lit.: George, IX, no. 11952

Lord Aberdeen is shown inviting a largely uninterested Society to examine a 'curious relique of Antiquity' inscribed 'K.I.S.S. / .M.Y. / Rs'. He had just succeeded as President Sir Henry Englefield who as a Catholic was disqualified from office (he is here identified by the rosary on his shoulder and is shown lusting over the bust of a negress). Before Englefield the Duke of Norfolk was a highly unsatisfactory President. He is shown fast asleep on the left. Knight, who is also on the left and identified by a reference to his work on Priapus, helped Aberdeen take control but in so doing referred to the great power exercised in all the learned societies by Sir Joseph Banks, who stands wearing his star on the left behind the stunted Flaxman who expounds the Bible to the Royal Librarian Frederick Barnard, then Vice-President. Knight mentioned that the Society was 'thoroughly gothicized' and among its most active members was the great historian of Gothic architecture John Carter (here identified by a 'scrap . . . for Gentleman's Magazine'). The opposition of Flaxman and Knight may be intentional. Flaxman did not admire Knight's bronzes (Farington, 22 Dec. 1795) and Knight did not esteem Flaxman (Farington, 3 April 1816) — although his kinsmen the Knight's of Wolverley employed him, also his father

[THE SICILIAN EXPEDITION]

Charles Gore (1729–1807)

97 *Syracuse from the Ruins of Olympeion, with the Remains of the Temple of Jupiter*

Watercolour over pencil: pen and ink: 37.2 × 18.8
Inscribed in pen and ink by Knight (?): *Syracuse*
Prov.: Payne Knight Bequest (Oo.4–3)

The silhouette of the city in the background is carefully outlined in pen and ink and seems to support the status of no. 97 as a finished work, despite the sketchy execution in foreground and sky. Two similar views (Oo.4–24, 25) of the ruins at Agrigentum and a finished watercolour of the scene shown here (Weimar, Goethe-Nationalmuseum, Th.Scr.2.2³, no. 73) are less evocative of the melancholy associations of the scenery, described by Knight in his diary (ff. 60–1)

Charles Gore (1729–1807)   Plate 8

98 *The Lipari Islands from the North*

Watercolour over pencil: 44.9 × 17.1
Inscribed in pen and ink by J. Ph. Hackert: *L'isles de Stromboli, Panaria, La Saline: prise de côte de Nord douze Miles de distance en voyant la Stromboletta. 1777*
Prov.: Payne Knight Bequest (Oo.4–5)

This view of the Lipari Islands is one of the two which Payne Knight chose as illustrations for his diary (Oo.4–5, 6). Twelve related watercolours are today preserved in the Goethe-Nationalmuseum, Weimar (Th.Scr.2.2³ 2–13), together with Gore's other collections. It must have been in the period of close co-operation on the Sicilian drawings after the party's return to Rome (see Chapter Two, note 69) that Hackert inscribed Gore's views, presumably to record their place in the context of Knight's diary

Jakob Philipp Hackert (1737–1807)

99 *Temple at Segesta*

Watercolour over pencil; gouache: 44.5 × 33.1 (including a 68 mm wide additional strip on the right side)
Inscribed in pen and ink by the artist: *Temple à Segeste en Sicile 1777 Ph. Hackert f.*
Prov.: Payne Knight Bequest (Oo.4–7)
Lit.: Kronig, 1979, p. 367

Hackert enhances the monumentality of the temple by a close viewpoint and a deliberate omission of the surrounding hills (which were painted over in gouache). His colouring is lively. The detail is meticulous — his attitude is

99

obviously akin to that of the figures he includes, measuring and recording the temple. Gore's view of the building (Oo.4—5) is in subdued colours, carefully executed, emphasizing spatial and atmospheric effects rather than topographical and archaeological facts and the monumentality of the central motif, so important to his companion

? John Robert Cozens (1752—97)

100 *Temple at Segesta*

Watercolour over pencil; pen and ink: 37.0× 22.8
Prov.: Payne Knight Bequest (Oo.4—8)
Lit.: Bell and Girtin, no. 105 and introduction p. ii
The attribution of this watercolour to J. R. Cozens based,

according to the 1845 catalogue, on an inscription on the original mount has been questioned by Francis Hawcroft. The weak execution, ill-defined spatial relations and clumsy composition are, indeed, not convincing when compared with Cozens's finished Swiss views (which may, however, have been completed much later than the original sketches of 1776) (see cat. nos. 129—32). Also, the fourteen columns of the long side of the temple have here been increased by three, an archaeological error probably due to a misinterpretation of a watercolour of the same subject by Gore (Weimar, Goethe-Nationalmuseum Th.Scr.2.2.3, no. 55), where the columns are indistinctly drawn. Both versions would presumably have been made after a common model, probably in Rome, when Cozens's style was not yet homogeneous. If this was a later discarded sketch for the view, which Knight may have kept for the motif rather than its quality, the attribution to Cozens could well be correct

Thomas Hearne (1744–1817)   Plate 9

101 *Ruins of the Great Temple at Selinus with Two Male Figures*

Watercolour over pencil: 37.6 × 23.2
Signed by the artist at L.L. border: *Hearne*
Prov.: Payne Knight Bequest (Oo.4–13)

The fragments seen here are the same as on the right-hand side of Gore's *Ruins of Selinus* (cat. no. 103), as can be gathered from the two upright column stumps in the centre. The view is unlikely to have been deliberately reversed for engraving. They appear, rather, to be seen from the opposite direction, from the West. The broken capital in the front may well have been introduced into the scene as a picturesque motive. It appears separately in another of Gore's sketches, (Oo.4–11) and was also copied and combined with other fragments in Hearne's *Ruins* with one figure (Oo.4–12)

TRUSTEES OF THE BRITISH MUSEUM

Jakob Philipp Hackert (1737–1807)

102 *Ruins of the Great Temple at Selinus with Two Goats in the Foreground*

Watercolour over pencil: 23.6 × 38.7
Prov.: Payne Knight Bequest (Oo.4–14)
Lit.: Wilton 1971, no. 27; Krönig, 1979, p. 374, ill. 14

Hackert produced several similar views of the ruins at Selinunte (see Krönig, ill. 12–15), in pencil, pen and ink and watercolour. The motifs were presumably first recorded after nature and the pencil outlines later reworked in the studio, where he also used them in various combinations for his paintings (see cat. no. 105). The position of the fragments depicted here is controversial (Wilton, Temple F; Krönig, Temple G)

TRUSTEES OF THE BRITISH MUSEUM

Charles Gore (1729–1807)

103 *Ruins of Selinus with Two Oxen in the Foreground*

Watercolour over pencil: 37.0 × 22.0
Inscribed in pen and ink by Hackert (?): *Les Ruines de Silinus. 1777*
Prov.: Payne Knight Bequest (Oo.4–16)

The Great Temple (Temple G) is here seen from the north-east. The continuation of the scene and the site of the eastern Temples to which it belongs is shown in an appropriate watercolour by Gore (Oo.4–15). Both formed a single view as in the still coherent views of the same scene by Gore in Weimar (Goethe-Nationalmuseum, Th.Scr.2.2.³, no. 57), and a copy by Thomas Hearne (Oo.4–29). The site is also shown in three large illustrations (up to 90 × 35) by Gore (Oo.4–19/20) and Hackert (Oo.4–17/18) from different directions and including the ruins of the Acropolis

and details like the column stumps on the right appear in several other views (see cat. no. 101). All testify to the great care with which the party recorded the complicated archaeological evidence

TRUSTEES OF THE BRITISH MUSEUM

Thomas Hearne (1744–1817)

104 *Sepulchre at Agrigentum*

Watercolour over pencil; pen and ink: 44.7 × 27.0
Signed in pen and ink by the artist, L.L. corner: *Hearne*
Prov.: Payne Knight Bequest (Oo.4–23)
Lit.: W. Ehrlich, p. 117–36.

Payne Knight discusses the controversial date of the Sepulchre shown on the left, in his diary (ff. 44–5). It is here seen from the west, with the temples of Concord and Juno Lacinia (cat. nos. 105–7) on the hills in the background. Two finished watercolours by Charles Gore (B.M. 1927–7.12.4 and Weimar, Goethe-Nationalmuseum, Th.Scr.2.2³, no. 63) illustrate exactly the same view – with slight alterations to the foreground and the figures in the British Museum version. It cannot be determined whether Gore produced two finished watercolours, one of which was given to Hearne to copy, or whether all three were made after a common model. In the latter case Gore probably produced his second version after Hearne's and including the artist's 'improvements' of his own view

TRUSTEES OF THE BRITISH MUSEUM

Jakob Phillipp Hackert (1737–1807)

105 *Temple of Juno Lacinia at Agrigentum*

Watercolour over pencil, pen and ink; squared: 45.2 × 33.9
Inscribed in pen and ink by the artist: *Temple de Junon Lucine à Girgenti. 1777 f. P. Hackert*
Prov.: Payne Knight Bequest (Oo.4–28)
Lit.: Krönig, 1979, p. 368

The watercolours are here applied over a pen and ink underdrawing. Hackert's characteristically bright colouring (see cat. no. 99) while appropriately illustrating the evenly-lit southern scenery, lacks Gore's atmospheric sensitivity (see cat. no. 107). The temple is seen from the north-east and the fragmented columns rise effectively against the sky. Hackert used the motive of the temple – from a slightly different angle – for several paintings, executed after the journey (see Krönig 1979, ill. 3–6 'View of Mount Etna', 1778 exh. J. Böhler, Munich, June–Sept. 1966; and later in: 'Italian Landscape, 1801', Sale Lepke, Berlin, 24–6 Feb. 1973). The motif also appears in F. Morelli's prints after Hackert

TRUSTEES OF THE BRITISH MUSEUM

Thomas Hearne (1744–1817)

106 *Temple said to be of Juno at Agrigentum*

Watercolour over pencil; India ink: 43.6× 27.3
Prov.: Payne Knight Bequest (Oo.4–29)

Hearne's watercolour shows the south-west corner of the temple, which is also depicted in Gore's version (cat. no. 107) but from a greater distance. Here the ridge of the hill on which the temple is situated is emphasized by the inclusion of the steep slope on the left and the reactions of the figures to the prospect. Hearne's characteristic use of contrasting areas of light and shade further enhances the picturesque scenery described in Knight's Diary (f. 41). The architectural details are at the same time carefully recorded – even stressed – as in the corrosion of the columns in the foreground, probably intended as an additional hint for the engraver. Although there is no proof that Hearne's watercolours were made for this purpose, a comparison with the similarly finished series of watercolours the artist produced for the *Antiquities of Great Britain* seems to support this conjecture

Charles Gore (1729–1807)

107 *Temples said to be of Juno and Concord at Agrigentum*

Watercolour over pencil: 41.8× 19.2
Inscribed in pen and ink by Knight (?): *Temple of Juno Lucina*
Prov.: Payne Knight Bequest (Oo.4–30)

The temple of Juno Lacinia (Temple D) is seen from the south-west, with the Temple of Concord (Temple F) in the far background on the left and Agrigento on the right. It is surprising that Gore, contrary to factual evidence and representations in a number of paintings by Hackert (see cat. no. 105) and a version of the view by Hearne (cat. no. 106) omitted the stepped base of the temple. Archaeological discrepancies like this are rare in Hackert's and Gore's oeuvre. It may, however, be that Gore made the watercolour after a sketch showing only the elevation of the temple and was uncertain of the foreground, as may also be indicated by its unfinished state

Charles Gore (1729–1807)

108 *Temple said to be of Juno Lacinia at Agrigento*

Watercolour over pencil: 42.0× 22.6
Prov.: Payne Knight Bequest (Oo.4–31)

Gore has chosen a slightly more distant viewpoint than Hackert (cat. no. 109) in order to define the setting of the temple. His colouring is – again – subdued, a fact, which may well be due to his extensive use of the camera obscura, testified to by several respective notes on the drawings in Weimar. The English Lord in Goethe's *Wahlverwandtschaften*, for whom Gore was the prototype, was '. . . occupied most of the day by taking picturesque views of the park with the help of a dark box, a practice he had followed for several years on his extensive travels . . .'. The foreground may have been left unfinished deliberately to allow Hearne to introduce figures or other picturesque motifs.

108

Jakob Philipp Hackert (1737–1807)   Plate 10

109 *Inside of the Cavern called the 'Ear of Dionysius' at Syracuse*

Sepia: 33.7×44.4
Inscribed in pen and ink by the artist: *L'Oreille de Dionise près de Siracuse. Ph. Hackert f. 1777*
Prov.: Payne Knight Bequest Oo.4–33
Lit.: Krönig, 1968

The 'Ear of Dionysius' (see pp. 25–6) is also illustrated in two watercolours by Thomas Hearne (Oo.4–34, 35), one of them in conjunction with Hackert (Oo.4–35). The latter shows the outside of the cavern and is listed as being 'begun by Hackert and finished by Hearne'. A sepia drawing of the latter also by Hackert is today in Berlin (Kupferstich-kabinett, Staatliche Museen Preussischer Kulturbesitz, Berlin-Ost, Hackert no. 229). While the artist's sepias may well have served as models for watercolours, like Hearne's, they must also have been sold independently, which would agree well with Hackert's notorious commercial acumen (see Jones, p. 118)

TRUSTEES OF THE BRITISH MUSEUM

John Robert Cozens (1752–97)   Plate 11

110 *Mount Etna from the Grotta del Capro*

Watercolour over pencil and scratching out: 47.8×35.4
Prov.: Payne Knight Bequest (Oo.4–38)
Lit.: Bell and Girtin, no. 107, pl. VIII a, b; Wilton, 1980, p. 42, no. 95

The watercolour was first published by Bell and Girtin together with a sketch by Charles Gore (Weimar, Goethe-Nationalmuseum Th.Scr.2.2³, no. 93), upon which it is based. The differences between original and copy show the complete freedom with which Cozens transformed his models: the scale of the figures is diminished, that of the surrounding landscape and the distant mountain exaggerated, and the moonlight effect is strongly emphasized. An outline drawing in pencil (Soane Museum, Cozens Album, no. 13) represents the intermediate stage. Cozens presumably made it after Gore's sketch, when the party had returned to Rome and produced the finished watercolour later. The scene shows the travellers' nocturnal rest in the 'Grotta del Capro' during the ascent of Mount Etna as described in Knight's Diary (f. 76)

TRUSTEES OF THE BRITISH MUSEUM

Charles Gore (1729–1807) and   Colour Plate I
Thomas Hearne (1744–1817)

111 *Mount Etna from the Convent of Nicolosi*

Watercolour over pencil: 44.1×27.9
Prov.: Payne Knight Bequest (Oo.4–39)

According to the 1845 catalogue of the Payne Knight Bequest where an inscription from the original mount is quoted, this scene was 'taken May 28th 1777. C.G. delin. foreground finished by T. Hearne'. Compared with a finished watercolour by Gore of the same subject in Weimar (Goethe-Nationalmuseum, Th.Scr.2.2³, no. 106) in which the left foreground and the group of figures are different from this version, this watercolour seems to have been outlined and partly coloured (in the background) by Gore, while the foreground up to the stone wall was left for Hearne to finish. This must have been common practice, as another view begun by Hackert (Payne Knight Bequest, Oo.4–35) was also finished by Hearne and the left foreground in Gore's *Temple of Juno* (cat. no. 108) may also have been left unfinished for this reason

TRUSTEES OF THE BRITISH MUSEUM

Jackob Philipp Hackert (1737–1807)

112 *Mount Etna from Taormina*

Watercolour: 56.8×38.6
Signed and dated by the artist at the lower border: *Ph. Hackert 1777* and top left-hand corner: *L'Etna prise à Taormine*
Prov.: Payne Knight Bequest Oo.4–48
Lit.: Bell and Girtin, no. 106

It was this watercolour – compared with Cozens's *Mount Etna from a Rock of Lava* (Oo.4–9) – which convinced Bell and Girtin that Hackert must have influenced Cozens's method of colouring and initiated the younger artist's 'first attempts in full colour' (p. 24). It is more likely that Cozens was influenced by Hackert's 'handling of landscape masses seen across a wide space', as Andrew Wilton has suggested (1971, p. 54, no. 147)

TRUSTEES OF THE BRITISH MUSEUM

Thomas Hearne (1744–1817)

113 *Citadel of Cefalù*

Watercolour over pencil: 44.9×27.1 (cut on right margin)
Inscribed in pen and ink by Knight (?): *View of Cephalu North Coast of Sicily between Milazzo and Pale(rmo)*
Prov.: Payne Knight Bequest (Oo.4–41)

The watercolour may well have included a massive tree on the left which must have been cut off (see inscription). This tree appears in a version of the same scene by Charles Gore (Goethe-Nationalmuseum, Th.Scr.2.2.³, no. 24) which seems to have been made from the same model as Hearne's. Knight describes his unsuccessful search for the ruins of 'Alusa & Cephaladis', mentioned by Fazello, in his Diary (f. 20)

TRUSTEES OF THE BRITISH MUSEUM

[THE LANDSCAPE AT DOWNTON CASTLE]

Thomas Hearne (1744–1817)

114 *The 'Alpine Bridge' on the Teme at Downton*

Pen and ink with grey and brown wash: 32.1×34.9

Prov.: W. Smith by whom bequeathed December 1876

Hearne was apprenticed in 1765 to the engraver William Woollet and whilst still employed by him exhibited, between 1766 and 1770, one print and a number of watercolour drawings at the Free Society. He travelled to the Leeward Islands in the West Indies as a draughtsman to the Governor in 1771, sending back drawings of Antigua for exhibition at the Society of Artists. On his return in 1774 he established a reputation as a skilled topographical artist with the *Antiquities of Great Britain* published in parts from 1778 onwards and collected in two volumes in 1807 for which he supplied fifty-two of the eighty-four illustrations (most of which were engraved by William Byrne) — original watercolours for this were exhibited by Hearne at the Society of Artists between 1777 and 1783. He was in the same period engaged by Knight in connection with the making of copies (surely in preparation for publication) of views made in Sicily (see no. 106). Hearne exhibited watercolour drawings regularly at the Royal Academy between 1781 and 1793 (thereafter only once, in 1806) and in this period became an intimate friend of Dr Monro and Sir George Beaumont, and was revered by the younger watercolour artists, especially Edridge. In 1785 he exhibited a 'View upon the River Teme at Downton, the Seat of R. P. Knight Esq.' (586) which must have been at least based on a drawing made in 1784. In 1786 he showed four other views under the same title (453, 469, 574, and 588) and in subsequent years views of Bredwardine, Moccas Court and Ludlow Castle all in the same neighbourhood. This drawing clearly relates to a watercolour made at Downton (cat. no. 115, x). The bridge is discussed on p. 47

VICTORIA AND ALBERT MUSEUM

Thomas Hearne (1744–1817)

115 *Twelve Views of the River Teme at Downton*

Watercolour with pencil

Prov.: R. P. Knight; by descent to the present owner. Denis Lennox has kindly supplied the following topographical descriptions:

(i) The Castle Bridge viewed from downstream on the south bank of the Teme. The foreground oak tree may still be seen
33.8×49.3
Signed (L.L.): *Hearne 1784*

(ii) Downton Castle viewed from the south bank of the Teme immediately downstream from Castle Bridge Plate 13
34.0×48.5
Signed (L.R.): *Hearne 1785*

(iii) 'The Rock' viewed from near the 'Roman Bath' on the north bank of the Teme. The path on the bank on the right survives and some steps mark the site of the building which appears by the river bank here
49.3×33.5
Signed (L.L.): on contemporary mount: *Hearne 1785*

(iv) The Castle Bridge seen from the north bank above the Ladies' Dingle, with the Clee Hill in the distance
34.2×48.8
Signed (L.L.): *Hearne 1785*

(v) View of the west end of the gorge from near where it is now crossed by the aquaduct
34.0×49.5
Signed (L.R. of centre): *Hearne 1785*

115(iii)

115(i)

115(vi)

(vi) The overhanging boulder (visible amongst the rocks in the distance of (v)) with the Bow Bridge beyond. This bridge, still in use today, was the old packhorse bridge serving the main road between Leintwardine and Ludlow. It replaced the ford, shown here by wading cattle, downstream
34.8 × 49.5
Signed (L.R.): *Hearne 1785*

(vii) View from below Pool's farm on the eminence above the 'Roman Bath' looking south-east
34.6 × 49.8
Signed (L.L.): *Hearne 1785*

(viii) The Castle Bridge seen from beneath the Castle from near the postern gate on the north bank of the Teme
31.2 × 33.4
Signed (L.L.) on contemporary mount: *Hearne 1786*

(ix) The view upstream towards the gorge from the south bank a little upstream from the Castle Bridge near where the path enters the cave which Knight made. The brook which runs down Ladies' Dingle joins the river in the middle distance   Colour Plate VIII
48.6 × 34.4
Signed (L.L. of centre): *Hearne 1786*

(x) The 'Alpine Bridge'. The exact location of this structure is uncertain but it must have been downstream from the Haymill and it appears below the 'Roman Bath' in Owen's watercolour (cat. no. 117), and may also be discerned in a watercolour of 'the Gorge at Downton' by Lady Harriet Clive (daughter of Knight's neighbour the hon. Robert Clive) which hangs at Scotney Castle, Kent (reproduced, in reverse, *Country Life*, 10 May 1979, p. 1441)   Plate 28
30.5 × 33.5
Signed (L.L.) on restored patch of paper: *Hearne*

(xi) The Haymill previous to its extension
33.1 × 49.4
Signed (L.L.): *Hearne 1784*

(xii) The Haymill after extension. The old stone building seen in (xi) remains but the lean-to is now replaced by a handsome wing with ample windows adorned with flower-pots and birdcages. Frolicking dogs remain but not the washing, the woman feeding chickens and the man axing logs. The mill was still active in this century but is no longer standing
33.5 × 49.2 (sight)

For Hearne and for his watercolours of Downton shown at the Academy see cat. no. 114. There are others apparently from the same series: one dated 1785 and of similar size (33.0 × 49.5) in Knight's bequest to the British Museum (Oo.5–38) and for another see cat. no. 116. The Philadelphia Museum of Art possess a watercolour drawing of the Iron Forge at Downton – this seems to be related to an etching by Pouncy entitled *An Iron Work at Downton*, and

dated 1796. There are also autograph repetitions and variations of some of the works exhibited above. A version of (i) but measuring 21.0 × 30.0 was sold at Sotheby's, 28 Nov. 1974; one of (iii) in a private collection is reproduced as plate 12 of Andrew Wilton's *British Watercolours 1750 to 1850*, London 1977

D. P. H. LENNOX, ESQ.

Thomas Hearne (1744–1817)

116 *An Oak Tree*

Brown pen and watercolour: 50.6 × 34.3
Inscribed in ink L.L.: *Hearne*
Prov.: Payne Knight Bequest (Oo.5–37)
Possibly a view at Downton, see cat. no. 115

TRUSTEES OF THE BRITISH MUSEUM

116

William Owen (1769–1825) Plate 24

117 *The 'Roman Bath' near Downton Castle*

Watercolour: 29.5×40.0
Signed (L. Centre): *Wm. Owen 1790* (possibly
1796 or 1798)
Prov.: R. P. Knight; by descent

Owen was the nephew of Knight's butler. As a portraitist
he was patronized by the Towneley family. He also painted
portraits of Thomas Andrew Knight and his wife. The
curious building shown here, which still hangs precariously
above the Teme gorge due south from Pool's Farm, is the
most important piece of landscape architecture associated
with Knight. It consisted of three interconnected chambers.
The principal one here in which the pensive traveller rests
has now fallen in: the massive curved stones forming an
arch may be seen on the ground. The other two chambers
were beehive domes. The oldest (it has a wooden hat here),
made of stone with spars lining the interior, served as a
bath house with steps down to a basin into which the
spring once ran but now trickles. The other was presumably
more recent because it is of brick. It has fallen in so that
there is no trace of the gothic window just visible here (the
chimney stack, however, survives). The surrounding em-
bankment has broken up and the vegetation is much
denser. The stump of the large overhanging tree may still
be seen

D. P. H. LENNOX, ESQ.

[OTHER DRAWINGS AND WATERCOLOURS]

Sir George Beaumont, Bart. (1753–1827)

118 *Album of Drawings entitled 'Sketches from Nature'*

Prov.: Presented by Lady Beaumont in 1829 to
Anne Sturges Bourne; presented to the
Whitworth by Lady Bonham-Carter 1974

The volume consists of drawings in black chalk on blue/
grey paper (some with white hightening). Several are from
'fancy' (one of these is inspired by Wordsworth's *Peter Bell*)
but most are composed after sketches made out of doors
at or near Benarth, Conway, the house they took for the
summers of 1800 (when Knight was one of their guests),
1801 and 1802 and at Coleorton, their country seat – but
also in the Lake District and elsewhere. They display
Beaumont's skilful mimicry of both Gainsborough and
Richard Wilson. The volume is open at f. 58, one of several
views of a dramatic waterfall, 'Between Llanwrst and
Conway' – perhaps the very one about six miles from
Llanwrst which Price mentions in a letter to Beaumont as
having been especially admired by Knight (Coleorton
Papers MA 1581–99). This is inscribed 'Coleorton Wednes-
day Aug. 1/1804'. F. 27 (not displayed) is a drawing made
at Cheltenham in 1802 of a yew tree sketched at Foxley,
Uvedale Price's seat, for which see cat. no. 139

WHITWORTH ART GALLERY, MANCHESTER UNIVERSITY

John Brown (1752–87)

119 *Charles Townley*

Black chalk on vellum: 12.2×8.5
Prov.: Presented by K. M. Guichard 1972

Brown was a Scottish miniaturist and engraver whom
Townley may have first met in Italy. Susan Bourne has
discovered (in the personal account book of Charles
Townley, Towneley Hall Papers, DDTo) the records of
payments to Brown for 'drawings from my marbles' made
in 1785 and 1787 by Townley. The marble bust might
be the Homer which is placed behind the sitter in Zoffany's
portrait but if this is Townley he is at least ten years
younger here

NATIONAL GALLERY OF SCOTLAND

Agostino Carracci (1557–1602)

120 *Sheet of Caricatures*

Brown pen and ink: 20.1×13.5
Prov.: J. Richardson Senr. (Lugt, no. 2185);
Benjamin West (Lugt, no. 419); Payne Knight
Bequest (Pp.3–11)

This drawing, comparable to other sheets of caricatures
and studies of limbs by Agostino, would have been an
interesting acquistion for a collector of Old Master drawings
who intended to show something of the history of 'carica-
tura' in his collection

TRUSTEES OF THE BRITISH MUSEUM

Annibale Carracci (1560–1609)

121 *Cartoon of a Helmsman*

Charcoal on blue paper: 45.8×44.4 (made up of
three pieces of paper and repaired)
Prov.: Lord Spencer; his sale Philipe's, 11 June,
1811, lot 146 as Annibale Carracci, *A Man
Rowing a Boat*, part of a cartoon, bt. Knight for
£1 2s 0d; Payne Knight Bequest (Oo.3–6)
Lit.: Martin, p. 246, no. 28

This is a cartoon for the helmsman in the lunette fresco of
Ulysses and the Sirens in the Farnese Palace, Rome.
At least three other drawings can be identified for this
composition – Royal Library, Windsor (for the three
Sirens); Louvre, Paris (for the oarsman); Louvre, Paris (for
the helmsman – which seems to be a study from the life on
which this is based). Subsequent to entering the British
Museum it was reattributed to Tintoretto until correctly
identified by Popham

TRUSTEES OF THE BRITISH MUSEUM

Claude Gellée le Lorrain (1600–82)

122 *View with Trees*

Chalk, brown and pink wash: 21.6 × 32.3
Prov.: Payne Knight Bequest (Oo.6–114)
Lit.: Roethlisberger, no. 177
Dated by Roethlisberger 1635–40
TRUSTEES OF THE BRITISH MUSEUM

Claude Gellée le Lorrain (1600–82)

123 *Trees in Vigna Madama*

Chalk, pen, brown and grey wash: 33.0 × 22.5
Inscribed at bottom:
*Claudio fecit / facto a Vigne
Madama* and 22
Prov.: Payne Knight Bequest (Oo.7–224)
Lit.: Roethlisberger, no. 295
A nature drawing, dated by Roethlisberger to *c.* 1638 and
stated to be from the Campagna book
TRUSTEES OF THE BRITISH MUSEUM

Claude Gellée le Lorrain (1600–82)

124 *Coast with Sailing Boats*

Pen and brown wash: 23.6 × 17.5
Prov.: Payne Knight Bequest (Oo.6–100)
Lit.: Roethlisberger, no. 281
A nature drawing, dated by Roethlisberger *c.* 1638
TRUSTEES OF THE BRITISH MUSEUM

Claude Gellée le Lorrain (1600–82)

125 *Landscape*

Pen, brown, grey and pink washes: 32.0 × 22.2
Inscribed L.R. *Claudio fecit*, followed by 4 *(2?)*
Prov.: Payne Knight Bequest (Oo.7–230)
Lit.: Roethlisberger, no. 395
The drawing is from Claude's Campagna book, dated by
Roethlisberger 1638–9. The recto is an exceptionally
beautiful nature drawing, the verso contains several
sketches of the port at Civita Vecchia
TRUSTEES OF THE BRITISH MUSEUM

123

125

Claude Gellée le Lorrain   Colour Plate IX
(1600–82)

126 *Wooded View*

Pen, brown, grey and pink wash on blue paper:
22.4 × 32.7
Inscribed in pen, verso: *Claudio fecit Roma*
Prov.: Payne Knight Bequest (Oo.7–190)
Lit.: Roethlisberger, no. 587
Dated by Roethlisberger, who describes it as 'characteristic
of drawings done as an end in themselves', to *c.* 1645
TRUSTEES OF THE BRITISH MUSEUM

Claude Gellée le Lorrain (1600–82)

127 *View of La Crescenza*

Pen and brown ink: 19.6 × 25.7
Lit.: Roethlisberger, no. 669; Kitson, pp. 126–7
This sheet (LV 118) is the first of five pure pen drawings in
the Liber Veritatis, Claude's celebrated book of 195
drawings recording most of his major compositions. Under
the terms of the artist's will the book remained with the
artist's heirs; after they had died out it was briefly in the
possession of a Parisian jeweller in the early eighteenth
century and by 1728 was in the collection of the second
Duke of Devonshire, from whom it passed by descent until
it was allocated to the British Museum in 1957 in lieu of
death duty. The painting (Plate 21) which this drawing
records was acquired by Knight in 1806 and remained at
Downton Castle until 1978, when it was sold to the
Metropolitan Museum, New York. As Kitson and others
have noted, the view depicted of the Casale della Crescenza
(a property belonging to the Crescenzi family to the north
of Rome) bears a curious resemblance to Downton Castle,
and its acquisition must have been exceptionally satisfying
to Knight, who was a lifelong admirer of Claude
TRUSTEES OF THE BRITISH MUSEUM

Claude Gellée le Lorrain (1600–82)

128 *Coast View with Aeneas Hunting*

Chalk, grey and brown wash, pen, white
heightening: 24.1 × 35.6
Inscribed L.C.: *CLAVDIO G / F.IV. Rom /. 1669*
Prov.: Payne Knight Bequest (Oo.8–256)
Lit.: Roethlisberger, no. 991.
One of four surviving preparatory drawings for the painting
of 1672 of the same subject (LV 180, Brussels, Musée des
Beaux-Arts)
TRUSTEES OF THE BRITISH MUSEUM

129 *over page* →

John Robert Cozens (1752–97)

129 *The Reichenbach between Grindelwald and the Valley of Oberhasli*

Black pen, grey wash and watercolour: 21.1 × 35.6
Numbered 20 on verso
Prov.: Payne Knight; John Towneley, sale, 1–15
May 1816 (394) bt. Woodburn; Hon. Rowland
Allanson-Winn
Lit.: Bell and Girtin, no. 20; Hawcroft, 1971, no. 5
This and the following three drawings belong to a problema-
tical group which probably belonged to an album executed
by Cozens as a record for Knight of his journey through
Switzerland in 1776 en route to Italy and Sicily. Two
pieces of unsubstantiated evidence point to Cozens and
Knight travelling together on this Swiss tour. Roget
(I, p. 161), without having seen the volume of fifty-seven
Swiss views formerly in the John Towneley Collection,
claimed that it bore the inscription 'Views in Swisserland,
a present from R. P. Knight, and taken by the late Mr.
Cozens under his inspection during a tour in Swisserland
in 1776'. John Towneley of Chiswick was a noted collector
of prints and was the uncle and heir of Knight's close
friend Charles Townley. He was certainly known to Knight
and in close contact with him after Charles Townley's
death, as both men were involved in discussions concerning the purchase of the Townley marbles for the nation.
Henry Angelo (*Reminiscences*, II, 1884 ed., p. 126) stated
that Knight 'took Cozens with him to Switzerland to make
drawings'. Oppé, who discusses the drawings' provenance
in full (p. 127) was somewhat cautious in accepting this
evidence but, more recently, Andrew Wilton (1980, pp.
38–9) has seen little reason to doubt it and has written
of the Swiss drawings, 'They may have been worked on as a
set for presentation to Payne Knight after Cozens arrived
in Rome, or perhaps during the journey.' Despite their
almost monochromatic appearance, Wilton considers that
'the drawings are too elaborate and carefully executed to
have the character of sketches made on the spot', and in
this respect he echoes Oppé's earlier evaluation of the
series. Twenty-four of the album's drawings were purchased in 1900 by the British Museum; others are in
numerous other collections. The drawings in the British
Museum have now been laid down, making it impossible to
verify the numbering on the versos noted earlier by Bell
and Girtin. When Cozens's health deteriorated in the
1790s, causing him to be placed under the care of Dr
Monro in 1794, the artist was not forgotten by Knight.
Farington (22 June) recorded, 'A subscription for Cozens
has been raised sufficient to support him for at least a year,
witht. applying to professional men. Mr Knight & Sir
George Beaumont have been the principals in effecting it.'
(Knight subscribed 2 guineas towards the total of 30
guineas raised by Beaumont.) Knight's conduct was in
marked contrast to that of William Beckford, who had
employed Cozens as his travelling artist on an Italian tour
of 1782–3, but who declined to subscribe to the fund
TRUSTEES OF THE BRITISH MUSEUM

129

John Robert Cozens (1752–97)

130 *View on the Reichenbach*

Black pen, grey wash and watercolour: 35.5×
23.2
Numbered 23 on the verso
Prov.: see cat. no. 129
Lit.: Bell and Girtin, no. 22
A Monro School copy is in the Whitworth Art Gallery
(Bell and Girtin, pl. ivb)
TRUSTEES OF THE BRITISH MUSEUM

John Robert Cozens (1752–97)

131 *View of Oberhasli*

Black pen, grey-blue wash and watercolour:
23.4× 35.2
Numbered 29 on verso, inscribed in pencil verso:
*Lower part of the Valley / of Oberhasley from the /
Southeast*
Prov.: see cat. no. 129
Lit.: Bell and Girtin, no. 27.i
Another version is in the Victoria and Albert Museum,
signed and dated 1778 (Bell and Girtin, no. 27.ii: Haw-
croft, 1971, no. 8)
TRUSTEES OF THE BRITISH MUSEUM

John Robert Cozens (1752–97)

132 *View on the Linth*

Brown pen and watercolour: 23.2× 35.5
Numbered 46 on verso
Prov.: see cat. no. 129
Lit.: Bell and Girtin, no. 39.i
Two other versions are known – Bell and Girtin 39.ii
(1971 in the collection of Brigadier W. D. Tighe-Wood);
Hawcroft, 1971, no. 11, signed and dated 1778 (J. Leslie
Wright Collection, City Museum and Art Gallery, Birming-
ham)
TRUSTEES OF THE BRITISH MUSEUM

John Robert Cozens (1752–97)

133 *Grand Tour Sketchbook*

Volume II
Prov.: William Beckford; by descent to 15th
Duke of Hamilton by whom sold Sotheby's
29 Nov. 1973; Leger Galleries, from whom
purchased 1975
Lit.: Bell and Girtin, no. 249; Hawcroft, 1978
The volume is one of a group made in 1782 and 1783 by
Cozens on his second visit to Italy when he accompanied
William Beckford (just as he had, it seems, accompanied

Knight on his first visit – see cat. no. 129). It is open at f. 20, a characteristic sketch in pencil with grey wash dated August 30 and inscribed 'At Sir W. Hamilton's Villa – Portici'. Hamilton, who received almost all English travellers to the Neapolitan Kingdom – including perhaps Knight on his first Italian tour – welcomed Beckford, who was a remote cousin. The villa was close to the Royal Palace which then contained the museum of antiquities from Herculaneum and it looked out upon Vesuvius, which Hamilton studied

WHITWORTH ART GALLERY, MANCHESTER UNIVERSITY

John Robert Cozens (1752–97)
134 *Grand Tour Sketchbook*

Volume IV
Prov.: as in cat. no. 133
Lit.: Bell and Girtin, no. 298; Hawcroft, 1978
This volume, another in the set described in cat. no. 133,

130

is open at f. 11, a sketch in pencil with grey wash, squared for transfer and annotated. It is dated 7 November (1782), and shows 'the three Temples at Paestum', seen from the south-west – some of the Greek Doric remains which a few years earlier Knight had surveyed with enthusiasm on his way to Sicily

WHITWORTH ART GALLERY, MANCHESTER UNIVERSITY

Henry Edridge (1769–1821)
135 *Thomas Hearne Sketching*

Pencil, oval: 15.2× 13.0
Inscribed verso, in Dr Monro's hand: *T. Hearne / Author of the Antiquities / of Great Britain / Sketched by h / his friend / Henry Edridge*
Prov.: Dr Thomas Monro; Mr and Mrs Cyril Fry
Lit.: Victoria and Albert Museum, 1976, no. 81
Edridge was, of the younger generation of watercolourists, the one most attached and indebted to Hearne. Knight's patronage of Hearne is discussed at cat. no. 114. Monro was a celebrated amateur watercolourist who treated J. R. Cozens for insanity in the 1790s and also ran his own 'Academy' where promising young artists, including Turner and Girtin, could copy from drawings by J. R. Cozens, Canaletto and Hearne amongst others. Roget (I, p. 77) wrote of Monro, 'As a leader of connoisseurship, he was looked upon in his day much in the same light as Sir George Beaumont and Mr Payne Knight . . . none seems to have taken more effectual means to promote the education of young artists than Dr Thomas Monro'

MR & MRS CYRIL FRY

Henry Edridge (1769–1821)
136 *Amelia Long, Lady Farnborough*

Pencil and watercolour: 15.0× 14.7
Prov.: The Fine Art Society; Mrs Judy Egerton
Lit.: Sidey, no. 60
Executed *c.* 1820; see cat. no. 147

MRS JUDY EGERTON

Adam Elsheimer (1578–1610)
137 *Evening Campagna landscape with a Castle and Shepherds around a Fire*

Black, white and grey gouache on brown ground paper: 10.8× 15.5
Prov.: Payne Knight Bequest (Oo.10–134)
Lit.: Möhle, no. 55
Knight also owned an important painting by Elsheimer (see p. 108)

TRUSTEES OF THE BRITISH MUSEUM

Thomas Gainsborough (1727–78)

138 *A Man Holding a Claude Glass*

Pencil: 18.4 × 13.8
Prov.: Gainsborough sale, Christie's, 11 May
1799 (85) (a sketchbook), bt. Payne Knight; his
Bequest (Oo.2–27)
Lit.: Hayes, no. 10

A study from the life, dated by Hayes to the early to mid
1750s. A 'Claude glass', essentially a darkened, slightly
convex mirror, was a popular drawing device in the
eighteenth century. The sketchbook from which this is
taken was one of ten offered for sale at Christie's by the
artist's daughter, Margaret. Two were bought in, Colnaghi's
and Payne Knight bought one each, and Messrs. Hibbert
and Pugh three each. According to Farington (11 May
1799), Hibbert, a print and book collector, divided one of his
sketchbooks with Sir George Beaumont

TRUSTEES OF THE BRITISH MUSEUM

Thomas Gainsborough (1727–88)

139 *Beech Trees at Foxley with Yazor Church in
the Distance*

Brown chalk, watercolour and bodycolour over

pencil: 27.7 × 38.9
Signed and dated: *Tho: Gainsborough / del 1760*
on a fragment of paper now pasted on the back
of the frame
Prov.: Sir Robert Price; John, 2nd Viscount
Bateman; Bateman Sale, Christie's 11 April 1896
(20) bt. Agnew; Walker's Galleries; A. E.
Anderson by whom presented 1931
Lit.: Hayes, no. 248

According to old labels stuck on the back of the frame this
view of 'some famous beech trees' at Foxley, the Herefordshire seat of the Price family, was a 'study from nature'
(but this need not mean painted out of doors) made by the
artist when on a visit there. Gainsborough was known to
three generations of the Price family. This drawing was in
the collection of his friend Sir Robert, the father of Uvedale
Price, and there is also a portrait by Gainsborough perhaps
of Sir Robert's father, Uvedale Tomkyns Price (Neue
Pinakothek, Munich). Uvedale Price recalled the excursions
he made with Gainsborough into the countryside near
Bath: 'he was a man of an eager irritable mind, though
warmly attached to those he loved; of a lively and playful
imagination, yet at times severe and sarcastic' (Price, II,
p. 368)

WHITWORTH ART GALLERY, MANCHESTER UNIVERSITY

141

Benozzo Gozzoli (1420–97)

140 *The Entombment*

Pen and ink and orange-vermillion bodycolour
on paper tinted pink, heightened with white:
13.3× 10.2
Inscribed in ink close to the lower edge: *Giotto
fiorentº* / *13 ? (1)5*
Prov.: G. Vasari; P. J. Mariette (Lugt, 2097);
sale, Paris, 1775, 15 Nov. (228); Abbé Tersan,
Paris (purchased from him by Knight, 28 April
1791): Payne Knight Bequest (Pp.1–2)
Lit.: Popham and Pouncey, no. 88

The attribution to Giotto (which is followed in the B.M.
manuscript Catalogue) may have been taken from Vasari,
whose ownership is stated on Mariette's mount. Popham
and Pouncey date the drawing to late in Benozzo's development. They suggest the main composition is for an
altarpiece, whilst the figure in a roundel is for a *Risen Christ*
in the upper part of a tabernacle immediately above the
altar

TRUSTEES OF THE BRITISH MUSEUM

Giovanni Francesco Barbieri, called Il Guercino
(1591–1666)

141 *Landscape with Angelica and Medoro*

Brown pen and ink: 30.8× 46.2
Inscribed in ink L.L.: *Guercino* and *ANGELICA E /
MEDORO* on stone in front of the two figures
Prov.: Payne Knight Bequest (Pp.4–63)
Lit.: Mahon, pp. 51–2 under no. 26

The subject is taken from Ariosto. As Mahon points out,
this is not connected with Guercino's two large paintings
of the same subject of 1642 and 1647. It can be grouped
with a number of highly finished drawings by Guercino
(such as the group at Chatsworth), and possibly dates from
the first half of his career

TRUSTEES OF THE BRITISH MUSEUM

George Perfect Harding (died 1853)

142 *Thomas Bruce, Seventh Earl of Elgin*

Pencil, pen and grey wash: 19.1× 14.9
Signed: *G P Harding fec.*
Prov.: Purchased 1898
Lit.: A. H. Smith, 1916, p. 164

Like many miniaturists Harding copied other, larger,
portraits: his original in this case was by Anton Graff and
dates from the mid 1790s. Elgin was appointed Ambassador
to the Porte in 1799. Having been persuaded by his
chaplain to remove the sculpture from the Parthenon in
Athens (rather than simply take casts as had been his
original intention) and having transported it at enormous
cost and trouble to London he understandably expected to
be applauded for his public spirit in offering it on generous

142

terms to the nation. But his action was controversial, the
financial circumstances not fully understood, the treasury
unconvinced, and a campaign had to be mounted by his
supporters to the success of which the lack of enthusiasm
for the sculpture expressed by Richard Payne Knight was,
for nearly a decade, one of the major impediments. There
was another version of this drawing exhibited at the Fine
Art Society, London, *The Rediscovery of Greece*, 1979 (215)

TRUSTEES OF THE BRITISH MUSEUM

Benjamin Robert Haydon (1786–1846)

143 *Studies of the Horse's Head from the West
Pediment of the Parthenon*

Black chalk on grey paper with white
heightening: 55.5× 76.3
Dated: *1809* (the verso has similar studies)
Prov.: By descent to the artist's son F. W.
Haydon from whom purchased 1889
See cat. no. 145

TRUSTEES OF THE BRITISH MUSEUM

144

Benjamin Robert Haydon (1786–1846)

144 *Study of the so-called 'Fates' from the West Pediment of the Parthenon, with the Metopes Behind*

Black chalk on grey paper with white heightening: 55.5 × 77.0
Dated: *1809*
Prov.: As in cat. no. 143
See cat. no. 145

Benjamin Robert Haydon (1786–1846)

145 *Study of the 'Illissus' from the East Pediment of the Parthenon*

Black chalk on blue paper: 55.5 × 78.0
Dated 1809
Prov.: As in cat. no. 143

This was f. 13 and 143 and 144 were ff. 3 and 6 in an album of Haydon's work (C.100*). All three drawings testify to the diligence with which Haydon studied 'Lord Elgin's Marbles' when they were kept in a shed in Elgin's Park Lane home – his priority in this over West and Lawrence was something he was proud of (Haydon, 1846, p. 219). Their scale is also important for the grand style that Haydon hoped to learn from them. In his Diaries and in his foolhardy attack on Knight in *The Examiner* Haydon cast himself in the rôle of the poor artist who almost single-handed defended the merits and secured for the nation the masterpieces of Phidias against Knight – 'the leader of our Salons, to whose dictum everyone bowed, and against whose *ipse dixits* no one dared dispute, be he whom or what he might, in rank, station or talents' (*ibid.*, p. 215). He entertained fantasies of Knight dying in agony and was convinced that Knight was prejudicing patrons against him, for instance by informing Princess Caroline that his *Judgment of Solomon* was 'Distorted Stuff' (1853, I, pp. 326–7)

Philips Koninck (1619–88)

146 *Panoramic Landscape*

Watercolour: 13.5× 21.0
Prov.: Possibly (according to Gerson) J. Witson
sale, Amsterdam, 16 August 1790 (30), sold with
no. 31 for 7 florins to Heemskerk; Payne Knight
Bequest (Oo.9–83)
Lit.: Gerson, no. Z50

The painterly qualities of this drawing point to a dating in
the later part of Koninck's career

TRUSTEES OF THE BRITISH MUSEUM

Amelia Long, Lady Farnborough (1772–1837)

147 *In the grounds at Bromley Hill*

Pencil: 24.8× 38.9
Inscribed, signed and dated L.R.: *Bromley Hill /
Amelia Long 1895*
Prov.: Payne Knight Bequest (Oo.5–55)
Lit.: Sidey, no. 5

Amelia Long was the daughter of the great collector Sir
Abraham Hume, and niece of the still greater collector the
Earl of Bridgewater. She was one of the most distinguished
of English lady amateur artists and was described by Roget
as Girtin's 'favourite pupil'. In 1793 she married Charles
Long (see cat. no. 66) and they settled at Bromley, Kent, in
1801. This drawing was executed in the grounds of their
house, Bromley Hill Place, where Knight was a frequent
guest. The Longs visited him at Downton in the late
summer of 1809. Farington (6 Feb. 1808) records a dinner
party at Charles Long's 'at the Pay Office, Whitehall' at
which Knight was present – 'Before dinner we adjourned
to another room & saw a drawing of a view of buildings at
Cambridge made by Mrs Long; also some sketches of trees
made by her with black lead pencil. All far superior to any
that I have seen made by an Amateur artist.' Knight owned
a number of drawings by other English amateurs, most of
them presumably presented to him as personal gifts –
Heneage Finch, 4th Lord Aylesford (Oo.5–62), Sir George
Beaumont (Oo.5–56), Sir William Elford (Oo.5–57–88),
Charles Gore (see p. 20)

TRUSTEES OF THE BRITISH MUSEUM

Michelangelo Buonarroti (1475–1564)

148 *The Holy Family with the Infant St John*

Black chalk: 31.7× 19.1
Trimmed at the top and on the right, a strip
stuck on at the bottom
Prov.: P. J. Mariette (Lugt 1852); Marquis de
Lagoy (Lugt 1710); Payne Knight Bequest
(Pp.1–58)
Lit.: Wilde, no. 65

Dated by Wilde *c.* 1534–41, this was the only drawing by
Michelangelo in the Knight bequest which he accepted as

148

autograph. It is possible that Knight acquired the drawing
from the dealer Samuel Woodburn who purchased, in
1820, 138 of the Marquis de Lagoy's finest drawings and
sold most, but not all, of them to Thomas Dimsdale (see
Lugt, p. 309)

TRUSTEES OF THE BRITISH MUSEUM

Pier Francesco Mola (1612–66)   Colour Plate X

149 *Head of a Man Wearing a Hat*

Black and red chalks: 25.3× 21.6
Indecipherable inscription, brown ink, L.R.
Prov.: J. Richardson, sen. (Lugt, no. 2184);
J. van Rijmsdijk (Lugt, no. 2167); Sir J. Reynolds
(Lugt, no. 2364); Payne Knight Bequest
Pp.4–89)

The head resembles in reverse that of Nicodemus in
Barocci's *Entombment* (S. Croce, Senigallia), except that in
Barocci's painting Nicodemus wears a turban, whereas the
man in Mola's drawing wears a wide-brimmed hat

TRUSTEES OF THE BRITISH MUSEUM

150

John Hamilton Mortimer (1740–79)

150 *Banditti Returning*

Pen and ink: 35.2× 41.0
Prov.: Payne Knight Bequest (Oo.5–9)
Lit.: Nicolson, no. 53

Knight must have acquired this drawing by 1780 as an
etching after it by R. Blyth was published in November
1780 with the inscription 'From an Original Drawing of
J. Mortimer in the Collection of Richard Payne Knight
Esq.... by J. Mortimer 1775'. The drawing is a companion
to *Banditti Going Out*, also owned by Knight (Oo.5–10). Two
paintings with same titles were exhibited by Mortimer at
the Society of Artists, 1775 (unnumbered) and the drawings probably reflect their compositions. Knight's Bequest
included 9 drawings by Mortimer (Oo.5–(9–16)) and an
album containing another 37 (1975–U1591)

TRUSTEES OF THE BRITISH MUSEUM

Adriaen van Ostade (1610–85)

151 *Interior of an Inn, with Numerous Figures*

Brown pen and watercolour: 15.9× 24.2
Signed and dated, brown ink, L.R.: *A. Ostade.*
1673
Prov.: Payne Knight Bequest (Oo.10–162)

Knight found space in *the Landscape* to praise Ostade's
paintings, of which he owned at least one example

TRUSTEES OF THE BRITISH MUSEUM

Francesco Mazzola, called Il Parmigianino
(1503–40)

152 *Studies of St John the Baptist Preaching*

Pen and brown ink and brown wash, heightened
with white, over black chalk and stylus

151

152

underdrawing: 15.5×20.9
Prov.: Cavaliere F. Bajardi; M. Cavalca; J. Richardson sen. (Lugt, no. 2184); N. Hone (Lugt, no. 2793); Sir J. Reynolds (Lugt, no. 2364); Payne Knight Bequest (Pp.2–131)
Lit.: Popham, no. 82

Popham traced the early provenance of this drawing. He noted a description of it occurring in an inventory of the effects of Francesco Bajardi drawn up probably shortly after the latter's death in 1561. Vasari relates that the drawings in his collection were inherited by Bajardi's grandson, Marcantonio Cavalca. There is a possible connection between this drawing and the *Madonna and Child with SS. John the Baptist and Jerome* in the National Gallery, London

TRUSTEES OF THE BRITISH MUSEUM

Gaspard Dughet, called Gaspard Poussin (1613–75)

153 *Interior of a Wood*

Black chalk, brown pen and wash: 25.5×18.5
Inscribed in ink L.R.: *119*
Prov.: Crozat; G. Huquier (Lugt, no. 1285); P. J. Mariette (Lugt, no. 1852); Payne Knight Bequest (Pp.4–71)
Lit.: Friedlaender and Blunt, IV, no. G8, as by Gaspard Dughet

TRUSTEES OF THE BRITISH MUSEUM

Gaspard Dughet, called Gaspard Poussin (1613–75)?

154 *A Stream*

Pen, black chalk, grey wash and bodycolour, heightened with white: 26.8×40.2
Prov.: Charles Rogers; Payne Knight Bequest (Pp.4–77)
Lit.: French, no. 34

Accepted by most authorities as by Dughet, Anne French dates this drawing to early in Dughet's career, though Michael Kitson, reviewing the Kenwood *Dughet* exhibition (*Burlington Magazine*, Sept. 1980, p. 651) considers 'the uncharacteristically detailed drawing of "A Stream" (No. 34) in the British Museum should perhaps have a question mark attached to it'

TRUSTEES OF THE BRITISH MUSEUM

Raphael (1483–1520)

155 *Head and Right Forearm of an Angel: Study for the 'Coronation of the Virgin'*

Metal-point on warm white prepared ground: 27.6×19.6
Prov.: J.-B.-J. Wicar?; W. Y. Ottley (sale anon.,

London, T. Philipe, 1804, 13 Apr., (348)); Payne Knight Bequest (Pp.1–67)
Lit.: Pouncey and Gere, no. 4

A study for the angel on the extreme right of the *Coronation of the Virgin* (Vatican, Rome), probably completed by September 1503. It can be grouped with six other leaves in a similar technique from an 'Umbrian silverpoint sketchbook'. Knight's admiration of Raphael's drawings is evident in his discussion of the artist's studies after the antique — 'the firmness and dexterity which the drawings of the former [Raphael] display, prove either immense practice, or most extraordinary talent' — [Knight], 1810, p. 301

TRUSTEES OF THE BRITISH MUSEUM

156

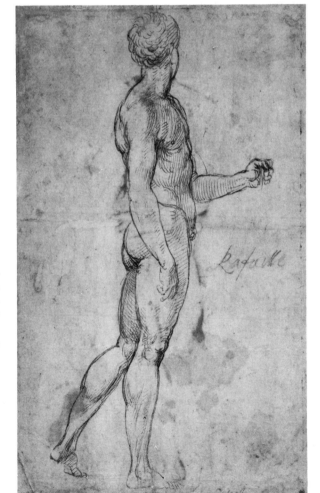

157

Raphael (1483–1520)

156 *Nude Man Advancing to Right*

Pen and brown ink: 27.9 × 16.9
Inscribed recto and verso in same hand in black
chalk: *Raffaelle* and in ink on lower edges (on
verso twice): *Raffaello*
Prov.: P. Crozat; P. J. Mariette (Lugt, no. 2097)
by 1741; Payne Knight Bequest (Pp.1–65)
Lit.: Pouncey and Gere, no. 14

On the verso is a nude study for a saint (Peter?) and studies
for his leg and foot. Pouncey and Gere consider both recto
and verso to be studies from the life. The recto can be
connected with another of Knight's Raphael drawings
(Pouncey and Gere, no. 15) in that the poses of both are
derived from Michelangelo's *David*, erected in June 1504

Rembrandt van Rijn (1606–69)

157 *The Lamentation at the Foot of the Cross*

Pen, brown ink and wash with grey oil colours
over red and black chalks: 21.6 × 25.4
Prov.: J. Richardson, jun. (Lugt, no. 2170);
Sir J. Reynolds (Lugt 2364); Payne Knight
Bequest (Oo.9–103)
Lit.: Benesch, no. 154

The drawing has been cut and reassembled several times.
Jonathan Richardson jun., in a lengthy inscription on a
piece of paper formerly on the old mount (now laid on the
back of the present mount) noted, 'My Father and I counted,
I think, seventeen different pieces of Paper'. James Northcote (*The Life of Sir Joshua Reynolds*, 2nd ed., London 1819,
vol. I, pp. 261f) recalled buying it at Richardson's sale for
Reynolds, who also owned the painting of this subject
(National Gallery, London; Sir George Beaumont Gift) for
which cat. no. 157 is a study

Rembrandt van Rijn (1606–69)

158 *Study of a Chained Lioness*

Black chalk, grey wash, white heightening:
12.6× 18.1
Inscribed in ink U.L.: *?o*
Prov.: Payne Knight Bequest (Oo.9–75)
Lit.: Benesch, no. 774

Travelling circuses may have provided the sources for Rembrandt's animal studies of lionesses and elephants. Both cat. nos. 158 and 159 were probably used by Rembrandt as preparatory studies for the chained lioness in his painting of 1641, *The Concord of the State* (Bredius, no. 476, Rotterdam Boymans Museum)

Rembrandt van Rijn (1606–69)

159 *Study of a Lioness Eating a Bird*

Black chalk, brown wash, white heightening:
12.7× 24.0
Prov.: Payne Knight Bequest (Oo.9–71)
Lit.: Benesch, no. 775

See cat. no. 158

Rembrandt van Rijn (1606–69)

160 *Life Study of a Man Standing*

Pen and brown ink, grey wash, white heightening, traces of red and black chalk underneath: 25.2× 19.2
Prov.: Payne Knight Bequest {Oo.9–94)
Lit.: Benesch, no. 710

A life study, in reverse, for the standing figure in an etching by Rembrandt (Bartsch, no. 194). Cat. no. 160 is closely related to a drawing in the Albertina, Vienna (Benesch, no. 709), also a life-study from the same model

? Rembrandt van Rijn (1606–69)

161 *Landscape with a Cottage, Canal and Trees*

Pen and brown wash: 10.2× 14.0
Prov.: Payne Knight Bequest (Oo.9–110)
Lit.: Benesch, no. C55

Benesch relegates this to copy status on grounds of execution; otherwise he compares it to the landscape drawings of the late 1640s. 'Rembrandt', Knight wrote, 'seems . . . to have given himself no trouble in the selection of subjects. Extensive plains of barren down, bog, or fallow, intersected by rows of pollard trees, straight canals, mounds, and ditches are so melted and blended together by this light, and so animated by the magic of his pencil, as to exhibit effects the most beautiful; though if seen or represented in the glare of a mid-day sun, they would be most disgustingly ugly' – 1805 (1808), p. 98; cf. 1794 (1795), pp. 88–9n

159

Humphry Repton (1752–1818) and others

162 *Album of Drawings*

Prov.: From the Colman Collection
Lit.: Stroud, p. 26

Repton was a protégé of William Windham, who was a friend of Fox, Price and Knight. He had decided on a career as a landscape gardener in 1788 and by March 1789 he had completed his first 'Red Book'. He certainly knew Knight by July of that year when he invited Anna Seward to join them in exploring 'the labyrinths of Hainault Forest'. In the event Knight and Repton went alone and on the lower of the two drawings (in grey wash, black chalk and pencil) displayed here Repton has written 'Epping Forest with Mr Knight cutting our joint names – & my low forest car & Captain', the latter, evidently, equine. In late September of the same year Repton travelled to Ferney Hall to advise Samuel Phipps, a friend of Windham, and it was then, according to Price that he consulted Knight who lived nearby, concerning the treatment of a rocky dell there; and at the same date he was introduced to Price (Price, III, pp. 89–90). In the following years Repton's professional success doubtless discouraged deference to Knight, and their friendship cooled

NORFOLK COUNTY LIBRARY

Salvator Rosa (1615–73)

163 *The Resurrected Christ*

Brown pen and ink with grey wash: 35.8 × 25.7
Inscribed in pen, by a later hand, in framing mount below: *Sal: Rosa* –
Prov.: Payne Knight Bequest (Pp.5–104)
Lit.: Mahoney, no. 66.13

According to Mahoney this is one of four surviving drawings for one in a series of five paintings by Rosa executed *c.* 1662 for Carlo de' Rossi, who installed them, probably in 1679, in Santa Maria in Montesanto, Piazza del Popolo, Rome. The paintings are now in the Musée Condé at Chantilly though, judging from a photograph, Mahoney considers that of *The Resurrected Christ* to be a copy of the missing original. Knight acquired eleven other drawings as by Rosa

TRUSTEES OF THE BRITISH MUSEUM

Sir Peter Paul Rubens (1577–1640)

164 *Study for the Figure of Christ on the Cross*

Black chalk, brown wash, white heightening: 52.8 × 37.0
Prov.: Payne Knight Bequest (Oo.9–26)
Lit.: Held, no. 82; Rowlands, no. 64

This magnificent life study is dated by Held 1614–15 and is therefore later than the preliminary work on the *Raising of the Cross*, 1609–10, for St Walpurgis, Antwerp. It cannot be linked with any known commission

TRUSTEES OF THE BRITISH MUSEUM

Sir Peter Paul Rubens (1577–1640)

165 *A Naked Man Dropping from a Wall, after Raphael*

Pen and brown ink with brown wash and white heightening: 22.5 × 11.1
Prov.: Payne Knight Bequest (Oo.9–23)
Lit.: Pouncey and Gere, under no. 87; Rowlands, no. 33

The drawing is after a figure in Raphael's fresco, the *Fire in the Borgo* in the Stanza dell'Incendio in the Vatican, but the differences in detail between this drawing and the fresco (drapery, position of the right arm and the shadow) point to the former being based on a lost copy of the fresco. Two similar copies from the composition, attributed to the Raphael school, are in the Albertina, Vienna and the Ashmolean Museum, Oxford. Rubens used the pose of the upper half of the man's torso in his large oil-sketch *The Miracles of St Benedict* (Brussels, Musée des Beaux-Arts)

TRUSTEES OF THE BRITISH MUSEUM

164

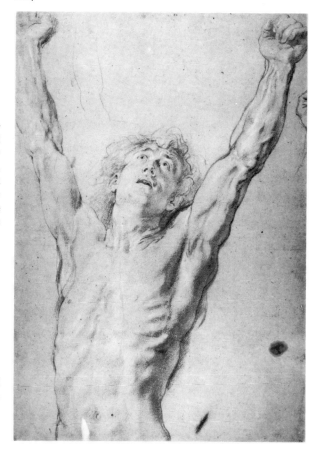

167

Copy after Giovanni Bellini (*c.* 1430–1516), retouched by Rubens

166 *Two Saints*

Drawn with the point of the brush on blue surface, heightened with white: 28.1×14.2
Prov.: P. P. Rubens (?); P. J. Mariette (Lugt, no. 1852: sale, Paris, 1775, 15 Nov., &c., lot 186?); Tersan (inscr. back of mount: *Bt. of Abbé Tersant at Paris April 28, 1791 for 250 livres*); Payne Knight Bequest (Oo.9–31)
Lit.: Popham and Pouncey, no. 20; Rowlands, no. 45

Probably an early copy of the figures in the right hand wing of Bellini's triptych of 1488 in the Frari Church, Venice. The reworking by Rubens is very extensive. Knight was certainly aware of Rubens's reworking of Old Master drawings: 'It is curious to observe how he has twisted and distorted them [bodies] in his attempts to improve the drawings of the old Roman and Florentine masters, whose meagre upright figures have their muscles swoln, and their limbs bent into all those flowing and undulating lines, which have been called the lines of grace and beauty . . .' (Knight, 1805 (1808), p. 184)

Paul Sandby (1730–1809)

167 *Landscape with Blasted Tree*

Black chalk and watercolour with white heightening on prepared blue/grey paper: 48.5×38.8
Signed and dated L.R. in black pen: *P. Sandby 1764*
Prov.: Payne Knight Bequest (Oo.5–39)

This splendid drawing is one of a small number of works from relatively early in Sandby's career which display the influence of Salvator Rosa (see *The Landscape*, 1795 ed., pp. 77–8 for Knight's comments on Rosa's trees). This influence can be detected in at least two other signed and dated works featuring similar trees – a watercolour of 1755 (*Woodcutters near a River*, exhibited *Paul Sandby 1725–1809*, Guildhall Art Gallery, 1960 (12), lent by the Corporation of London) and an etching (later aquatinted) of 1762 of figures in a landscape (example in the British Museum, no. 1904–8–19–730). Knight also acquired two other drawings as by Sandby, one of which (Oo.5–40) is now thought to be by Taverner, *c.* 1770. (Information kindly provided by Bruce Robertson)

Herman van Swanewelt (*c.* 1600–55)

168 *Hermes and Battus*

Brown pen, grey and brown wash with pencil underdrawing: 18.2×25.5

Inscribed in ink L.R.: *20*
An original study in reverse for the etching of the same subject (Bartsch 96); the story is told in Ovid's *Metamorphoses* (II.681–708). The acquisition of drawings by Swanewelt, by whom he owned three examples, would have been a natural step for Knight, given his enthusiasm for Claude's drawings

J. M. W. Turner (1775–1851)

169 *View of the North Front of Hampton Court, Herefordshire*

Pencil, watercolour and bodycolour: 32.0×42.4
Prov.: Viscount Malden; J. E. Taylor, by whom presented 1892
Lit.: Cornforth; Wilton, 1979, no. 182

Turner's visit to Hampton Court can be dated to 1795 from his sketchbooks in the British Museum, and this watercolour is one of a series recording the improvements made there by George, Viscount Malden (later 5th Earl of Essex), after his marriage in 1786, probably during the early 1790s and perhaps to designs by James Wyatt (who worked for the same family at Cassiobury). It is important, however, that this side of the house had not been much changed since it was tidied up by Lord Coningsby in the early eighteenth century – his architect (perhaps Talman) had left it with battlements to give it, in a phrase used by Vanbrugh, 'something of a Castle Air', so it provides a precedent in Herefordshire for Knight's battlements at Downton Castle

Sir Anthony Van Dyck (1599–1641)

170 *Study of Trees*

Pen, sepia, and watercolour: 19.5×23.6
Prov.: J. Richardson, Sen. (Lugt, no. 2183); Sir J. Reynolds (Lugt, no. 2364); Payne Knight Bequest (Oo.9–50)
Lit.: Vey, no. 303

Vey notes the similarity of the tree on the left of the main group in this drawing to the large tree in the background of Van Dyck's great *Equestrian Portrait of Charles I* (National Gallery, London), probably of the late 1630s

Jean-Antoine Watteau (1684–1721)

171 *Head of a Young Woman, studied in Profile and in Full Face*

Red and black chalks: 17.3×15.6
Prov.: Payne Knight Bequest (Oo.11–262)
Lit.: Parker and Mathey, no. 776

A study used for *Le Concert Champêtre, c.* 1717, this drawing was etched in reverse by Cars for Jean de Jullienne's *Figures de différents Caractères, de Paysages et d'Études* (Paris 1726–8). This was the first drawing by Watteau to enter the British Museum's collection and the only example of his work owned by Knight

TRUSTEES OF THE BRITISH MUSEUM

[OIL PAINTINGS]

David Allan (1744–96)
172 *Sir William Hamilton*

Oil on canvas: 236.1 × 180.3
Signed and dated (B.L.) 1775
Prov.: The artist, by whom donated to the British Museum 1775; transferred to the National Portrait Gallery 1879
Lit.: Thompson

This was an extraordinary tribute by the Scottish artist Allan to his 'Protector' Sir William Hamilton, who was at that time British Ambassador at the Court of Naples. The British Museum's purchase of the Hamilton Collection in 1772 for £8400 prompted Allan (in a letter from Rome dated 6 October 1775) to offer this portrait to Dr Matthew Maty, Principal Librarian at Montagu House (British Museum), in the hope that it might be hung with the Hamilton Collection. The portrait, in which Hamilton wears the insignia of the Order of the Bath, was duly accepted by the Trustees. Various objects in the picture

172

make overt reference to Hamilton's interests including, in the large open-fronted cabinet, an ornate Apulian vase from his collection (B.M. Dept. of Greek and Roman Antiquities: volute-crater F.284). The design of the decoration on the vase is in reverse, indicating that Allan copied it from the reversed plate in d'Hancarville's publication (see cat. no. 77). In 1782 Hamilton presented his own portrait by Sir Joshua Reynolds (studio) to the Museum (Waterhouse, 1941, p. 68) and Allan's portrait was relegated to the Store Room. Both portraits eventually found their way to the National Portrait Gallery. On Knight and Hamilton see p. 70

NATIONAL PORTRAIT GALLERY, LONDON

Archibald Archer (1789/90–1848)
173 *The Temporary Elgin Room in the British Museum*

Oil on canvas: 76.2 × 127.0
Signed: *A Archer 1819*
Prov.: Edward Hawkins; Dr J. E. Gray, by whom bequeathed 1872
Lit.: A. H. Smith, 1816, pp. 353–4

This picture provides an accurate record of one end of the simple accommodation run up by the Museum over the winter of 1816–17 to accommodate the Parthenon sculpture and which was replaced in 1831 by a more substantial and attractive room. The sculpture was arranged as shown here but 'the Elgin Eros, the metope on the end wall, the bronze, vase, and the horse's head' have been added, as Smith pointed out, 'to enrich the composition'. The *Illissus* and *Theseus* are placed on low pedestals with rotating tops — the former here has been turned. Behind the *Illissus* stands Haydon (see cat. no. 145). The old man seated on the left is Benjamin West. Archer himself appears in the foreground right. Other figures are identified by Smith

TRUSTEES OF THE BRITISH MUSEUM

Pietro Paolo Bonzi, also called 'Il Gobbo dei Carracci' or 'dei Frutti' (died 1636)
174 *Landscape with Erminia and the Shepherds*

Oil on panel: 37.4 × 53.4
Prov.: ? R. P. Knight; by descent to Denis Lennox by whom sold Christie's, 4 May 1979 (90)

The attribution to Bonzi rests on comparison with a very similar landscape in a private collection with an old inscription on the verso, and is supported by his taste, displayed in his etchings as well as his paintings, for the type of crippled tree that appears here (Pugliatti, plates iii, xiii). Martin Royalton-Kisch, who supplies this information, also notes that 'Knight' (not certainly R. P. Knight) acquired a painting attributed to Albano entitled 'Erminia, from Tasso' at Sir Joshua Reynolds's sale (Christie's, 14 March 1795, (30)) for £9 19s 6d.

MANCHESTER CITY ART GALLERIES

173

174

Nathaniel Dance (1735–1811)

175 *Lancelot 'Capability' Brown*

Oil on canvas: 76.2×63.5
Prov.: Warren Trevor Esq., from whom
purchased 1975

This is one of a number of copies after Dance's original portrait of Brown, *c.* 1769, on loan to the National Portrait Gallery from Mrs M. Morrice. Brown (1715–83) was an extremely important landscape gardener and horticulturist whose deliberately contrived landscapes were sharply satirised by Knight in *The Landscape* (see pp. 10, 47). At the same time that Knight was shaping the landscape at Downton Castle Brown was employed nearby at Berrington, a house built by his son-in-law Henry Holland

NATIONAL PORTRAIT GALLERY, LONDON

Studio of Domenico Fetti (1588/9–1623)

176 *The Good Samaritan*

Oil on panel: 61.5×43.5 (sight)
Prov.: Probably Payne Knight; by descent
Lit.: Askew, no. 7e

Fetti's celebrated series of Parables, of which he executed more than any other artist, was probably painted in the period 1618–22. Askew suggests two groupings for these, placing *The Good Samaritan* (Luke 10: 30–7) in the later group 1621–2, after Fetti's return from Venice to Mantua, where he had been court painter to Duke Ferdinando Gonzaga since 1613, as well as superintendent of his art collections. The first, horizontal, version is in the Gemäldegalerie, Dresden, with a variant in the Boston Museum of Fine Arts. The present example is one of a number of replicas of the third, vertical, version in the Metropolitan Museum, New York. In Askew's opinion 'It seems unlikely that Fetti had much personal share in the actual painting'. Interestingly, William Beckford also owned a similar version (Askew, no. 7d)

D. P. H. LENNOX, ESQ.

Thomas Gainsborough (1727–88)

177 *Self Portrait*

Oil on canvas: 74.9×61.0
Prov.: The artist; presented by his daughter,
Margaret, 1808
Lit.: Waterhouse, 1958, no. 292

Unfinished, probably the picture he was painting for his friend the musician Abel when the latter died in 1787. It was by this particular portrait that Gainsborough wished his likeness to be remembered. Knight purchased one of the artist's sketchbooks from his daughter Margaret (cat. no. 138)

ROYAL ACADEMY, LONDON

Nathaniel Hone (1718–84)   Plate 2

178 *Richard Payne Knight*

Oil on canvas: 66.0×55.0
Prov.: R. P. Knight; by descent

This portrait has been traditionally known as Richard Knight and the only member of the family in his twenties when this must, to judge by both costume and style, have been painted was Richard Payne Knight: it is quite compatible with his later likenesses, although he appears surprisingly meek. Hone signed a portrait of Knight's sisters Barbara and Ursula in 1775 (in the same collection) shortly before they both died and a date in the 1770s seems reasonable for this picture. Knight's cousin Edward recorded a payment of 6 guineas to Hone for a miniature on 22 April 1762 (Kidderminster MS 283) and purchased Hone's famous satire on Sir Joshua Reynolds, *The Conjuror*, for 15 guineas on 1 May 1790 (*ibid.*, 290)

D. P. H. LENNOX, ESQ.

John Hoppner 1758?–1810

179 *Sir George Beaumont, Bart.*

Oil on canvas: 77.5×63.9
Prov.: Bequeathed by Claude Dickason Rotch,
1962

Beaumont (1753–1827) was a close acquaintance of Knight's (see pp. 12, 98) and a principal benefactor of the newly founded National Gallery, to which he donated his collection in 1823–8 (see Gregory Martin, 'The founding of the National Gallery in London: part I', *The Connoisseur*, June 1974, pp. 280–7). This is probably the portrait for which he is recorded as sitting to Hoppner in 1806 (Farington, 31 May 1809). 'They [Beaumont and his son] said they were both sitting to Hoppner, — Sir George said He is the last Colourist since Sir Joshua Reynolds, but has too much red in his flesh, — and wants the *naturalizing* of Sir Joshua —'. The picture was exhibited at the Royal Academy, 1809 (54) and several replicas exist

NATIONAL GALLERY, LONDON

Angelica Kauffmann (1741–1807)

180 *Thomas Jenkins and his Niece Anna Maria*

Oil on canvas: 129.5×94.6
Signed and dated: *Angelica Kauffmann / Pinx
Roma / 1790*
Prov.: R. W. M. Walker; Christie's, 20 July 1945
(92); Philips, Son and Neale, 10 July 1972.
Anon. (44) bt. J. A. Lewin; Christie's, 20 June
1975 (113) bt. National Portrait Gallery
Lit.: Manners and Williamson, pp. 85 and 158

Jenkins, whose dealings with Knight are mentioned on pp. 65, 69 was discussed at length in an article by Brinsley Ford in *Apollo*, June 1974, pp. 416–25. The painting is recorded in Angelica Kauffmann's *Memorandum of Paintings*

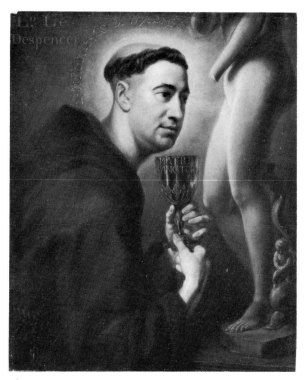

181

182

(MS. in the Royal Academy), according to which she painted Jenkins and his niece 'out of friendship'. In return for this portrait Jenkins presented Angelica with several objects of virtu. Knight also owned a drawing by Angelica (Pp.5–151, Manners and Williamson, p. 195)

NATIONAL PORTRAIT GALLERY, LONDON

George Knapton (1698–1778)

181 *Francis Dashwood, 15th Baron Le Despencer*

Oil on canvas 76.2×63.5
Lit.: Harcourt-Smith, pp. 52–3
See cat. no. 182

THE SOCIETY OF DILETTANTI

George Knapton (1698–1778)

182 *John Monckton, Viscount Galway*

Oil on canvas: 76.2×63.5
Lit.: Harcourt-Smith, pp. 58–9

Knapton, a pupil of Jonathon Richardson, who had been resident in Italy between 1725 and 1732, was elected to the Society of Dilettanti as their official 'limner'. He had painted portraits of twenty-three members by 1749 – an undertaking commenced in January 1740–1- which was accelerated by a system of fines ('face money') imposed

from 1744. Both this painting and cat. no. 181 date from 1742. Knapton resigned in 1763 and was replaced as 'limner' by James Stuart, who did nothing and who was replaced by Reynolds (see cat. no. 88). The paintings admirably convey the character of the Society in the years of its abortive patronage of Italian Opera and prior to its serious involvement in archaeology. Several members are shown in Roman armour but an equal number appear as gondoliers and a couple as Turks. Dashwood and Galway were both elected in 1736. Dashwood was perhaps the genius of the Society in these years, as Knight was to be half a century later – he designed the President's dress, the device for the seal and made plans for permanent premises (Dilettanti Papers I, ff. 18, 20, 105, 107, 109). Here he appears as a monk raising a Chalice towards the pudenda of a conveniently mutilated reduction of the Medici Venus. The future Chancellor of the Exchequer was a member of the notorious sham Franciscan Order at Medmenham. Hence this guise and the halo inscribed *San. Francesco di Wycombo* – West Wycombe being his seat. Lord Galway, a Commissioner of Revenue in Ireland and future Surveyor General of Woods and Forests, appears as a convivial Cardinal with a Pan leering behind his shoulder. The ridiculing of religion and the ribald humour survived in the Society to combine with their archaeological pursuits in the 1780s, when Hamilton solemnly announced to them his discovery of the survival of ancient phallic worship at a Roman Catholic festival

THE SOCIETY OF DILETTANTI

Sir Thomas Lawrence (1769–1830)   Plate 6

183 *Homer Reciting his Poems*

Oil on canvas: 94.0× 111.0
Inscribed: *TL 1790*
Prov.: R. P. Knight; by descent to Major
Kincaid-Lennox by whom sold through Thos.
Agnew and Son Ltd 1975
Lit.: Williams, pp. 122–3; *Tate Gallery 1974–6:
Illustrated Catalogue of Acquisitions*, pp. 32–3

Begun, according to Williams, in 1788, and dated 1790, this picture was exhibited, to a mixed reception in the press, at the Academy in 1791 (180), the year following the artist's tremendous success with his portraits of Queen Charlotte and Elizabeth Farren. The subject may have been suggested by Knight, whose *Analytical Essay*, his first contribution to Homer criticism, was published in the year this was exhibited. It is the first important painting by Lawrence which is not a portrait and the only early one to survive. His painting of Lady Hamilton ('a Lady of Fashion as La Penserosa') exhibited a year later represents an attempt to transfuse its sylvan poetry into portraiture. And in 1793 he exhibited *Prospero raising the Storm*, which is likely to have similarly combined landscape with history painting. His later, occasional, attempts at history subjects were single figures and with no landscape. One reason for Knight's early support for Lawrence was given by Marchant when gossiping with Farington (16 Jan. 1794) – 'Lawrence senior' had been of service to Knight in elections at Ludlow

TATE, GALLERY, LONDON

Sir Thomas Lawrence   Colour Plate VII
(1769–1830)

184 *Richard Payne Knight*

Oil on canvas: 127.0× 102.0
Prov.: R. P. Knight; by descent to Major
Kincaid-Lennox; accepted by the Inland Revenue
in lieu of duty on his estate 1970; presented by
H.M. Treasury 1975
Lit.: Garlick, p. 45

This extraordinary image of an inspired scholar – ridiculed by 'Antony Pasquin' as 'an irascible pedagogue explaining Euclid to a dunce' (Layard, p. 24) – was exhibited as a 'portrait of a gentleman' at the Academy in 1794 (181), by which date Lawrence had already painted several of Knight's friends – Lord Abercorn, Sir George Beaumont and Lady Hamilton. For the bronze vessel see cat. no. 40. The painting was placed in the library at Downton Castle (Lipscomb, p. 269)

WHITWORTH ART GALLERY, MANCHESTER UNIVERSITY

Sir Thomas Lawrence (1769–1830)

185 *Richard Payne Knight*

Oil on canvas: 93.0× 61.0

Prov.: Presented by the sitter
Lit.: Harcourt-Smith, pp. 74–5; Garlick, p. 45

In this portrait of 1805, painted for the Society, whose official painter Lawrence had become (in succession to Reynolds), Knight has a less animated pose than in cat. no. 184 – and Lawrence's brushwork is less animated too. The artist was by this date often critical of his sitter's opinions, although sometimes ready to defend him (see Farington, 24 Aug. 1805, 2 Feb. 1808, 6 March 1810)

THE SOCIETY OF DILETTANTI

Sir Thomas Lawrence (1769–1830)

186 *George Hamilton Gordon, 4th Earl of Aberdeen*

Oil on canvas: 77.4× 60.9
Prov.: By descent; acquired with Haddo House
Lit.: Garlick, p. 23

The painting was exhibited at the Royal Academy in 1808 (74). This is the period when Lord Aberdeen was closest to Knight. They first met in about 1800 probably through Lord Abercorn, who was Lord Aberdeen's father-in-law. They had different political allegiances but shared a passionate interest in Greek literature and arts (especially coins), Lord Aberdeen generally following his older friend, but not always agreeing, especially on the subject of architecture (see pp. 43–4). Knight visited Haddo House in the summer of 1812 and subsequently sent Herefordshire acorns there

THE NATIONAL TRUST FOR SCOTLAND

William Lonsdale (1777–1839)

187 *Dr Samuel Parr*

Oil on canvas: 76.5× 64.2
Prov.: Bequeathed in 1859 by Edward Maltby,
Bishop of Durham

Parr, who is here shown wearing a prebendary's coat over his cassock (he became Prebendary of St Paul's in 1783), was best known as a Classical scholar and a Whig churchman. He was a close friend of Knight, who deferred to him as to few others. It is probably the same painting as the one engraved by Skelton in 1823 which was in the collection of the Duke of Sussex (the only consistently Whig son of George III) and which was sold at Christie's after his death, 24 June 1843 (129)

FITZWILLIAM MUSEUM, CAMBRDGE

John Hamilton Mortimer (1740–79)   Plate 44

188 *Banditti Fishing*

Oil on canvas: 76.2× 61.0
Prov.: ? R. P. Knight; by descent; sold Sotheby's,
17 June 1981 (84) bt. present owner
Lit.: Nicolson, no. 70

185

Dated by Nicolson to *c.* 1775–7, this is likely to be 'small picture of Banditti fishing' exhibited by the artist at the Society of Artists in 1777 (89) – but cannot be the picture with the same title exhibited at the Academy in the following year (208) which included, according to the *General Advertiser*, 'two ladies, drest in the extremity of fashion'. For Knight's patronage of Mortimer see pp. 96–7

MORTON MORRIS & COMPANY LIMITED

William Nicholson (1781–1844)
189 *Benjamin Robert Haydon*

Oil on canvas: 58.5× 52.5
Prov.: 'Murray, Exeter' (advertised *Connoisseur*, Feb. 1927); acquired 1929 from Harmsworth and Sons

For Haydon, who was Knight's most dedicated enemy, see cat. no. 145. The portrait is likely to date from shortly before 1814 when Nicholson moved from London to Edinburgh

PLYMOUTH CITY MUSEUM AND ART GALLERY

? John Opie (1761–1807)   Plate 7
190 *Thomas Andrew Knight*

Oil on canvas: 127.0× 102.0
Prov.: ? R. P. Knight; by descent

This portrait was surely commissioned as a companion to hang opposite (not beside) Lawrence's portrait of Richard

193

Payne Knight which is the same size and similar in conception, although Thomas Andrew looks up with less excitement from his volume of botanical illustration – which reminds us that he was one of the leading horticulturalists of his day and hardly less eminent as a scientist than his brother was as a classical scholar. Knight considered Opie to be a victim of fashionable patronage, hailed as a genius when he was a novelty and then unjustly neglected: 'Thus artists are multiplied and art degraded' – [Knight], 1814, p. 274. If by Opie it must, to judge by the sitter's age, be a late work

D. P. H. LENNOX, ESQ.

? Bernard Van Orley (?1491–1542)
191 *The Annunciation*

Oil on panel: 10.5 (diameter)
Prov.: ? R. P. Knight; by descent
See cat. no. 192

PRIVATE COLLECTION

? Bernard Van Orley (?1491–1542)
192 *The Crucifixion*

Oil on panel: 10.5 (diameter)
Prov.: ? R. P. Knight; by descent

This painting, together with cat. no. 191, is contained in a round tortoiseshell case with silver lock, hinges and filigree knob. The attribution to Van Orley, which was first made earlier in this century, is not certain, but the paintings are Flemish and of the mid sixteenth century and of high quality, cat. no. 191 especially being in excellent condition with beautifully gilded highlights and the lighting of the chamber beyond as subtle as in the best Dutch or Flemish interiors of the subsequent century

PRIVATE COLLECTION

Thomas Phillips (1770–1845)
193 *Lord Byron in Albanian Costume*

Oil on canvas: 74.9× 62.2
Signed: B.L. with artist's monogram
Prov.: Purchased by the National Portrait Gallery from the artist's son, Henry Wyndham Phillips, 1862
Lit.: Hamburg, no. 532

Painted in the summer of 1813, this portrait depicts Byron in Albanian costume which he purchased in that country in 1809 whilst on his first extensive foreign tour. It was on this voyage that he became deeply interested in the causes of Albania and Greece, which were both under Turkish occupation. Knight wrote in 1812 that Byron's satirical verse was 'on the whole, tho' very unequal, the work of greatest Vigour both of Conception & Expression that has appeared since Milton'. He was referring to *English Bards*

194

and *Scotch Reviewers* (published 1811) and it must have
helped that he was one of the few prominent figures in the
literary world not ridiculed in the poem — it certainly
helped that Byron attacked Lord Elgin. And Knight also
admired *The Curse of Minerva*, Byron's 'brilliant invective'
against Elgin's removal of the Parthenon marbles. He had
met the poet and was struck by his melancholy (Aberdeen
Papers, 43230, ff. 108–9). In the following years the men
met occasionally and Byron was to enjoy, in London and in
Herefordshire, the 'autumnal charms' of Knight's old
favourite, Lady Oxford

NATIONAL PORTRAIT GALLERY, LONDON

Sir Joshua Reynolds (1723–92)

193a *Sir Joseph Banks Bart.*

Oil on canvas: 127.0×101.5
Lit.: Waterhouse 1941

This portrait, exhibited at the Royal Academy in 1773 (39),
alludes by the seascape, globe and Latin inscription to the
sitter's recent voyage on the *Endeavour*. For Banks and
Knight see cat. no. 63. Knight, who knew Reynolds
towards the end of the painter's life, described him as 'the

first artist of his time and scarcely inferior to any of the
Ancients'

PRIVATE COLLECTION

Jacob Van Ruisdael (1628/9–82)

194 *The Silent Pool*

Oil on panel: 42.0×39.0 (sight)
Prov.: ? R. P. Knight; by descent
Lit.: Rosenberg, no. 284

Knight in *The Landscape* found room to praise 'Rysdael',
together with 'meek Hobbima', Ostade and Waterloe.
This painting is dated *c.* 1648 by Seymour Slive because
of its clear relationship with etchings dated 1647 and 1649.

D. P. H. LENNOX, ESQ.

Richard Smith (*fl.* 1791–1811)

195 *Flower Piece*

Oil on canvas: 69.0×61.0
Signed L.L.: *Rich.d Smith Pinx.t*
Prov.: ? R. P. Knight; by descent

A signed and dated (1791) painting of fruits and flowers by this obscure artist was sold at Christie's, 4 Nov. 1960. He is probably identical with 'R. Smith (An Honorary Exhibiter)' who showed *A Group of Flowers* at the Royal Academy, 1811 (755). This piece either may have been bought by Payne Knight as an act of patronage towards a local (?) artist or, given its subject matter, it may have been purchased by his brother Thomas Andrew

D. P. H. LENNOX, ESQ.

Michael Sweerts (1624–1664)   Colour Plate XI

196 *Portrait of a Girl*

Oil on canvas: 43.0 × 37.0
Prov.: ? R. P. Knight; by descent to
Major Kincaid-Lennox; accepted by the Inland
Revenue in lieu of duty on his estate 1970;
presented by H.M. Treasury 1975
Lit.: Rotterdam, no. 49

This is comparable in handling to a *Portrait of a Young Man with a Hat* in the Wadsworth Atheneum (Rotterdam, no. 48) and *A Head of a Girl* (Christie's, 10 April 1970 (29)). Sweerts' work has frequently been confused with that of Vermeer, to whom cat. no. 196 was attributed when exhibited at Birmingham in 1934 (150)

LEICESTERSHIRE MUSEUM AND ART GALLERY

J. M. W. Turner (1775–1851)

197 *The Unpaid Bill, or the Dentist Reproving his Son's Prodigality*

Oil on panel: 59.4 × 80.0
Prov.: R. P. Knight; by descent
Lit.: Gage, 1965, pp. 76–7; Butlin and Joll,
pp. 43–4; *Life and Landscape in Britain*, pp. 37–8

'The figures here, like all the rest of this artist', wrote Robert Hunt, the critic of *The Examiner* (15 May 1808, p. 316) of this picture when it was displayed at the Academy in 1808 (116), 'are wretchedly drawn, but for a picture of colouring and effect, it is not only unexceptionable but inestimable. The blaze of sunshine bursting through the window receives increased splendour from the profusion of bottles and other apparatus of the dentist's shop. This is admirably qualified by a secondary sunshine seen through the door of another room. The piece is worthy of its destination, as a companion for the cradle-piece of Mr P. Knight's Rembrandt.' It has been ingeniously proposed that some polemical point was intended by patron or artist in this pairing, but although Knight was surely interested in Rembrandt's light effects, *The Examiner* may have been confused, for the picture makes a better pair with another painting in Knight's collection, the so-called *Alchemist's Laboratory* recently attributed to Gerard Thomas (Christie's, 4 May 1979, (99)) in which another elderly sedentary

197

male in a dim interior littered with potions and papers expostulates against his disordered household

D. P. H. LENNOX, ESQ.

Henry Walton (1746–1813)

198 *Rev. William Gilpin (1724–1804)*

Oil on panel: 25.4 × 20.3
Signed and dated L.L.: *H. Walton 1781*
Prov.: Rev. W. Gilpin; Edwin Bernard Benson (d. 1940); J. S. Maas & Co Ltd, from whom purchased 1964
Lit.: Barbier, p. 87n.5

Walton was a gentleman painter from Norfolk who studied under Zoffany in his mid-teens. He was also active as a connoisseur who advised on the formation of several notable collections including those of Lord Fitzwilliam and Lord Lansdowne. Gilpin's publications both reflected and promoted the fashion for touring areas of Britain such as the Wye, North Wales and the Lakes. He provided terminology with which his readers could express their admiration for such scenery, and formulae for composing sketches of it. His *Essay on Picturesque Beauty* which appeared in 1791 helped familiarize the educated public with the distinction between the beautiful and the picturesque which in following years Price elaborated and Knight confused

NATIONAL PORTRAIT GALLERY, LONDON

Benjamin West (1738–1820)

199 *Self Portrait*

Oil on canvas: 91.6 × 143.0
Inscribed: *B. West 179(?3)*
Prov.: West's sale, Robin's, 22 Jan. 1829 (88); presented by Joseph Neeld, 1830

The artist is shown with the volumes of English and Greek history from which he took his subjects and with the Royal Academy's premises in the Strand block of Somerset House behind him, a reference to his presidency (1792–1805, 1806–20). Knight in a note to *The Landscape* in 1794 referred to West as 'the great artist who now so worthily fills the President's chair' and in his *Inquiry* in 1805 he singled out West's famous *Death of Wolfe* for special praise as a superlative modern masterpiece. He did not, it seems, own any work by him but they were both connoisseurs and collectors of Old Master drawings. Uvedale Price in a letter to Sir George Beaumont of 21 May 1803 wrote of a tour he planned to make with Knight and West to Fonthill and Corsham and then on to see Ralph Willett's collection of drawings, at Merly House in Dorset (Coleorton Papers, MA 1581–40). Knight bought extensively at the sale of West's drawings held at Christie's 9–14 June 1820

ROYAL ACADEMY, LONDON

See cat. no. 197
? Gerard Thomas,
The Alchemist's Laboratory
(formerly Downton Castle)

Richard Westall (1765–1836) Colour Plate VI

200 *Harvesters in a Storm*

Oil on card, loosely mounted on canvas: 58.8×
78.0 (sight)
Signed L.L. on barrel: *RW/1795* (last digit not
entirely clear)
Prov.: R. P. Knight; by descent

Westall, who first exhibited at the Academy in 1784, was
elected ARA in 1792 and RA in 1794. His success in the
1790s was considerable and it seems chiefly associated
with this painting, or at least subject. The caption on a line
engraving of this picture, or rather one very similar, noted
that the 'original painting' was in watercolour and was
purchased by W. Chamberlayne Esq. The earliest version
in oils seems to be the *Haymakers in a Storm* exhibited at
the Academy in 1795 (607) which is likely to be identical
with this. Westall also exhibited *The Reapers* in 1798 (335).
In that year Charles Knight engraved a very similar but
smaller group of female figures in a similar (pathetic but not
painful) plight which seems to be based on Westall's
watercolour now in the National Gallery of Scotland and
dated 1794. Also related is the *Woman and Child in a
Storm – principal group of a Storm in the Harvest* exhibited in
1802 (62). Knight, who declared that Westall's *Harvesters
in a Storm* was one of the most outstanding productions of
modern art (1805 (1808), pp. 311–12), patronized him
more extensively and consistently than he did any other
contemporary artist, and entertained him at Downton
Castle (Farington, 5 Sept. 1806).

D. P. H. LENNOX, ESQ.

Richard Westall (1765–1836)

201 *Peasant at a Cottage Door*

Oil on canvas: 27.5× 20.5
Prov.: R. P. Knight; by descent
See cat. no. 202

D. P. H. LENNOX, ESQ.

Richard Westall (1765–1836)

202 *Young Woman Sewing*

Oil on canvas: 27.5× 20.0
Prov.: R. P. Knight; by descent

This picture and its pair, cat. no. 201, would seem to have
been those exhibited (under the titles we have employed
here) as nos. 38 and 39 at the Royal Academy in 1798.
They may well have been painted to hang beside Knight's
small seventeenth-century Dutch and Flemish pictures of
the picturesque poor in cottages and taverns

D. P. H. LENNOX, ESQ.

203

Richard Westall (1765–1836)

203 *Flora Unveiled by Zephyrs*

Oil on panel: 76.0× 58.5 (sight)
Signed L.R.: *R. Westall 1807*
Prov.: R. P. Knight; by descent

This picture has been identified as the *Una* shown at the
Royal Academy in 1807 (68) but it is quite impossible that
anyone could represent Spenser's chaste heroine exhibiting
herself in this manner, and it must be the *Flora unveiled by
Zephyrs* shown in the same exhibition (139). It seems to be
companion with two other paintings of the same size
painted for Knight: the *Orpheus* (121 at the Academy
exhibition of 1811) and the *Vertumnus and Pomona* (cat.
no. 204). Gods are surrounded by flowers here, by birds
and beasts in the *Orpheus* and by fruit in the *Vertumnus and
Pomona*. The approbation given by Knight to Westall's
Flora was considered 'an additional proof of his bad taste'
by Samuel Rogers, and also regretted by Beaumont
(Farington, 6 and 8 May 1807).

D. P. H. LENNOX, ESQ.

204

Richard Westall (1765–1836)

204 *Vertumnus and Pomona*

Oil on panel: 76.0× 58.0
Signed B.C.: R. Westall
Prov.: R. P. Knight; by descent

This painting has been described as *Venus and Adonis* but Adonis yearned for the pleasures not of Venus but of the hunt from which she kept him and he is never shown without his hounds. It surely represents Vertumnus enjoying the company of Pomona in her fruity bower, and must have been intended as a companion for cat. no. 203. Westall exhibited a painting with this title at the Academy in 1809 (127)

D. P. H. LENNOX, ESQ.

Richard Westall (1765–1836)   Plate 45

205 *The Sword of Damocles*

Oil on panel: 77.0× 61.0
Signed on base of throne: *R. Westall/1811*
Prov.: R. P. Knight; by descent

The painting was exhibited at the Academy in 1811 (127) and purchased by Knight for 150 guineas – as was the same artist's *Orpheus* exhibited in the same year (Waterhouse, 1953). It is typical of the subjects from Classical history and mythology which Westall was encouraged to take up by the patronage of antiquarians and connoisseurs such as Knight and Thomas Hope. In this case the subject is from the history of the elder Dionysius, tyrant of Syracuse, in whom Knight was especially interested and it involves a glittering array of ancient silver-ware of the sort he avidly collected. Farington noted that Thomas Hope commissioned a larger version, and this is likely to be the painting dated 1812 (and measuring 129.5× 104.0) sold at Parke-Bernet, New York, 9 Oct. 1974 (230) which is tighter in composition and gives a more commanding presence to the figure of Dionysius contemplating the discomfort of the obsequious flatterer, who, invited to experience the life of a monarch he had pronounced 'the happiest of men', is granted a vision of a naked sword suspended above him by a single hair

D. P. H. LENNOX, ESQ.

Richard Westall (1765–1836)   Plate 46

206 *The Grecian Wedding*

Oil on canvas: 95.2× 152.4
Prov.: R. P. Knight; by descent

Farington records on 8 July 1811 a recent visit made to Westall's studio by Knight, who commissioned an oil painting to be the same 'generally' as a drawing (doubtless coloured) which the artist had made for Mr Chamberlayne, but twice the size. For this he offered the astonishing sum of 1000 guineas – more than twice what Lawrence (then the leading portrait painter) asked for a whole-length portrait or Turner (then the leading landscapist) asked for a 'six-footer'. Farington recorded that Westall was still at work on the painting in November 1812 and it was described in Sept. 1814 as 'recently exhibited' – [Knight], 1814, p. 287 – no doubt at Westall's one-man exhibition in that year. The combination of Greek archaeology with picturesque lighting was more liable to appeal to Knight than the subject of matrimony

D. P. H. LENNOX, ESQ.

207

Sir David Wilkie (1785–1841)

207 *A Veteran Highlander who Served at the Battle of Minden*

Oil on panel: 35.6×29.2
Signed and dated 1819
Prov.: R. P. Knight; by descent to D. P. H.
Lennox, by whom sold 1978
Lit.: Cunningham, II, pp. 27–8; III, p. 526

Knight was a friend of some of Wilkie's earliest patrons — Lord Mulgrave and Sir George Beaumont for instance — but he acquired this work when the artist was well established and was beginning to develop a freer manner and to turn to heroic, as distinct from comic, low-life subjects. This one was no doubt suggested by the *Chelsea Pensioners* upon which he was then at work. Knight paid 35 guineas (including frame) for it in January 1820 when it was displayed at the British Institution, where Knight, as a prominent supporter, must have felt obliged to purchase

RENFREW DISTRICT COUNCIL MUSEUM AND ART GALLERIES, PAISLEY

Pieter Christoffel Wonder (1780–1850)

208 *Lord Aberdeen, Lord Farnborough and Sir Abraham Hume*

Oil on canvas: 54.6×57.8
Prov.: E. Joseph, presented to the National Portrait Gallery 1888
Lit.: Niemeijer

One of four preparatory sketches (all now in the National Portrait Gallery) for a painting entitled *Patrons and Lovers of Art* (now in a private collection), painted by the Utrecht artist Wonder between 1824 and 1827 for Sir John Murray, Bart., showing Murray himself and the leading collectors of the day in an imaginary art gallery hung with many of their own paintings — almost a nineteenth-century 'Kunstkammer'. (All four sketches and the final painting were recently exhibited at the Ferens Art Gallery, Hull, *Scholars of Nature*, 1981, 42–6.) The figures here were all important acquaintances of Knight's and are, from left to right, Sir Charles Long, 1st Baron Farnborough, his father-in-law Sir Abraham Hume (seated) and the 4th Earl of Aberdeen

NATIONAL PORTRAIT GALLERY, LONDON

Joachim Wtewael (*c.* 1566–1638)

209 *The Judgement of Paris*

Oil on copper: 17.0× 22.0
Prov.: Jean de Jullienne; probably Payne Knight; by descent
Lit.: Lindeman, p. 97

Engraved by Surugue when in the De Jullienne Collection, there is a copy of this painting in the Fitzwilliam Museum, Cambridge. This subject was painted several times by Wtewael (see the entry no. 127 in the exhibition catalogue *Europaische Landschaft-malerei, 1550–1650*, Albertina, Vienna, 1972, describing the Budapest painting — a smaller version of which is at Waddesdon Manor — and listing the others including that in the National Gallery, London, painted on wood)

D. P. H. LENNOX, ESQ.

Johan Zoffany (1733–1810) Plate 30

210 *Charles Townley and his Collection*

Oil on canvas: 127.0×99.0
Prov.: Presented to Charles Townley by the artist; by descent to the 3rd Lord O'Hagan by whom sold Christie's 19 May 1939 (92)
Lit.: Webster, p. 72; Cook

This picture, begun in 1781 and completed in 1783, celebrates the most famous collection of antiquities in London in the late eighteenth century — that assembled by Knight's friend Charles Townley, who is portrayed here seated on the right with his well-travelled dog Kam, in conversation with the erudite adventurer d'Hancarville. Behind the latter stands Charles Greville, the nephew of d'Hancarville's former patron, Sir William Hamilton. Greville had at this date just acquired Emma Hart (see cat. no. 61), whom later presented to his uncle, but here he points to Townley's 'wife', the chief beauty in this collection, *Clytie* (see cat. no. 59), and discusses her with the palaeographer and bibliophile Thomas Astle, whose researches on the origin of writing interested both Knight and d'Hancarville. The

208

collection, which was not, of course, originally arranged in this way (Brian Cook has identified each piece and noted its original location), was chiefly composed of carefully restored ancient marbles, most of them Roman portraits or Roman copies of Hellenistic and Classical works: an exception is the fifth-century grave relief of a seated man (Xanthippus) holding a votive foot bought from Athens in the 1740s by Dr Askew and acquired by Townley at his sale in 1775 for a mere £20. Earlier, in 1768, Townley acquired from the Barberini in Rome what was then a far more valued work, and cost him £400. This is the boy biting another boy's arm, here placed in front of the chimney piece, a group which was associated by Winckelmann with Polyclitus. This, however, Knight considered to possess 'neither grandeur nor beauty in the forms; nor grace or dignity in the action or character' and to be too extensively restored to merit inclusion in *Specimens*

(Knight, 1809, pp. xlii–xliii). As for the copy of the Discobolus of Myron which Zoffany added to the painting in 1792 at Townley's request (and to the detriment of the composition), Knight admired it but felt it his 'duty to the public' to point out that the head was an erroneous addition made under the direction of 'Mr Jenkins' which had deceived his friend, although his 'judgment in art was as nearly infallible as human judgment can be' (*ibid.*, plate xxix). Indeed Townley's notes show that he knew that the other copies showed that Myron had not placed the head looking forward, but he believed his version to be an antique improvement on Myron's work (Towneley Hall Papers, DDTo, box 46 for cost of marbles, and Box marked 'Antiq. Park St. Marbles' for Discobolus). The key to the painting was apparently drafted by Townley

BURNLEY BOROUGH COUNCIL, TOWNELEY HALL ART GALLERY AND MUSEUM

List of lenders